Scotland by Rail and Sea

The visitors guide to exploring Scotland by train and ferry

by Kevin Sinclair

www.britainbyrail.co.uk
www.acerleaf.co.uk

D1437569

Published by Kevin Sinclair.

Printed by Imprint Digital, Exeter, www.imprintdigital.net

ISBN: 978-0-9566846-0-8

Photographs by the author unless otherwise credited. The following organisations have kindly supplied photographs for use in this book and are credited as follows:

NF – Northlink Ferries
CM – Caledonian MacBrayne
NTS – National Trust for Scotland Photo Library. Contact: Photo Library, Wemyss House, 28 Charlotte Square, Edinburgh, EH2 4ET.
Tel: 0131 243 9300 email: irobertson@nts.org.uk

Cover photographs:

Front cover: The Strathspey Railway's Boat of Garten station in the Cairngorm National Park.
Rear cover: MV Hjaltland passes the Kirkabister Ness Lighthouse on the Shetland island of Bressay at the end of the journey from Aberdeen to Lerwick. Photo credit: Northlink Ferries.

Contents

Acknowledgements:

The author would like to thank everyone who has contributed to this book with information, ideas and thoughts to make it far better than it could otherwise have been. A huge thank you also goes to my friends and family for your patience, and proof reading!

Particular thanks is also given to Caledonian MacBrayne, Northlink Ferries and the National Trust for Scotland for the kind help they offered, and the supply of many of the images contained in this book.

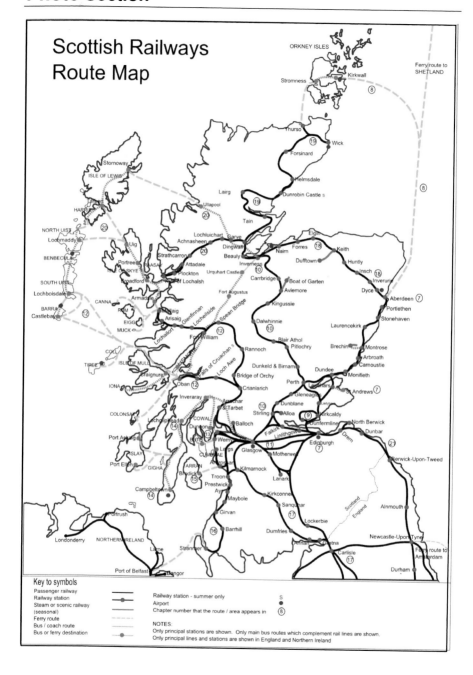

Above: Plocton and the scenic Inverness to Kyle of Lochalsh Railway.

Left: RRS Discovery of the Scott and Shackleton Antarctic expedition of 1901 – 1904, now a museum ship at Dundee.

Above: A typical Scottish train near Dingwall.
Below Left: Edinburgh Castle.
Below Right: A traditional cinema in historic St Andrews.

*Above:Caledonian MacBrayne ship MV Bute on the Wemyess Bay to
Rothesay route (CM).
Below: MV Isle of Mull sails from Oban (CM).*

Above: Culzeen Castle in Ayrshire (NTS / John Sinclair)

Below: The island of Canna (NTS / John Sinclair)

bove: Northlink Ferry, MV Hamnavoe passes the Old Man of Hoy on the crabster (near Thurso) to Orkney route (NF).

elow: The scenic Highland Mainline near Dalwhinnie.

Above: Eilean Donan Castle near Kyle of Lochalsh, Scotland's most photographed castle was a ruin until restoration in 1932.
Below Left: The Cairngorn National Park
Below Right: Glasgow Cathedral.

Above: the Royal Palace of Holyroodhouse is the official residence of the Monarch in Scotland.
Below Left: Elgin Cathedral
Below Right: Steam on the Strathspey Railway

1. Introduction

Scotland is a great small country to take a holiday or short break in. It is packed with a variety of landscapes which change around every corner and a rich history that is evident in almost every town and village. There is such a variety of places to go. City breaks offer world class attractions, shopping and cultural events. There are castles, grand houses and amazing landscapes all over the country. Many people enjoy hillwalking or other outdoor events. Don't forget the Scottish islands either, which each offer a different experience.

You may be planning a visit to Scotland as part of a larger itinerary, or perhaps it's your main holiday. Or maybe you live in Scotland and you are looking for days out and perhaps a short break or two. Whatever your aim, this guide is designed to help you get the most from your trip.

Much of Scotland is rural with a relatively small population. Yet, this often does not mean the need for a car to visit these areas. Possibly the best way to see Scotland is on foot or by bike. But if you don't have the time or you want to supplement these with something a bit quicker, the train is a great way to get you there. In addition to an excellent rail service from all parts of Britain, Scotland has a fantastic rail service within the country. The urban areas of Glasgow and Edinburgh with their surrounding settlements have frequent trains on suburban rail networks. Long distance routes connect all cities and major towns with well appointed long distance trains. Beyond these intensive networks, the railway reaches out into almost every area of the country with a network of lines taking you to the less well travelled areas. As a result of the routes the early railway builders took, even today there are stations in small villages and places of interest.

In addition to this comprehensive rail network there is an excellent ferry network run by Caledonian MacBrayne and Northlink, which is ideal for a country with over 700 islands! Trains and ferries link many locations throughout the country and where a connection is required, a good network of coaches and buses join the trains and ferries with other communities. Bus services, even in remote areas, offer modern vehicles and usually several services each day. Also linked into the rail network are long distance walking and cycling routes so that you can combine these modes of transport with your rail holiday.

Discovering Scotland by rail is not just possible, it's the ideal way to see the country. Trains offer splendid views and a hassle free way to travel. Despite so many visitors taking the train, guidebooks don't give good directions on how to reach visitor attractions by public transport. This book seeks to correct that. And, even if you are on a motoring holiday, you should find this an ideal guide to day trips by train and ferry.

So enjoy the book, and enjoy planning your next trip around Scotland by rail!

PART 1, General Information

2. Practicalities

Scotland is well appointed for the visitor with all the facilities you would expect from a modern country. Planning your visit in advance should mean that you have no unexpected problems once you arrive. This section details some practical advice for your visit.

Accommodation
There are many options for accommodation in Scotland. Throughout the country there are campsites, hostels, hotels, bed & breakfasts and guest houses. The costs of accommodation vary greatly. Camping is a good way to save money and can be relatively comfortable if staying on a serviced camp site. Youth hostels are another good budget choice and are not just for young people. The Scottish Youth Hostel Association (SYHA) runs an extensive network of quality accommodation for all ages and has many hostels with private rooms which are ideal for families (www.syha.org.uk). There are also private hostels, but be aware that the quality is not always as high as SYHA. In rural areas, bed & breakfast accommodation is often a great way to stay as you will be staying in private homes with families who are excellent hosts. Hotels tend to be the most expensive option, although sometimes good deals can be obtained. As with everything be flexible and try to avoid the peak times. Most accommodation is graded by Visit Scotland, the official tourist organisation to ensure that you have good quality accommodation (see www.visitscotland.com, which also has a booking service). Another good place to search for accommodation can be community websites which often detail all the local services in an area or village.

Avoiding the Crowds
Towards the end of term before the school summer break there will often be school visits, so it can be best to visit attractions after 14.30 at these times of the year. Weekends are always busier for visitor attractions as local people will also be visiting. Bank Holidays (the name given to public holidays) are another busy time for both attractions and travel. Avoiding travel on Bank Holidays could make your stay much more pleasant. Shops tend to be very busy on Saturdays and often Sundays too. Trains are busiest in the mornings before 09.00 and after 17.00 for commuter services and on Fridays and public holidays for long distance services. Although keep in mind that many long distance trains are used by commuters for part of their route!

Banking and Currency

Banks are generally open Monday to Friday between the hours of 09.30 and 16.30. Some will be open longer while in rural communities it is not uncommon for a bank to be open perhaps only two mornings per week. Many rural branches have closed and even cash machines have been withdrawn, so make sure you have sufficient currency when you visit a more rural area.

Cash machines are usually free to use when they are provided by banks themselves, although other companies will often charge a fee in addition to any exchange rate charges. The main banks in Scotland are Bank of Scotland, Clydesdale, Lloyds TSB and Royal Bank of Scotland, although other building societies and English banks also sometimes have branches in the larger towns.

Credit and debit cards are almost universally accepted. However, keep some cash on you for small transactions and any places that do not accept card payments. Local buses will take cash only and many require exact fares so keep a selection of coins. Coins come in 1, 2, 5, 10, 20, 50 pence and 1 and 2 pound sizes. The currency in Britain is the Pound while in most of Europe it is the Euro, so take some of both currencies if you are planning a visit to mainland Europe.

Disabled Visitors

All buildings where possible have disabled access and facilities. The only exceptions may be historic buildings where it has not been possible to fit disabled access. Even in these cases, call ahead to find out what is available. Many old castles for example may be partially accessible and some even offer a DVD presentation of areas that are not suitable for all visitors. Transport is also usually accessible with most bus services now being equipped with low floor buses or lifts. Check with coach and bus operators for details. Rail stations and trains are accessible to wheelchairs and have accessible toilets (where toilets are provided). Always call ahead to make sure the railway knows you are travelling so that staff will be ready with a ramp at your departure and arrival stations as most stations are not usually staffed.

Etiquette

Please and thank you go a long way along with general politeness, and those practicing such will normally receive better service. Also be aware that when people are waiting for anything, from cinema tickets to a bus, a queue (or line) is formed.

Opening Hours

Visitor attractions will tend to be open between 10.00 and 17.00. Of course some will open for longer, including evenings, and others may have shorter hours. The large attractions will tend to open seven days per week from

Easter until September or even year round. Others may have shorter opening hours or only open several days per week. Many attractions will close over the winter months, especially historic houses and castles. But others, such as larger museums will probably be open all year round. If there is a particular attraction you don't want to miss, be sure to check it is open when you plan to visit.

Shops will tend to open from 09.00 until 17.00. Some will have evening opening a few days per week. Sunday opening is now common, although many smaller shops will still take this as a holiday.

Immigration and Customs

European Union visitors enter the UK through the same channel as UK residents and do not have to declare items at customs. Checks for illegal substances are still made. Other nationals and those coming from outside the EU still have to declare items if over the allowed rates and will often need a Visa to enter the UK.

Personal Safety

Most areas are generally safe and you can usually rely on local people to be helpful if seeking directions or assistance. Thankfully, pickpockets and those targeting tourists are very rare, allowing you to relax during your break. Most city centres have television monitoring systems to reduce crime and are very safe.

One area to be careful of is city centres in the evenings and at night. Most British towns are popular areas for pubs and unfortunately are known for anti social behaviour especially on Friday and Saturday evenings. Avoid areas with high concentrations of pubs if you do plan to go out in the evenings and stick to the areas frequented by tourists.

Police forces have stations in most towns and villages and are on call for emergencies 24 hours a day in all locations. Dial 999 if you ever encounter an emergency and you will be able to be put in touch with fire, police, ambulance or coast guard as appropriate.

The UK rail network has its own police force, the British Transport Police (BTP). The BTP patrol stations and trains and have offices at many larger rail stations. In general all UK transport is safe and you are very unlikely to encounter any problems.

Postal Services

Letters are handled by the Royal Mail and a network of Post Offices. Be aware that mail is now priced according to size, in addition to weight and destination. It is probably best to visit a Post Office to buy stamps until you become familiar with what you need for various letters. Second and first class mail is available to all of the UK. First class aims to be at the destination next day. International mail may be sent surface or airmail, except for very small items that are always sent by airmail.

Smoking

Smoking is now illegal in all indoor public places in Scotland. There are fines for those breaking this law both towards the smoker and the owner of the establishment. Non-smokers will be glad to know they can now go anywhere and never need to seek out non-smoking venues.

Telephones

Public telephones are widely available. They are located at most railway stations and on streets and are usually in phone boxes although some will be located on station walls. Telephones are provided by British Telecom. New style boxes come in many styles, while the traditional red phone box is still in existence. Most, but not all phones accept coins and many will also take credit cards. Most will allow text messages and emails in addition to phone calls.

When to go

The busiest time is during the summer months from June to early September. Local school holidays occur in July and early August and make this the very busiest period. The weather during this time is usually fairly warm to hot and sunny. It is also important to note that weather is unpredictable at any time of the year. If you're going out, take an umbrella or rain jacket regardless of the time of year, forecast or even how hot it looks when you leave. Due to its position, Scotland enjoys long hours of daylight during the summer months where it almost seems never to get dark.

August in Edinburgh is Festival time, which dominates everything in the city and means accommodation is hard to come by. Elsewhere, events such as Highland Games, folk festivals or sporting events – most of which take place in the summer months – can tie up accommodation, though normally only in a fairly concentrated local area. If you're out and about in the Highlands throughout the summer, you won't be able to avoid the clouds of small biting insects called midges, which can be a real annoyance on still days, particularly around dusk. Buy some good insect repellent before venturing out, and remember not to leave windows open with the light on in the evening.

It is common for May and September to throw up weather which is every bit as good as, if not better than, the months of high summer. You're less likely to encounter crowds or struggle to find somewhere to stay, and the mild temperatures combined with the changing colours of nature mean both are great for outdoor activities, particularly hiking.

The spring and autumn months of April and October bracket the season for many parts of rural Scotland. A large number of attractions, tourist offices and guest houses often open for business on Easter weekend and shut up shop after the school half-term in mid-October. If places do stay open through the winter it's normally with reduced opening hours; this is the best time to pick up special offers at hotels and guest houses.

Winter days, from November through to March, occasionally crisp and bright, are more often cold, gloomy and all too brief, although New Year has traditionally been a time to visit Scotland for partying and warm hospitality. While even tourist hotspots such as Edinburgh are notably quieter during winter, a fall of snow in the Highlands will prompt plenty of activity around the ski resorts. Also during the winter, be aware of dark days. In December and January daylight may be around 09.00 and darkness at 16.00, if not earlier.

3. Overview of Scotland

The land area of Scotland occupies the northern third of the island of Britain. It has a land mass of 30,414 square miles and a population of just over 5 million inhabitants, who are mainly concentrated in the central area between the largest cities of Glasgow and Edinburgh. There are over 700 lakes, known as lochs, and over 790 islands of which 92 are inhabited. Large areas of the country comprise highly scenic countryside of mountains, lochs and rivers. Being surrounded by the sea, Scotland is bordered by the North Sea to the east, the Atlantic Ocean to the west and the Irish Sea to the south west. To the south the land border is with England.

Politically, Scotland is one of four countries that make up the United Kingdom, which is a member of the European Union, although has not joined the Euro currency. The main parliament is in London while Scotland has its own government based in Edinburgh. As with the rest of the UK, it is a constitutional monarchy with Queen Elizabeth II as head of state. There are also local authorities, known as councils, which provide local services over large areas as there are no longer any town councils or assemblies.

A Brief History of Scotland

It is believed that the first hunter-gatherers arrived in Scotland around 11,000 years ago after the last ice age. Prior to that time there is no evidence of human habitation as the ice removed all traces of any people who may have lived there. These first peoples were hunter-gatherers. Later the first villages were built around 6000 years ago as people began to settle and grown crops. In the Neolithic Period (which means new Stone Age) from 4000 to 2000 BC many hunter-gatherers lived alongside other peoples who had settled in villages. On the Scottish Islands with a lack of large trees, their villages were constructed almost entirely of stone. In 1850 on Orkney a storm uncovered an early settlement which has turned out to be a village from this time period. The village of Skara Brae on the Mainland of Orkney is now under the care of Historic Scotland and is open to the public. Other Neolithic habitation, burial and ritual sites are particularly common and well-preserved in the Northern Isles and Western Isles due to their stone construction. In other areas the habitations were likely to have been constructed from less durable materials which have long since decayed.

The next period was what is now known as the Bronze Age (2100 to 750 BC) when people began to make tools and weapons from bronze and tin which of course was a huge advance on the stone previously used. The Iron Age followed where people were able to smelt iron. During this time the main peoples in Scotland were the Celts and Picts, who were described by the Romans as painted people due to their painting of designs on their bodies.

Scotland as we know it could be said to begin at Hadrian's Wall, both geographically and historically. It was with the arrival of the Romans that written history was first recorded resulting in a great deal of knowledge about all the centuries since then and the peoples of that time including the Picts and Celts. Although the Romans mainly occupied England and Wales which were called Britannia, they did occupy areas of Scotland over the years. Hadrian's Wall was built on what is roughly the border between England and Scotland today. What is less well known is that north of this wall was the territory of Caledonia. Over the years the Romans had varying degrees of control over the land. Until 87 AD when troops were withdrawn for the Danube battles, the 'Gask Frontier' of wooden forts took control of land as far north as Perthshire. At sea, the Roman fleet sailed right around Scotland. This was followed by a retreat to the Antonine Wall along the valley between what is now Glasgow and Edinburgh in 142 AD. The Romans finally withdrew from Britain in 410 AD after a period of nearly 500 years. Roman soldiers, like the Picts and Celts, believed in a variety of gods and set up shrines over the countryside to them. However what is less well known is that is after the execution of Jesus Christ in another part of the Roman Empire in 33 AD, many Roman soldiers became followers of Jesus (one of the first is actually recorded in the Bible as saying "Surely this man was the Son of God!"). His followers became known as 'Christians' and with Roman soldiers based in Scotland, word of Jesus spread here also and many people came to follow him here too. What is better known is that in 400 AD Ninian arrived in Scotland again with news of Jesus and many Picts became followers also, as is evidenced in the many Christian symbols on Pictish stones of that time. Regardless of the origin it is clear that the desire to become followers of Jesus was to shape Scotland for the next two thousand years. Eventually as more people became followers, formal churches were established and Scotland was known as a 'Christian' country.

Returning to Pictish times, between the 6th and 8th centuries Scotland became the Pictish Kingdom and this was essentially the formation of Scotland as a country. From 843 until 1058 Scotland was ruled by the House of Alpin. Kenneth MacAlpin is regarded at the first Scottish Monarch, although he was never crowned as such. He did most of the work to unite the Scots and Picts and create a nation of Scotland.

By 1124 Scotland had become a fully functioning kingdom under David I and prospered in relative peace. Systems of government were introduced and many of the institutions of a nation were established. This new House of Canmore ended in 1290 with the death of the Queen of Scotland, Margaret Maid of Norway at only seven years old. A time of turmoil followed. John Balliol was a candidate for kingship of Scotland and was supported over Robert Bruce by Edward I of England. However shortly after becoming king in 1292 he infuriated Edward I of England by seeking an alliance with France. This was signed in 1295 and known as the Auld Alliance. It was a diplomatic agreement aimed at containing England's expansionist ambitions. In response Edward I invaded and took castles as far north as Elgin. He also took the Stone of Scone to Westminster Abby where it was placed under the Coronation Chair. The Stone's significance is that it was the Coronation Seat of Scottish kings since Kenneth MacAlpin. The stone remained there until 1996 when it was returned to Scotland by Prime Minister John Major.

Balliol was imprisoned in the Tower of London and was released on the agreement he leave for France. Edward I died and was replaced by Edward II, while Robert Bruce became King of Scotland. What followed was a further war. Robert Bruce besieged Stirling Castle in 1314 and a battle followed at nearby Bannockburn. Stirling Castle and Bannockburn can still be visited by those interested. Robert Bruce won and declared the Declaration of Arbroath in 1320 which declared Scotland as an independent country.

The 16th century is perhaps best remembered for the Scottish Reformation. In 1517 Martin Luther nailed his Ninety-Five Theses to the door of the castle church in Wittenburg, Germany. He was a priest who spoke out against abuses of power in the church and wanted reform. In Scotland Patrick Hamilton of St Andrews took up the cause. He believed in the Bible rather than traditions which had become part of the church. The Bishop at St Andrews organised a trial of Hamilton, who was convicted and burnt on the street in St Andrews (the spot is still marked outside the University). Eventually the Reformation was successful and a new system of church was established.

An interesting period began with King James VI of Scotland also becoming King James I of England after the death of Elizabeth I in 1604. Effectively this resulted in two separate nations with the same leader and was known as the 'Union of the Crowns'. Although both countries had the same monarch, they were still functioning as two separate countries. James came into conflict with Oliver Cromwell who eventually overthrew him and declared himself Lord Protector of England. He also created the Commonwealth, which Scotland was part of and effectively again Scotland and England shared political leadership. The Commonwealth ended in 1660 and the Monarchy was restored. Scotland remained a separate state. In 1707, however, following English threats to end trade and free movement across the border, the Scots Parliament and the Parliament of England enacted the twin Acts of Union, which created the Kingdom of Great Britain.

From here the history of Scotland is intertwined with that of England. The new country of Britain proved to be a highly successful entity. From peasant subsistence based economy developed a highly advanced industrial leader. The change occurred in only a few hundred years. The industrial revolution changed the entire country. Essentially this meant mechanisation. Factories with machines that could produce far more than home cottage industries sprang up. This was the catalyst which led to the building of most of the cities. In Scotland, Glasgow and Dundee especially became major industrial centres. Steam power is what gave factories the ability to product huge quantities of goods. This was initially transported by sea and inland, by canal. However when steam was harnessed for use by railways, the growth became apparently unstoppable.

Alongside this industrial growth the Empire became an economic and political powerhouse. The Royal Navy became one of the greatest, if not the greatest, in the world, needed to protect all the overseas territories and shipping routes. Scotland benefited from all of this UK activity. Industry changed the 'central belt' to become a prosperous and industrialised area to rival any in the rest of the country. In Victorian times this new wealth combined with rail travel opened up the Highlands to sporting and fishing holidays for the wealthy.

Through the 20th century Scotland developed into a modern country alongside the rest of the UK. A major development that perhaps was unique to Scotland was the discovery of North Sea oil in the 1970s. Aberdeen especially, but other areas of Scotland too benefited from construction and serving of these resources. Industry has declined all over the UK and Scotland is now a service based economy. Thankfully there is much for the visitor to see and do. A rich and long history has left relics and buildings across the nation which, for the most part, survive for you to visit. Also the countryside which first attracted the Victorians as a leisure pursuit remains to this day probably the biggest draw to Scotland.

4. Getting to and from Scotland

Getting to Scotland couldn't be easier with excellent rail, air and sea links to the rest of Britain, Europe, North America and the rest of the world.

By Rail

There are frequent high-speed train services from all parts of England to Scotland. The East Coast route runs along the east coast of England from London, Peterborough, York and Newcastle to Edinburgh, Glasgow, Aberdeen and Inverness, plus numerous other smaller stations. The West Coast mainline from London and west coast towns (including Birmingham and Crewe) to Glasgow is the alternative route along the other side of the country. Finally, the cross-country network takes services direct from the South West of England to Scotland. If time is an issue or if you would just like the experience, Scotrail have overnight services (known as the Caledonian Sleeper) from London direct to over forty Scottish towns.

If travelling from Europe, Eurostar offers an international rail service direct to London. It is now possible to travel from over 100 destinations throughout Europe connecting with Eurostar. On arrival at the impressive St Pancras station in London, simply walk to the next door Kings Cross station for trains to Scotland.

By Sea

From Europe, DFDS Seaways operate a daily service between Holland and Newcastle (in northern England). On arrival at Newcastle, transfer from the ferry terminal at North Shields to the central railway station in the clearly marked DFDS bus.

From Northern Ireland, special 'Rail and Sail' tickets to Ireland (Belfast) are available via Stranraer (with ScotRail and StenaLine). Trains from Stranraer to Glasgow Central take a little over two hours. Sailings between Stranraer and Belfast take around 1 hour 45 minutes, arriving at Belfast Port. See the ferry company's website at www.stenaline.com for details.

By Air

Iceland Air operates direct to Glasgow from Iceland and North American cities. From the USA, Continental operates direct to Edinburgh and Glasgow from Newark, New Jersey. Their airport at New Jersey has its own Amtrak inter city rail station allowing easy access from across the USA. There is a dedicated bus link from Edinburgh Airport to the rail stations in Edinburgh (Haymarket and Waverley Stations). Glasgow Airport also has a bus link to both city centre railway stations. Other airlines, including Flybe, operate services to London and Manchester, and there are easy rail connections from all UK airports to Scotland. If flying from Europe, there are numerous direct services to Scottish airports.

5. Scotland's Railways – General Information

Train Operating Companies

Until rail privatisation there was a single UK national rail operator – British Rail. This was a state owned organisation and through its subsidiaries operated all of the UK rail routes. The Scottish Region was named Scotrail, while long distance services were operated by the InterCity sector. Since privatisation rail services have been operated on a franchise basis.

In Scotland the largest operator is Scotrail. The company has 350 stations, 4000 staff and operates almost 2000 services each day. Each year 75 million passengers use its trains. Their trains are reliable, frequent and comfortable. The staff are usually friendly and take their time to assist those unfamiliar with the area. The services range from local suburban routes around the cities of Glasgow and Edinburgh, to longer distance routes linking the major towns and scenic rail journeys. The company is also famous for its overnight Caledonian Sleeper services to London from over 40 Scottish towns and cities.

Scotrail is the only domestic rail operator, but it shares services to England with East Coast, Virgin and Cross Country. East Coast operates its services from London, York, Newcastle and right along the east coast to Edinburgh, Glasgow, Stirling, Perth, Dundee and Aberdeen. Virgin trains provide services from London along the west coast of Britain to Glasgow. These are high-speed InterCity trains with all the amenities expected of long distance travel. Cross Country trains start from Aberdeen, Dundee and Edinburgh to cities right across England including Manchester, Birmingham, Bristol and as far south as Brighton and Penzance. Finally, Transpennie Express operates a direct service between Glasgow, Edinburgh and Manchester Airport.

There are good links between operators (so you can travel out with one company and return with another) and with other modes of transport including buses, ferries and air. Aside from these main railway operators there are a number of excursion and private railways in Scotland providing tourist train services.

Railway Tickets Explained

Depending on where and when you wish to travel there are a wide variety of railway tickets available. There are set railway fares between any two railway stations in Britain. Longer journeys will have cheaper 'Advance' tickets, the price of which will vary according to demand. While this means you know in advance what your ticket will cost, it also makes the selection of tickets (designed to take account of quiet periods) can be confusing. However with a little thought you can make easy sense of them and get the best possible value. As a general rule if you can be flexible with your travelling times, you will usually be able to get a better value fare.

The most common ticket types are:

- Anytime. These are the most expensive tickets, but also the most flexible. You can break your journey, travel on any train or any train company. They are available as single or return options. With return tickets you must come back within one month.

- Off Peak. These tickets may require travel on a certain route or train company. They are available as single or returns, and the return journey must be used within one month. However the main difference is that you must travel on off peak services, usually these are after 09.30 Monday to Friday and are sometimes restricted in the evening peak time also. A break of journey is usually possible. Both Anytime and Off Peak are refundable less an admin charge.

- Advance. These are the cheapest tickets but have the most restrictions. Breaks of journey are not allowed and you must travel on the specific trains booked in advance, otherwise you lose your ticket. These fares are not refundable.

- Rover and Ranger Tickets. These fares allow unlimited travel within a specified area and are ideal for touring. They can be useful for budgeting (you know in advance how much you will spend on travel), should be cheaper than buying tickets on the day of travel, and allow complete flexibility in travel plans. For those wishing to tour, these are the ideal option. There are also international versions called 'BritRail' for overseas visitors.

- First class. First class tickets are flexible and usually allow travel on any train at any time with the return journey within one month. They are also refundable. Discounted first class tickets are available on some operators (but not Scotrail).

All standard class tickets can be used with a Railcard to gain discounts of around 30% and qualify for child discounts also which are usually 50% for those up to 16 years old and free places for under fives (two per fare paying adult). If travelling with a family, the Family and Friends Railcard allows further discounts for both the adult and child fares.

Where and How to Purchase Tickets

For overseas visitors to Britain, tickets can be purchased before you leave from BritRail and their international representatives. This probably represents the best value fares for the overseas visitor.

For UK travellers, tickets can be purchased from any staffed rail station or rail appointed travel agent. You don't need to buy the ticket from the station you intend to travel from and purchasing in advance or on the day of travel are both possible. It is also possible to buy your ticket online either from the Trainline or various rail company web sites. For the UK traveller the main thing to keep in mind is to buy your ticket as early as possible to get the best value fares. Also by deciding which trains you will travel on, you get the best fares. If you do need to be flexible, it will cost a little more. Also look into single tickets. There are many new bargain singles and they can often work out cheaper than a standard return. Use Railcards where ever possible as this will gain considerable savings.

Trains and On Board Facilities

Trains and the facilities they offer vary enormously from company to company and route to route. It is impossible to describe every train in use but certain features are common to most. Even by using the timetable you can find out the basic services available, such as whether the train has first class, a trolley service or if seat reservations are available. The types of trains used on a particular route don't tend to vary often so once you have travelled a journey once you will know what to expect for the next time.

All trains will offer as a minimum standard class accommodation. Very short suburban journeys may not have toilet facilities but all journeys of slightly longer length will have at least one toilet per train or often per carriage. Seats will vary from basic commuter type seating with three seats on one side of the aisle and two on the other to comfortable long distance seating offering spacious leg room, overhead luggage racks and even sometimes entertainment plug in points. Generally trains are provided with the type of journey in mind. So luggage space etc should reflect the type of journey on that route, although modern trains have less luggage space and toilet facilities in favour of more seats!

Overnight sleeping car trains are described in their own section. They offer both berths and seated service.

Catering is very often provided on longer distance trains. Usually this is by way of a trolley service, similar to that on an aircraft, and hot and cold drinks and snacks are provided. InterCity trains have better facilities and provide a buffet car. This can offer a much better selection of hot and cold refreshments. A few trains have a full restaurant service with an on board kitchen for the preparation of fresh meals.

Types of Train in Use Today

Most trains in Scotland today use multiple unit vehicles. These self propelled trains are either diesel or electric and come in two, three and four coach versions. There are various types, known as classes. On diesel routes the class 156 trains work the longer distance services in the West Highlands and Southwest to Stranraer. They have opening windows, space for six bikes and usually have a trolley catering service. Trains on the North Highland lines, in central Scotland and the northern express route between Inverness and Aberdeen use the class 158 Express trains. These are similar to the class 156 being two coaches long and have a bike area in the centre but have the addition of air conditioning and first class, although the seating in first class is almost identical to that of standard and not worth the supplement! The newest diesel train is the class 170 Turbostar. These three coach air conditioned trains are used on the Glasgow to Edinburgh service as well as trains to Perth, Inverness and Aberdeen. They have first class compartments with nine seats each at either end of the train, are air conditioned, have bike space and are generally the most comfortable train on Scotrail today. On scenic routes they are popular for their large picture windows. There is also a version for local services in central Scotland which is almost identical but has no first class accommodation. On electric routes similar trains are used and are either three or four coaches long. The routes from Glasgow to the coast (Gourock, Wemyss Bay, Largs, Ardrossan Harbour, Prestwick Airport and Ayr are benefiting from new class 380 electric trains. These have more spacious seats, bike space, air conditioning and power points for laptops.

High-speed Trains (HST) run on the Edinburgh to Aberdeen (three daily) and Inverness (once daily) routes from London. These large locomotive hauled trains have six standard class coaches, two first class, a restaurant / café car, luggage vans for bikes and air conditioning. They are the most comfortable trains running within Scotland today and are popular with holiday makers heading north from England.

Scotrail Sleeper Trains. These overnight trains offer comfortable accommodations to travellers overnight from Scotland to England. They used coaches hauled by locomotives, so there is no engine noise from under floor engines (perfect for sleeping!). The trains use modern sleeping cars each with 12 or 13 cabins. In standard class cabins have two berths, a wash basin, coat hangers, individual reading lights, bottled water and fresh bed linen. First class cabins are identical however they have only one berth and offer a private cabin for the single traveller. First class passengers also have access to the lounge car. This coach is also open to standard class when space is available. Also on offer is a coach car with reclining seats for overnight travel. The seating is similar to that used in first class for day time trains.

Stations

Railway stations in Britain all have a level platform for easy boarding, timetable information, a waiting shelter and usually some kind of live train running information either via a display board or free telephone link. Some also have ticket machines. Larger stations will have a proper waiting room, toilets and staffed ticket office. Where there is no ticket office or machine you may purchase your ticket on the train from the conductor. However should there be ticket facilities you must purchase your ticket prior to boarding, or you will be charged the full fare without being able to take advantage of the cheaper tickets. The largest stations and terminals have the best facilities with a range of shops and places to eat, together with the full services you would expect from a large station.

Rural railways often have what are known as 'request stops'. These are most often found on the routes to Kyle of Lochalsh, Thurso, Wick and the West Highlands. At these stations the train will not stop unless you specifically request to alight or board. If you are on the train, just ask the conductor when you board, and they will make arrangements for the train to stop. If you wish to join the train, stand on the platform where you can be clearly seen by the train driver and signal by holding out your hand that you wish to board. These stops are marked as 'request' in timetables and at the station, and once you know how they work, you will have no trouble using them.

Seat Reservations

Seat reservations are usually always a good idea if you are travelling on a longer journey and should be taken if available. You may reserve a seat for free up to 18.00 the day before travel or when booking your ticket. If you are travelling with a rail pass you may book seats for journeys separately at any ticket office once you know when you wish to travel. Seat reservations are printed on card labels, which are attached to the seat, or more recently by electronic displays. You can find out which trains provide seat reservation services when you book your ticket. In general local services in the Glasgow, Clyde Coast, Edinburgh, Central Scotland and Fife areas do not provide reservations while those in the rest of the country do, with the exception of any local trains.

Cycles

You can take your bike or folding bike on almost any rail service. However the space available on trains for bikes is often limited so it's a good idea to book a bike reservation in advance. When your train arrives, look out for the bike symbol on coaches to know where to load your cycle. Folding bikes may be taken on any service and do not require a reservation.

Luggage and Pets

Passengers are allowed up to three items of personal luggage free of charge. This includes two larger items such as suitcases or rucksacks and one smaller item of hand luggage such as a briefcase. Some trains have a facility for leaving luggage in a luggage van for certain destinations on the route. This is not common and restricted to only a few InterCity routes (usually East Coast services and sleepers). In the most cases passengers must take care of their own luggage. However trolleys are normally available to assist at larger stations. Excess luggage and more bulky luggage may be carried subject to space being available and an excess charge will be applied.

Pets can normally be carried on most trains and free of charge so long as they do not disturb other passengers or sit on seats. Sleeper services require the owner to pay a supplement to cover the extra cleaning costs of the cabin. Also pets can only be carried when the owner has sole occupancy of the cabin. Special arrangements are always available for guide dogs. Eurostar and Heathrow Express do not allow the carriage of animals.

Railcards

Significant savings can often be obtained if you fall into certain categories which are eligible for reduced rate travel. The reductions are most often available by way of a Railcard. These can be purchased by post or at most ticket offices and rail appointed travel agents. The cards are usually valid for a year and give discounts off almost every UK rail fare. The main exceptions are particularly busy periods and private railways. There are three types of Railcard, these being the Senior Person's Railcard, 16–25 Railcard and the Family Railcard. The Senior card gives anyone over 60 around 1/3 off most rail fares, including first class. The 16–25 card is available to anyone within that age range and also full time students and gives 1/3 off most fares while the Family card gives up to 2 adults and up to 4 children travelling together 1/3 off the adult fares and 60% off the children's fares (which are already half price). Children are those aged 5 – 15, while over 15s use a 16–25 Railcard. There is no requirement for the group to be related but the adults must be travelling with a child. Under 5s always go free and do not need a ticket.

Rail Passes (including BritRail, Rover Tickets and Travelpass)

For visitors to Scotland a number of rail passes are available. For those unfamiliar with the concept, the rail pass allows a traveller to make unlimited journeys within a specified area for a set price. This can often work out much cheaper than buying individual point to point tickets. It also means that you don't have to book your journeys in advance but can just turn up and go where you want. Of course if you do want to book the longer journeys you can still make seat reservations along with the rail pass while still retaining the benefit of saving you money. For travellers who want to be spontaneous and go where they feel like, the rail pass offers even better value. This is because turn up and go tickets often cost more than tickets purchased in advance for travel on particular trains.

In Scotland passes sometimes come with additional value in the form of ship and coach travel for when the rails end. Travelpass and Rover tickets can be purchased by anyone, while BritRail products can only be purchased by international visitors.

Freedom of Scotland Travelpass

Valid: Any four out of eight consecutive days travel or Any eight out of fifteen consecutive days travel for a higher price.

The Freedom of Scotland Travelpass is a great way to roam across Scotland by train, coach and ferry – all with just one ticket. Most of the services covered are included in your price, while some others offer a substantial discount. Travelpass tickets include:

- Rail travel on all scheduled daytime passenger trains for journeys wholly within Scotland, including Scotrail, East Coast and Virgin trains to/from Carlisle and Berwick-upon-Tweed. (Travelpass tickets cannot be used to travel before 09.15 Mondays to Fridays, except between Glasgow-Oban/Fort William/Mallaig and Inverness-Kyle/Wick/Thurso.) There is also a 10% discount also available on Caledonian Sleeper Standard fares (from London to Scotland) when travelling to and from Scotland to use your Travelpass.

- Coach travel (on routes not served by rail). Scottish Citylink bus travel between Oban/Fort William and Inverness; Kyle of Lochalsh - Uig; Inverness - Ullapool; Oban - Campbeltown; and Wick - Thurso. Stagecoach in Fife services between Dundee and Leuchars / St. Andrews. Inclusive bus travel on the Isle of Mull with Bowmans Coaches. Inclusive bus travel between Thurso - Scrabster; Wick - John O'Groats; and Thurso - John O'Groats with Stagecoach. First Edinburgh services to/from the Scottish Borders (Kelso - Melrose - Galashiels - Peebles - Edinburgh (No 62); and Carlisle - Langholm - Hawick - Galashiels - Edinburgh (No X95). Inclusive bus travel on the Isle of Skye with Stagecoach.

- Ferry travel. Valid on all Caledonian MacBrayne scheduled ferry services within Scotland. For full details of ferry times please contact 01475 650100 or www.calmac.co.uk. On Northlink Ferries a 20% discount on standard fares between Scrabster-Stromness; Aberdeen-Lerwick; and Aberdeen-Kirkwall-Lerwick (Valid only on day of sailing, and applies to reclining seat fares only, not cabin inclusive).

You can get your Travelpass ticket at staffed railway stations throughout Britain; rail appointed travel agents; ScotRail Telesales (08457 550033); British Visitor Centre, Regent Street, London, and BritRail outlets in Europe and North America or online.

Central Scotland Rover

Valid: three out of seven days unlimited travel

With a Central Scotland Rover you can visit some of the most famous spots in Scotland's central belt. With the Rover you could visit Edinburgh with one of the finest skylines in Europe and the world's best international festival. There are numerous other places too including Stirling with its ancient castle or the Abbey and Abbot House of Dunfermline in Fife.

The Central Scotland Rover Ticket includes:

- Rail travel between Edinburgh, Glasgow Queen Street, North Berwick, Bathgate, Dunblane, Bridge of Allan, Stirling, the Fife Circle, Markinch, Falkirk and all intermediate stations. Also valid between Edinburgh Waverley, Brunstane and Newcraighall.

- Unlimited travel on Glasgow Underground (on presentation of their Central Rover ticket, customers will be issued with an exchange ticket).

Central Scotland Rover tickets are also available from staffed railway stations throughout Britain, rail appointed travel agents, and ScotRail Telesales (08457 550033).

Highland Rover

Valid: any four out of eight consecutive days travel

The Highland Rover is a great way to explore the West Highlands or the North Highlands of Scotland. The Rover allows unlimited travel and lets you go when you want rather than having to book tickets in advance. These lines cover some of the finest scenery in the UK and have lots of options for walking, cycling or sightseeing.

The Rover ticket includes:

- Rail travel. Travel between Glasgow and Oban, Fort William and Mallaig. Travel between Inverness and Wick, Thurso, Kyle of Lochalsh, Aberdeen, Aviemore and intermediate stations (Highland Rovers are not valid on trains arriving before 09.00 at Aberdeen or Inverness on Mondays to Fridays).

- Coach travel. Inclusive bus travel on the Isle of Mull with Bowmans Coaches. (Some services are seasonal – check before travelling on 01680 812313). Scottish Citylink bus travel between Oban/Fort William and Inverness. Inclusive bus travel between Thurso and Scrabster (for ships to Orkney), and on the Isle of Skye with Stagecoach.

- Ferry travel. Inclusive ferry travel between Oban - Mull and Mallaig - Skye with Caledonian MacBrayne. For full details of ferry times please call direct on 01475 650100 or visit www.calmac.co.uk. There is also a 20% discount on Northlink Ferries standard fares between Scrabster-Stromness; Aberdeen-Lerwick; and Aberdeen-Kirkwall-Lerwick.

You can also get your Highland Rover ticket at staffed railway stations throughout Britain when you arrive, rail appointed travel agents or ScotRail Telesales (08457 550033).

BritRail Scottish Freedom Pass (Only available to non UK residents)

The BritRail Scotland Pass is only available to non UK residents and offers a similar type of ticket to the Scottish Travelpass. It also covers the entire Scottish rail network, key bus links, ferries and offers discounts on some connecting services. If you plan to only visit Scotland, compare prices and terms with the Travelpass to determine which one suits you better, and remember if you do wish to buy the BritRail pass, you must do so before arriving in the UK.

Pass Features:

- Unlimited travel from morning until night throughout Scotland on all rail services (not special trains or private railways) including ferries to the various islands and buses to explore sites off the beaten path.
- Discounts for children travelling with adults or seniors.
- Available in standard class only.
- Allows you to explore by hopping on and off the trains as you wish.
- This pass also gives an additional 33% discount on Northlink Ferry Routes (Scrabster – Stromness (Orkney).

Pass holders are not be allowed to travel before 09.15 Monday to Friday and the Pass must be validated within six months of the date of purchase. The BritRail Scottish Freedom Pass may be validated at main stations within Scotland (Aberdeen, Dundee, Edinburgh Waverley, Fort William, Glasgow Central & Queen Street, Inverness, Oban, Paisley, Perth & Stirling). Other BritRail Passes are available to cover the entire UK.

6. Travel by Ferry, Coach, Bike, Car and Air

There are two main domestic ferry companies in Scotland, Caledonian MacBrayne, often referred to as CalMac, and Northlink. CalMac operates ferries in the Clyde and Hebrides, these being the islands off the West Coast of Scotland. Northlink provides service from the mainland to the northern isles of Orkney and Shetland. Coach services are provided by Scottish Citylink, Megabus and West Coast Motors. All these services are well connected with the rail network.

Travelling with Caledonian MacBrayne

As with the train, ferries offer wonderful views, good amenities and a relaxing way to travel. CalMac ships vary in size from the largest vessels with a choice of lounges, places to eat and large open decks, to small ferries with room for only a few cars and some passengers on the short routes. Most people enjoy getting out on deck for a while, especially for the views while passing close to land. Inside time may be spent using the comfortable lounges, catering and other services. Foot passengers can take advantage of not needing to make a reservation in advance and all routes are included in the Freedom of Scotland Travelpass rail ticket. While most ferry terminals are rail or coach connected, often passengers worry about not taking a car to the remote Scottish islands. Thankfully there are good bus links on the Western Isles for foot passengers, and for those who want everything included, CalMac offer a great range of day trips including ferry travel and guided coach tour of selected islands. Check with CalMac for details of what is currently on offer. Motorists may also take their cars with them on most CalMac sailings, while everyone has the chance to opt for day trips or longer stays, perhaps returning via an alternative route to the mainland.

Reservations and Tickets

Rail passengers may opt to purchase a Freedom of Scotland Travelpass which includes ferry travel in the fare. However if you are not using this ticket, or don't wish to use a day's travel for a short and inexpensive ferry fare, then tickets are available from CalMac's website at www.calmac.co.uk, by telephone from 08000 665000 or from any of the company's terminals. On the mainland these are located at Ullapool, Uig, Mallaig, Oban, Gourock, Wemyss Bay, Largs and Ardrossan. All of these are located close to railway stations or bus links. Rail passengers may also find the town centre booking office in Inverness and the CalMac office at Fort William railway station useful. Reservations may be made at the same time as booking tickets. For foot passengers there is usually no need to book in advance, so you may book on turning up at the ferry terminal. Motorists however should always reserve in advance as space fills up quickly, especially during the summer months. Rail passengers also have the option of buying through tickets including rail fares and ferry tickets to most CalMac destinations. These are available from all staffed Scotrail stations. Children under 5 travel free on all CalMac routes, and those of 5 to 15 years of age travel half price.

Boarding and Luggage

The numbers of passengers and crew on board are counted under law and on longer routes passengers must also complete a registration card. Check in is usually ten minutes prior to departure on the shorter routes, and 30 minutes on the longer routes. Check individual timetables for the route you plan to travel on and also remember to allow sufficient time for connections to other transport, allowing for delays if possible. The weight limit for luggage is 40kg but you must be able to carry it on board yourself in one trip, although there are no specifics on how many bags you may take. Elderly or infirm passengers may seek assistance when taking luggage on board, however there is no checked baggage service offered, with the exception of the Ullapool to Stornoway route for Citylink passengers. Bikes may be taken on all ferries free of charge, and these are loaded onto the car decks by the rider.

On Board

The ships of Caledonian MacBrayne vary in size and facilities offered. All ships have deck space, an enclosed passenger lounge and toilet facilities. The larger vessels have extra facilities such as a choice of comfortable lounges, shop, bar, café and self service restaurant. Ships are allocated to routes so that longer distance journeys have more facilities appropriate to the length of journey. CalMac ships do not offer first class accommodations on any route, nor overnight cabins as all sailings are covered in daylight hours.

Travelling with Northlink Ferries

Northlink Ferries operate the longest domestic ferry routes in Scotland to the northern isles of Orkney and Shetland. Their ships are larger than those of CalMac and offer greater amenities appropriate to the longer journeys, including overnight cabins. There are three routes to choose from. If travelling to Thurso there is a short bus link from the railway station to the pier for the sailing to Orkney. This is a short 90 minute crossing, although the ship has excellent facilities. At Aberdeen there is a choice of sailings to Orkney or Shetland. The ships are modern and extremely comfortable for these scenic journeys to the north.

Reservations and Tickets

These longer distance sailings often fill up quickly in the busy season so reservations are recommended for foot passengers on the routes from Aberdeen. Also anyone wishing a cabin should always make a reservation as they can sell out quickly. It is possible to book online at www.northlinkferries.co.uk or by telephone on 0845 6000449. There are also booking offices at both the Scrabster (Thurso) and Aberdeen ferry terminals. There are no through rail tickets offered but holders of Freedom of Scotland Travelpasses may obtain a 20% discount off all seated fares on all routes. Reservations are not so important for foot passengers on the Scrabster to Orkney route as the ship has a large capacity.

Boarding and Luggage

All passengers are required to have photographic ID, which includes passports, national identity card or photographic driving licences. You will also receive a unique booking number which you must have with you to check in. Check in times are available from the company and vary for each terminal. Remember also to factor in transport and walking times to each of the terminal buildings, advice is available from Northlink. The check in closes 30 minutes prior to departure on all routes and passengers arriving after this time cannot travel. Bikes are carried free on all sailings. They are not classed as hand luggage and must be taken on board to the vehicle decks. Northlink offers a checked luggage service on all routes so passengers should only take items they require for the crossing onto the ship with them. Remember to take a coat or jacket if you are planning going out on deck. Other luggage is checked in and may be collected at your destination.

On Board

The purpose built ships offer a very high level of service. Upon boarding at Aberdeen passengers may choose from the self service restaurant or enjoy a beautiful meal in the ship's à la carte restaurant which is open during the summer season. There are also comfortable lounges, shops, play areas, a bar, cinema and plenty of open deck space from which to enjoy the ever changing coastline, wildlife and sunsets over the North Sea. More detail on the crossings is provided in the main entries for Orkney and Shetland.

Travel by Coach

Long distance coaches are operated by Citylink or Megabus over most of the Scottish mainland, while West Coast Motors provides service along the west coast of Scotland from Glasgow north through Argyll and the islands to Oban. Coaches usually have around 50 reclining seats with individual settings for fresh air, tray tables and reading lights. Some modern coaches are also air conditioned and most have a basic toilet on board. They offer a comfortable way of getting around locations which might not be rail connected and many routes are included in the Freedom of Scotland Travelpass. Coach services can get very busy so ideally you should make a reservation in advance for the journey you intend to make. Luggage is usually limited to one larger item and a carry on item. Bikes are not carried on coach services, so you are best to cycle these parts of your journey. Tickets may be booked online or from large bus stations. For people touring Scotland, the Citylink unlimited travel tickets offer excellent value for money and can offer savings over touring by train. Contact Citylink (www.citylink.co.uk) or see their website for details. Some journeys may be booked as part of a rail journey, ask when booking your ticket.

Local bus travel can often be included in your train ticket with Plusbus (see www.plusbus.info). Using this system saves having to carry change and as the tickets offer unlimited local bus travel are often much cheaper than buying a ticket on the bus.

Travel by Car

In remote areas, such as the north west, rural Aberdeenshire and the islands, car travel can be an attractive option with free parking and quiet roads. Car hire is available from many Scottish railway stations. Local car hire companies will almost always collect and deliver to the local railway station so just check that there is a car hire company close to the station you intend to use.

Those wishing to hire a car from their arrival station should be aware that a valid driving licence is required. A foreign licence is usually valid if from the EU or North America and many other locations. Driving is on the left and a copy of the 'Highway Code' should be purchased to familiarise yourself with local rules and laws. Also note that petrol is expensive in the UK and keep in mind that congestion is a problem in almost all areas, even in many rural towns and locations. Parking is almost always charged and expensive in all sizes of towns. If on a motoring holiday, most stations provide parking which is sometimes free to railway travellers. Tourist railways and many ferry terminals will offer free parking for motorists taking day trips.

Air Travel

Although Scotland is a small country it can take a relatively long time to travel between places, especially the islands. It is rarely an issue for the visitor who will be keen to enjoy the scenery. However if you would like to visit a location but don't have the time, travelling even one way by air may make your visit possible. Domestic airline services are a Flybe franchise which is operated by the Scottish airline, Loganair. There are services from Inverness, Aberdeen, Glasgow and Edinburgh to the Scottish Islands and between Edinburgh and Wick on the mainland. Air fares can be expensive so book ahead for the best deals. One useful thing about air tickets, is that they tend to be sold as single fares, so there is no cost advantage in buying a return ticket. This can be useful for visitors who might wish to travel by ferry one way, and air the other.

Timetables

Public transport operators in Scotland do not tend to co-ordinate their services and make it hard for passengers to plan journeys by not providing details of services provided by other operators. However the Scottish Government has an excellent website called Traveline Scotland. The journey planner will provide a personal timetable between any two locations or postcodes in Scotland, making use of rail, bus, coach, subway, ferry and air services. You can use Traveline at the website, www.travelinescotland.com or telephone their 24 hour call centre on 0871 2002233. You can also get bus times for any bus stop in Scotland direct to your mobile phone. See www.nextbuses.mobi.

Part 2. Journeys by Rail and Sea

7. The East Coast – Edinburgh to Aberdeen

Scotland's east coast overlooks the North Sea; a large shallow sea surrounded by landscapes which are largely the result of ancient glacial activity. The east of Scotland is fertile farm country with old historic towns and rolling hills. Here you will find most of the oldest buildings and towns in Scotland. The railway from Edinburgh north to Aberdeen hugs the coastline for most of the route with the resulting spectacular sea views. It connects the Capital with the Scotland's oil capital – Aberdeen. Along the way there is the chance to visit Arbroath (famous for the Declaration of Arbroath, and the Arbroath Smokie), historic Montrose, St Andrews – home of Scotland's oldest university – and Dundee with Captain Scott's ship 'Discovery'. The total journey time from end to end is only around two and a half hours.

The journey takes you over the world famous Forth Railway Bridge which has probably taken part in more product endorsements than many celebrities. It also takes in coastline, farmland, pleasant small towns and some of the world's most famous golf courses including those at Carnoustie. The journey's end at Aberdeen could just as easily be the start of another adventure as it is also the beginning of the northern line to Inverness via Elgin and the departure point for ferries to the northern isles of Orkney and Shetland which is described in chapter eight.

Journey Summary

Route:	Edinburgh – Kirkcaldy – Leuchars – Dundee – Arbroath – Montrose – Aberdeen.
Operator:	Scotrail with some East Coast and Cross Country services.
Trains:	Scotrail with standard and first class. Most trains have a trolley service. East Coast trains have standard and first class coaches, a café / restaurant car and luggage vans at each end of the train.
Trip Length:	2 hours 25 minutes.
Frequency:	19 trains each way daily over entire route. Additional trains over parts of route.
Links:	From Edinburgh, East Coast and Cross Country trains to England and the overnight sleeper service to London. Ferry service from Aberdeen to Northern Isles. Bus link from Edinburgh Waverley and Haymarket stations direct to Edinburgh Airport. Local bus services at all towns along the route. Bus link from Leuchars station to St Andrews.

Edinburgh

We start our journey through Scotland in Edinburgh. This is a beautiful city which is filled with distinctive Scottish architecture and history. When you step off the train and emerge from Waverley station, you will find yourself in the very heart of the city. The large park outside the station is Princes Street gardens, a public park surrounded by many of the city's greatest buildings and views. To the north of the Gardens are the main shopping streets while to the south is 'The Mound' and Castle looking down over the city from its hill top position behind the railway. The city centre has two distinct parts, divided by Princes Street Gardens. To the north is the New Town with its dignified Georgian Houses and well laid out streets which are a lasting testimony to the city's desire to improve conditions. To the south is the Old Town, which unusually, rather than being demolished to make way for the new, survives. The Old Town, in contrast to the New Town, consists of alleys and tightly packed closes. It is associated in popular imagination with the body snatchers Burke and Hare, and Deacon Brodie, inspiration for Stevenson's novel 'Dr Jekyll and Mr Hyde'.

Edinburgh is Scotland's capital city and home to the Scottish Royal Palace of Holyrood and the Scottish Parliament. The city is large enough to take on the feel of a capital city but small enough to remain easy to explore. The city centre has Princes Street and the Royal Mile as its focal points and is easy to explore on foot. Alternatively the city has an excellent bus service. Open top tour buses are also available allowing visitors to hop on and off all day at places of interest.

Practicalities

Waverley Railway station is located in the city centre and within walking distance of all the main attractions. Taxis are located inside the station while local buses leave from outside on Waverley Bridge and Princes Street. Waverley Station is a busy terminal with all facilities provided including a booking office, toilets, showers, shops, cash points, left luggage, information and places to eat. Another station, Haymarket, is located slightly to the west of Waverley and some travellers may find this station more convenient depending on their destination. Haymarket is an attractive Georgian style building and also has taxis and buses available outside. Being a smaller station it lacks most of the facilities of Waverley, although does have a booking office.

Local Transport. Local bus services are mainly provided by First Bus and Lothian Transport. The Edinburgh bus network is excellent and inexpensive to use. Look out for day tickets. A special bus operates between the airport, city centre, and both railway stations and departs up to every 15 minutes all day. Plusbus railway tickets are valid on Edinburgh buses. Unlimited travel is available on Lothian Buses, First, Stagecoach, MacTours, MacEwan Coaches, Munro's of Jedburgh and E&M Horsburgh. The only excluded services are the Airlink 100 (the airport bus), sightseeing buses and 'N' night services. Telephone Traveline on 0871 2002233, or see www.lothianbuses.co.uk for information.

Tourist Information. There is a tourist information centre located on Princess Street (EH2 2QP) near the Waverley Railway Station – telephone 0845 2255121. Another is located at Edinburgh International Airport (EH12 9DN). Both are open year round.

Places of Interest – City Centre

The best way to explore the city centre is on foot, although open top sightseeing and regular buses do run to all parts. Open top sightseeing buses depart from Waverley Bridge, above Waverley Station while local city services depart from stances along Princes Street, outside the station.

On leaving the Station, visitors are in the heart of the city and the famous shopping street of **Princes Street**. Jenners, the famous Edinburgh department store, is close to the Station entrance. The Street however is particularly pleasant having shops on only one side. On the opposite side is **Princes Street Gardens**, a large open park right beside the Station. The Gardens are one of the most popular outdoor spaces in the city with views to the Castle which stands on a rock overlooking them. Just inside the Gardens entrance is a large monument in honour of the Scottish writer, Sir Walter Scott. The **Scott Monument** has a series of viewing platforms which visitors may climb to finally reach a height of 61 metres. Continue on a little further through the Gardens to find the **National Galleries of Scotland** including the **National Portrait Gallery**. The National Gallery houses part of the national collection, which includes works by almost every major figure of Western art, from the Early Renaissance to the end of the 19th century. The Portrait Gallery displays paintings of many of the most significant people in Scottish life over the years. Both offer free admission except for special exhibits and are open year round.

In the opposite direction to Princes Street Gardens is **Calton Hill** which is easily climbed for views over the city and out to the Firth of Forth and Fife. As well as the beautiful view there are a number of interesting buildings on the Hill. The **Nelson Monument** is designed in the shape of an upturned telescope and is in honour of Admiral Lord Nelson's victory at Trafalgar. The structure with the large columns is the **National Monument**, built in honour of those who died in the Napoleonic Wars. It is modelled on the Parthenon in Athens but appears incomplete. It is uncertain whether this was intentional or whether it was intended to complete the building. Continuing from Calton Hill down into the city again you may make your way towards Holyrood and Arthur's Seat.

Holyrood is the home of the new **Scottish Parliament** building which is open for tours on most days. The building was completed in 1994 and makes extensive use of wood and concrete to resemble something of an upturned boat. Opposite is **Holyrood Palace**, the official residence of the

Monarch in Scotland. A palace was completed here in 1501 and gradually developed over the years until the final reconstruction between 1671 and 1679 which gave the building its present form. Holyrood is still used today when the Queen is in Scotland on State business. The elegant building is a great photo opportunity while the interiors, including the Royal apartments, are open to the public when the Royal Family are not in residence. There is also a Royal art gallery located opposite the Palace which was opened in 2002 and displays works from the main Royal collection. See www.royalcollection.org.uk for opening times and admission charges. The Palace is a 15 minute walk from the Station. Adjacent to the Palace are the ruins of **Holyrood Abbey**. The Abbey was founded in 1127 by King David I but has been a ruin since 1768 when a hurricane damaged the roof leading to its collapse. The Abbey has hosted many royal coronations and weddings over the years prior to its abandonment. Admission is included in tickets to the Palace. A visit to the area should be combined, time permitting, with walking in **Holyrood Park** which is also known as the Queen's Park. This former hunting estate is a 600 acre public park in the centre of Edinburgh which is very popular with walkers. **Arthur's Seat,** a 250 metre high hill, is the most famous geological feature of the Park. However there are many other hills, cliffs, glens and three lochs within the Park. There are a number of recommended walking routes (see boards when you arrive) and it is easy to spend an entire day enjoying its features. The Park is managed by Historic Scotland and is open year round with free admission. There is a park ranger service.

Holyrood Palace and Park are at the end of the famous street to Edinburgh Castle, known as the **Royal Mile**. This straight mile long street heads uphill past the Station to the Castle through an area known as the **Old Town**. This part of the city retains its tenements, closes, courtyards and medieval atmosphere. This was Scottish city life for hundreds of years. The area is a popular tourist destination now, not only for the Old Town but also for some of Scotland's most important buildings, including the Scottish High Courts, Edinburgh University and the city library, which have been constructed in the area. To experience domestic life 400 years ago in this part of the town, visit **Gladstone's Land** (477b Lawnmarket, EH1 2NT). The ground floor is a recreated 17th century shop while the upper stories show what housing would have been like for a merchant family in this part of town where space restrictions meant the buildings were built upwards as the first 'high rise' housing developments. The National Trust owns this property, and it is open all year with an admission charge.

The area is also home to most of the city's museums. Edinburgh City Council has two significant museums on the Royal Mile. The **Museum of Edinburgh** (142 Canongate, Royal Mile, EH8 8DD) has many fascinating exhibits including the National Covenant and fine Edinburgh glass, while the **Museum of Childhood** (42 High Street, Royal Mile, EH1 1TG) tells the story of childhood through the years. It is known as the nosiest museum in the world! Both are open year round with free admission.

Stay in the Old Town area for one of the country's best national museums, the **National Museum of Scotland** (Chambers Street). This is the new name for what were once the Royal Museum and the adjacent Museum of Scotland. The original building was completed in 1888 in the Venetian Renaissance style and contrasts with the glass roofed main hall which was inspired by the Crystal Palace in London. There are collections on geology, archaeology, natural history, science, technology and art from across the world, including an ancient Egyptian hall. It is truly a museum which will fascinate both children and adults with an interest in the world. The rest of the museum houses the collections on Scottish history, people and culture. Both museums offer free admission.

Mid point on the Royal Mile is the amazing **St Giles Cathedral**. The four central pillars are said to date from 1124 and it is known that the church was the focal point of the church in Edinburgh for 900 years. Today visitors may explore the church daily, enjoying its architecture, stained glass windows and traditional crown topped spire. Significantly, it was the church of John Knox during the Reformation and it is filled with history to be explored. There are daily services which are open to all. Outside is a large square. Many of these squares were the site of markets in past times. Located at the top of the Royal Mile is Edinburgh Castle.

Edinburgh Castle. Perched on an imposing volcanic crag, the Castle dominates the Capital and overlooks Princes Street Gardens. Although the most famous of Edinburgh's castles, there are in fact another two which are also open to the public – read on to find out about them. Its role in Scottish history over hundreds of years may be discovered inside. The castle is perfectly preserved and today still holds the Scottish Crown Jewels. The three main items are the Crown, the Sceptre, and the Sword of State. Another Edinburgh tradition is the one o'clock gun. At one o'clock each day a gun (formerly cannon) is fired to announce the time. In the past a real cannon ball was shot over the city!

To the north of the Castle is Princes Street, which marks the start of the **New Town**. Built in stages from 1765 this is an excellent preserved area of neo classical design and urban planning and is designated as a world heritage site along with the Old Town. **The Georgian House** is situated in Robert Adam's masterpiece of design, Charlotte Square. This Georgian Square of houses is in contrast to the Old Town already mentioned. The National Trust has restored the House to be as near as possible to its original condition, complete with interior furnishings and it now shows a typical 17th century house in this part of town when those who could afford to escaped from the cramped Old Town conditions. It is open year round and has an admission charge.

Places of Interest – Other Areas of Edinburgh

Edinburgh's other castles are Lauriston Castle and Craigmillar Castle. **Lauriston Castle** (2a Cramond Road, EH4 5GD) is in fact a 19th century mansion built around a 16th century traditional tower castle. Set in 30 acres of parkland and overlooking the waters of the Forth, it has a wonderful location. Inside, its Edwardian interiors remain as they were in 1926 when the last owners left and it was gifted to the nation. It is open year round and there is an admission charge. See www.edinburgh.gov.uk for information. Regular city buses run from Princes Street to the Castle and fares are included in Plusbus tickets. The third castle in Edinburgh is **Craigmillar Castle**. Craigmillar was begun in the 15th century and is an impressive structure and one of the best preserved medieval castles in the country, despite being ruined. Highlights of a visit include the Great Hall, Chapel and the views over Edinburgh city centre including Holyrood and Edinburgh Castle from the top of the tower. It is open year round and has an admission charge. See Historic Scotland for details. City buses run regularly from the city centre and are included in Plusbus rail tickets to Edinburgh.

The Royal Botanical Garden (Inverleith Row, EH3 5LR) is one of the world's premier botanical gardens set in 72 acres. The site is so large it is hard to imagine that you are actually just one mile from the city centre. Visitors may enjoy the Victorian Palm House which is the tallest in the world, other tropical glasshouses, stroll amongst Giant Redwoods and enjoy the Chinese Hillside. The Garden is open all year and has free admission. The Garden is a half hour walk from Waverley station or catch a city bus which is included in Plusbus train tickets. See www.rbge.org.uk. Staying with the theme of nature but moving to the west end is **Edinburgh Zoo**. The Zoo is owned by the Royal Zoological Society and has been educating visitors since 1913 when the Zoo opened. There are currently over 1000 animals on the 82 acre site. It is the only UK place where it is possible to view koalas, but is perhaps most famous for its penguins and the daily penguin parade where you may meet them up close. It is open year round and has an admission charge. Regular buses run from Princes Street (Waverley Station) and outside Haymarket Station to the Zoo and are included in Plusbus tickets.

Britannia. The former Royal Yacht Britannia is now permanently moored in the Port of Leith. During the life of the Yacht, heads of state and others were entertained on board. However it was firstly the floating home of the British Royal Family. All parts of the ship are now included on the tour including the State rooms, the Family's private rooms, the bridge, engine room and the behind the scenes areas where the yachtsmen of the Royal Navy busily kept the ship working. There is an admission charge and it is open year round. To get there take a city bus (included in Plusbus tickets) or open top tour bus from city centre. www.royalyachtbritannia.co.uk.

The Journey to Aberdeen

Departing Edinburgh the train begins its journey north, first crossing the famous Forth Railway Bridge before making a scenic coastal journey through Fife. The tracks are 46 metres (150 feet) above sea level giving wonderful views along the waters of the Forth as the train crosses. To find out about places to visit and stations on this section of railway see Chapter 9 'The Fife Circle', which shares this section of railway.

Markinch Station. The first stop after Kirkcaldy (described in Chapter 9) is Markinch. The Station at Markinch is staffed with a ticket office open Monday to Saturday, has a public phone, toilet facilities and waiting shelters. The Station is a modern building but with a traditional pitched slate roof. It is located on the town's High Street and regular bus services depart from the Station for Glenrothes (which has its own station on the Fife Circle Line) and Leven.

Ladybank for Falkland. Ladybank Railway Station is situated on Commercial Road in Ladybank (KY15 7JS). The station has waiting shelters and a ticket office staffed for the morning peak hours only. This station is useful for reaching the nearby village of Falkland. There are several bus routes, but the most convenient is number 64A for Falkland. It departs from outside the Station and takes about 19 minutes, dropping you off only 100 metres from Falkland Palace and times allow for you to depart mid morning from Ladybank and return in the late afternoon. **Falkland** is nestled at the foot of the attractive Lomond Hills and was the first village in Britain to be designated a conservation zone due to the large number of historic buildings. There are a total of twenty eight listed buildings in the village and almost every street and building is character filled. The Village also boasts Britain's oldest tennis courts, Falkland Palace Tennis Court (1539), and an old horse market.

It is for **Falkland Palace** (KY15 7BU), however, that most people journey here. The Palace is the only former Royal residence under the care of the National Trust for Scotland. Built between 1450 and 1541 by James IV and James V it was a country residence of the Stuart monarchs of Scotland for over 200 years. Today it dominates the main street of Falkland, but once inside the Palace gardens nestled in the hills you would be forgiven for thinking that you are in the country. The Palace is an impressive Renaissance building and unlike many other buildings of this date in Scotland is almost fully restored and furnished giving a perspective which others such as Linlithgow cannot now offer in their ruined, but preserved, condition. The interior has many fascinating rooms including the keeper's apartment, bake house, chapel and the tapestry gallery. Outside, the gardens have beautiful lawns, trees and borders. The Palace is open from early March until late October. There is an entry fee and it has toilet facilities and a shop. See the National Trust website for details – www.nts.org.uk or telephone 0844 4932186.

Return to the train to continue to the next stop at **Springfield Station** (KY15 5QY). The Station offers useful bus connections to several nearby villages, although most train services do not stop here. The train travels beside the River Eden between Springfield and just after Cupar Station. There are some attractive low level hills on the right hand side of the train while the countryside is predominantly farmland through this part of Fife.

Leuchars (for St Andrews)

Leuchars Station (Junction Road, KY16 0AA) comes as almost a surprise to the traveller with its location apparently set in the fields. However, on the other side of the Station is RAF Leuchars and the village it is named after. The station is staffed for most departures, has a ticket office, ticket vending machine, pay phone, waiting room and toilets. Since the short-sighted closure of the railway line to St Andrews, Leuchars is now the nearest station for the popular university town. Buses depart from a dedicated bus stance at the Station every 15 minutes during the day for St Andrews Bus Station six miles away. Through rail and bus tickets are available to the town, and the St Andrews bus station has a full railway ticket office.

Shortly after leaving the station, the bus turns to travel alongside the River Eden Bay leading out to the North Sea. On the opposite shore is RAF Leuchars. Soon the spires of the ancient university town of St Andrews come into view and the bus arrives at the central bus station.

St Andrews as a settlement has existed since the Dark Ages. By 1150 it was established as the centre of the Scottish Church. In 1413 Scotland's first university, and the third oldest in the English speaking world, was established here. The University of St Andrews has existed continually since then and is the oldest university in Scotland. The town is also known throughout the world as the home of golf. The origins of golf may be in ancient Roman or Chinese culture, but the current most popular belief is that it began in Scotland at St Andrews. In 1754 the first golf club was established which became the Royal and Ancient Club in 1834 and is the first landmark you will see as you arrive into the town. Today St Andrews is a historic and largely unspoilt resort on the shores of St Andrews Bay. The small size of the town, with three main streets, makes exploring on foot easy.

Places of Interest

St Andrews University. Established in 1413 and proud of its status as Scotland's first University, St Andrews hit the headlines in recent years when the heir to the British throne, Prince William, decided to take his undergraduate studies there. After spending any length of time at all in the town it soon becomes apparent that the very layout of the town is built around the University. While still a functioning university and therefore not open to the public, there are many fine buildings that visitors may enjoy viewing externally. St Salvator's College was established in 1450 and the college chapel, tower and a tenement building (adjoining to the west of tower) and are still in use today. St Salvator's is also the location of the attractive 1930's university hall of residence of the same name. The College was merged with the 1511 St Leonard's College in 1747 when the University was in decline. However the University still owns the **St Leonard's Chapel** dating from the 1400's, a small intimate chapel in the grounds of the St Leonard's school in South Street. Before leaving the St Salvator's site though take some time to visit the St Salvator's Chapel, often open for visitors during the day. The impressive building with spire visible for miles around was completed in 1450 and is the highlight of North Street. See www.st-andrews.ac.uk for details of church services. If you are visiting on Sunday look out for the traditional after service Pier Walk from St Salvator's down the St Andrews Pier by students dressed in their gowns. Arts and science students wear bright red gowns while the divinity students wear dark gowns. The pier wall is rather narrow for a walk on windy days but no student has been lost yet! Located on 'The Scores', behind North Street, is the University's new Museum opened in 2008 to display some of the University's collection of over a hundred thousand artefacts. It is open year round and has free entry. The Museum will also let you know about other significant sites around the town belonging to the University.

Patrick Hamilton Memorial. Patrick Hamilton was an able student of the University who by the age of 24 had become Abbot of Fern Abbey, studied at Paris University and became a member of the University of St Andrews. While he was on the Continent he heard the teaching of the reformer, Martin Luther, and his preaching of the Gospel that anyone could know God without needing to go through the priesthood and church. This was truth, but it challenged the power of the establishment, and so he was burned on the spot now marked outside St Salvator's Chapel between 12 noon and 6 pm on the 28th of February 1528.

St Andrews Cathedral. Appropriately after hearing the story of Patrick Hamilton continue to the end of North Street and St Andrews Cathedral which fell into disuse after the Reformation of 1560. The Cathedral was established in 1158 and continued until the Reformation although storms and fires resulted in it being reconstructed several times. It was Scotland's largest cathedral and the museum today shows what it would have looked like when complete. Within the grounds there is a square tower. This is St Rule's Tower, the only surviving part of the 1127 St Rule's Chapel built to house the relics of St Andrew. The Cathedral is open all year and there is an admission charge. See www.historic-scotland.gov.uk or telephone 01334 472563 to find out more. The postcode is KY16 9QL. The Cathedral has a joint entry ticket with St Andrews Castle, located on the Scores, around the corner from the Cathedral.

St Andrews Castle is situated on a rock overlooking St Andrews Bay. It was the main residence of the Bishops and Archbishops of St Andrews Cathedral. Highlights include The Hamilton Façade on the entrance, a testimony to the power and wealth of its owners. Inside there is a mine and counter mine, giving an impression of medieval siege warfare. There is also the most infamous bottle dungeon where it is thought that John Knox and George Wishart may have been imprisoned who also suffered along with Patrick Hamilton for teaching the truth and challenging those in power at the time of the Reformation. The Castle was therefore a key site in the playing out of the Scottish Reformation. It is open year round and has a joint entry ticket with the Cathedral.

At the other end of town is **The West Port** on South Street, one of the few surviving city gates in Scotland, built in 1589 and renovated in 1843.

Botanical Gardens. The Gardens extend over seven hectares with many different climatic zones represented between the outdoor areas and greenhouses. There are numerous rare plants at this internationally recognised facility which is also a beautiful place to walk around and take photographs. The Gardens are located at Canongate (KY16 8RT), near the Bus Station. They are open year round and there is an admission charge. See www.st-andrews-botanic.org for details or telephone 01334 476452.

St Andrews Museum. The Museum tells the story of St Andrews including major displays on golf, tourism and the University. The displays therefore are wider ranging regarding local history than those of the St Andrews University Museum. It is located in Kinburn Park, next to the Bus Station, and has free entry and a café.

The **St Andrews Aquarium** (The Scores, KY16 9AS) has a wealth of marine life for visitors to come face to face with. From seahorses to frogs, the Aquarium not only displays these amazing creatures but also educates visitors about them. Perhaps the cutest residents though are the seals and the two resident adult seals on permanent display. Children in particular never forget their first visit with these creatures. See www.standrews aquarium.co.uk or telephone 01334 474786 for details of opening times and admission charges.

West and East Sands. Located at opposite sides of St Andrews with the town in the middle the two long sandy beaches of West Sands and East Sands offer a pleasant place for families to enjoy beach activities and relaxation. Both have toilet and café facilities and are located only 15 minutes walk from the Bus Station.

Returning to the train at Leuchars, the journey continues north and after a few miles the train crosses the long **Tay Bridge**. The Bridge over the Tay is approximately three and a half kilometres long and crosses the attractive Firth of Tay. This is a much more modest bridge than the Forth crossing but still awards the passenger fine views. The present day bridge is a replacement for an earlier one which collapsed in 1879 during a storm with a train on it. Over seventy people drowned when the train sank into the Tay. The remains of the piers of that bridge may still be seen in the water to the right of the train. Immediately after crossing the bridge the train arrives at Dundee Station.

Dundee

The city of Dundee has a long industrial past. Famous for the Discovery ship, the D.C Thomson Publishers, jam and jute, the City now has much to offer the visitor. The restored and pedestrian friendly city centre is focused on City Square with the impressive Caird Hall as its focal point. Streets radiate out from here with shops and most of the city's notable buildings. When walking east along the High Street, look out for the former tram lines now embedded as history in the new paving.

Practicalities

Dundee Railway Station on South Union Street (DD1 4BY) is the main station for the city. It has a ticket office open for most departures, ticket vending machines, toilets, café, newsagent, toilets, payphones, British Transport Police office and waiting rooms.

The Tourist Information Centre is located at Discovery Point, next to the RRS Discovery, outside the Railway Station. Most attractions are within walking distance, but Plusbus may be added to your train ticket if required.

Places of Interest

Without wishing to spoil the surprise that would otherwise greet you on arrival at Dundee's Railway Station, it would be useful to know that the **RRS Discovery** ship is right across the street from the Station. This area is known as Discovery Point. The RRS Discovery, apart from being a beautiful fully rigged tall ship, is the ship in which the heroes Captain Scott and Ernest Shackleton set sail for the Antarctic for in 1901, the same year as the ship was launched. They arrived in January 1902 and were to remain ice bound for two years before breaking free to return in 1904. At great personal risk they and their team charted the Antarctic, discovered it was a continent and accumulated enough scientific research to fill ten volumes. The ship returned to Dundee in 1986 and is now the highlight of the Discovery Point Exhibition Centre. The Centre itself is housed in a modern but very attractive building built for the purpose. Visit displays and information in the Centre before boarding the ship itself to see round almost its entire structure to get a real insight to what life must have been like on board. The Ship is open all year round and there is an admission charge. See www.rrsdiscovery.com or telephone 01382 309060 for details.

Verdant Works (West Henderson's Wynd, DD1 5BT). By 1883 50,000 people were employed in 100 jute mills in Dundee. The City was the jute capital of the world and made its fortune through this natural substance. Jute is a natural material and extremely versatile. It had an almost unlimited number of uses from bags to shoes, ropes to sacking. Verdant Works was one of those jute mills. In an age when women did not tend to have jobs, the mills employed almost exclusively women and children. This resulted in the men of the city looking after children at home. By 1950 there were only 39 mills left and in 1998 the last mill closed. Perhaps in this environmentally friendly age it is ironic that this natural, sustainable and biodegradable product has been replaced by plastic. Perhaps you might be inspired and 'discover' this material for another generation with your visit! The works is a great family day out and is open year round and has an admission charge. Find out more at www.rrsdiscovery.com (Verdant Works and RRS Discovery are owned by the same trust and share a website) or telephone 01382 309060. The Works are an 18 minute walk from the station. There is a bus route but it takes about 14 minutes so is not worth using unless it's raining!

McManus Galleries (Albert Square, DD1 1DA). The extravagant Gothic Revival style building comes as a surprise at the end of an otherwise normal pedestrian shopping street. Opened in 1867, it was named after Prince Albert, Queen Victoria's late husband, and was originally called the Albert Institute. The Galleries house collections of fine and decorative art together with history displays. The main Galleries are free to visit. See www.mcmanus.co.uk or telephone 01382 432350 for details. The Galleries are a 12 minute walk from the Railway Station.

Dundee Rep Theatre (Tay Square, DD1 1PB). The Theatre is home to Scotland's only resident ensemble company of actors. It is a popular venue for theatre, dance, music and comedy. The Theatre is a two minute walk from the Railway Station. Seat prices vary according to seat and performance. There is a restaurant and bar on site. See www.dundee rep.co.uk, or telephone the box office on 01382 223530 to find out about current performances.

Caird Hall (City Square, DD1 3BB). The magnificent Caird Hall was sponsored by the jute manufacturer, Sir James Caird, and constructed between 1914 and 1922. The grand concert hall is restored to its period splendour complete with the great organ. Today opera, ballet, comedy, choral, classical, pop/rock and traditional concerts are programmed throughout the year. To find out what is on see www.cairdhall.co.uk or telephone 01382 434451. The Hall is in the heart of the pedestrian friendly city centre and is a six minute walk from the Station.

Mills Observatory (Glamis Road, Balgay Park, DD2 2UB). John Mills was a linen manufacturer and keen amateur scientist. Using funding from a bequest he made, the observatory was opened in 1935. It is notable as being the only observatory in the UK to be built with the sole intention of encouraging public interest in science. It is also the only one which is regularly open to the public. The Observatory is in Balgay Park. Take city bus 2A from Union Street (two minutes from the Station) to the Park. Bus fares are included in Dundee Plusbus train tickets. Admission is free and the dome is open each weekday evening between October and March for stargazing.

The other railway station in Dundee is **Broughty Ferry** (DD5 2DX). The station consists of just a platform and a public phone. Unfortunately few trains call here, so you are probably better to travel to Dundee Station in the city centre and take a bus out. These journeys are included in Plusbus train tickets so you don't need to buy a separate bus ticket.

Broughty Ferry is now a suburb of Dundee and is a strange mix of former jute mill owners' mansions on the hill and small former fishermen's cottages by the sea. There are lots of good pubs and restaurants and it is a popular place to head out to on summer evenings. The main attraction is **Broughty Castle and Museum** (Castle Approach, DD5 2TF), situated right by the shoreline. It is a few minutes walk from the bus stop or station. The Castle sits on a rock on the mouth of the Tay. Architecturally pleasing, it was constructed in 1496 and today houses a museum with displays on local history, environment and wildlife. The Castle is a free attraction and is open year round. Check www.dundeecity.gov.uk for opening times.

The train continues through the stations at Monifieth and Balmossie, both of which are communities effectively joined to Dundee now. Look out for the large sandy expanses of Monifieth Sands on the right. After these settlements the line begins to curve north again and travels alongside the North Sea with great views from the right side of the train for most of the remainder of the journey to Aberdeen. On the left side of the train are farms and mainly pastoral country scenes. Look out for **Barry Links Station**. Since local rail services were withdrawn in 1990 it has become the least busy station in the United Kingdom which is not surprising since only one train a day stops here. Hopefully one day a better service may be restored. The train will also probably rush through the next station, Golf Street, which serves the nearby Carnoustie Golf Links which sometimes hosts the Open Championships. There are usually special trains to this station on these occasions, although the nearby main Carnoustie station is also convenient.

Carnoustie

The station at Carnoustie (DD7 6AY) is unstaffed but has a ticket vending machine and waiting shelters. Carnoustie is most famous as a golfing centre. Carnoustie Golf Links are located right outside the station and are the most convenient of the four local links for the rail traveller. They are also the home of the Open Championship when it is in town. See www.carnoustiegolflinks.co.uk for details.

On leaving Carnoustie Station the train travels alongside the rocky shoreline which then turns sandy. On a clear day there are fine views out over the North Sea again at this point.

Arbroath

The town of Arbroath is perhaps most famous for the Declaration of Arbroath, the Abbey and the Smokie. The Declaration of Arbroath was a letter signed by 53 nobles and magistrates on the 6th of April 1320 declaring Scottish independence. The Declaration is dated at Arbroath Abbey, however the link is not to an actual meeting having taken place there, but that the writer was the Abbot there and it was drafted at his office. The Arbroath Smokie is a haddock preserved in salt and then prepared over a hardwood fire to give it the unique taste. What better place to try this famous fish than in its hometown! Today Arbroath is a pleasant and well preserved historic town situated beside the sea with a fine stone harbour which is a pleasant place to spend some time.

Practicalities

Arbroath railway station, Keptie Street, DD11 1RQ, is located in the heart of the town. The station was built in 1848 and has an attractive stone building with traditional slate roof. The station is staffed with a ticket office, waiting room, luggage trolleys, pay phone, ticket vending machine and toilets. Until November 2008 it was still possible to see the old goods yard and substantial goods shed. At one time almost every station had these facilities for transporting almost every item coming into or leaving a town. Even the old loading gauge still survived. This is a wooden post suspended over the tracks so that unusual loads could be checked to make sure they would not foul bridges along the route. Unfortunately the shed was demolished and the relics cleared and a piece of history disappeared.

Places of Interest

Arbroath Abbey. Founded in 1178 by King William the Lion, the Abbey's most famous hour came in 1320 when the Declaration of Arbroath was written there. The Abbey was inhabited at first by Tironensian monks from Kelso Abbey in the Borders area of Scotland. Over the years it continued to be an important religious site until after the Scottish Reformation. Although monks still lived at the site they gradually died off and the building became a quarry for stone. By 1700 it reached the ruined condition it remains in today. Still impressive today is the Abbey's twin towers and the Abbot's House, the best preserved structure of its kind in Britain. The Abbey is six minutes walking from the railway station, in fact just a couple of streets away. It is owned by Historic Scotland and there is an admission charge. It is open year round. See www.historic-scotland.gov.uk or telephone 01241 878756 for details.

Arbroath Museum and Signal Tower (Ladyloan, DD11 1PU). The Signal Tower was constructed as the shore base of the Bell Rock Lighthouse. The Bell Rock is famous as being perhaps the most difficult lighthouse ever to have been built and as such is known as one of the seven industrial wonders of the world. It also holds the distinction of being the oldest sea washed lighthouse in existence. The Signal Tower provided a shore base and residences for the keepers. On top of the building there is a large ball which can be hoisted up or down to signal to the lighthouse located 12 miles offshore. The building today houses a museum with displays on the lighthouse and the local area. It has free admission and is open all year round. Telephone 01241 875598 for details. The Tower is located beside the Harbour, a five minute walk from the Station.

If visiting with children, take a visit to the Links, a large grassy area with beach which is ideal for family picnics and games. It is also home to **Kerr's Miniature Railway**. This miniature railway has operated since 1935 and is popular with children. See www.kerrsminiaturerailway.co.uk for details.

On leaving Arbroath the train heads inland and north. Look out for the remains of the old railway to Forfar on the left of the train. The train heads through a narrow valley and over the Lunan Water River before returning briefly to the coast and then in to Montrose. The station at Montrose and the line at this point travels alongside the **Montrose Basin**, a large bay which is linked to the sea through a narrow channel running under the railway. The Basin is a popular place for bird watching.

Montrose

Montrose is a busy east coast town with an attractive town centre with some fine buildings. Look out for the Library, Town Hall and Montrose Old Church with its 220 foot spire. The town has been a harbour for 900 years and continues to serve in this function today. There is also an attractive beach and grassy areas for games and family fun.

Practicalities

Montrose station is located in the town centre on Western Road, DD10 8LW. It is staffed with a ticket office, ticket vending machine, waiting room, toilets, pay phone and self help luggage trolleys. The building itself is a modern panelled design with a tiled roof and is functional rather than beautiful to view. The view of Montrose Basin from the station however makes up for its lack of architectural merits.

Tourist Information Centre. Montrose Tourist Information Centre is now located inside the Museum on Panmure Place, Montrose, DD10 8HE (Telephone 01674 673232). The Centre is a ten minute walk from the Station.

Places of Interest

Montrose Museum. The Montrose Natural History and Antiquarian Society opened their new museum in 1842 making it one of the first purpose built museums in Scotland. It was designed as a 'temple of learning' with its neo classic columned building and the word 'Museum' in gold above the front door. Even today it is a remarkable museum for a small town. The original collection of geology, natural history, ethnography and fine art has gradually been expanded over the years and now fills the spacious atrium, mezzanine and galleries. The Museum is open Monday to Saturday all year and has free admission. It is a ten minute walk from the station on Panmure Place (DD10 8HE).

Montrose Basin Visitor Centre and Wildlife Refuge. The Basin is a large expanse of water behind Montrose. It is popular for bird watching with the thousands of migrating birds visiting this reserve during the seasons. Two of the most poplar walks actually start from the Caledonian Railway Station or Bridge of Dun bus stop (see below) so if you would prefer this countryside experience use the bus or train mentioned below. The Centre on the other hand is best reached from Montrose town centre itself. The Centre is open all year, daily from March to November with restricted winter hours. It is about one mile south of the Station and may be reached in about 30 minutes. Much of the walk is alongside the Basin so your walk may take longer if you are interested in viewing wildlife and landscapes along the way. Remember to take firm footwear as paths are muddy. Binoculars are also recommended. The Basin website is www.montrosebasin.org.uk while the Visitor Centre is run by the Scottish Wildlife Trust who also run a related webpage at www.swt.org.uk.

Nearby Places of Interest

From Montrose station walk to the High Street (five minutes walk) and catch bus number 30 for two excellent nearby attractions, the House of Dun and Caledonian Railway at Brechin. Buses run hourly and take ten minutes to reach the House of Dun (stops at end of driveway) and fifteen to reach Brechin (stops outside the Caledonian Railway Station).

The House of Dun. This Georgian family house was designed by William Adam for David Erskine, the 13th Laird of Dunin in 1730. Its main attraction is the plasterwork interiors by Joseph Enzor. There are also fabulous Victorian gardens overlooking the Montrose Basin. The Estate consists of Lady Augusta Walk, adventure playground, Victorian walled garden, terraced gardens, woodland walk and farm land. The house is under the care of the National Trust for Scotland and is open from Easter to October. See www.nts.org.uk or call the house on 01674 810264 to find out more.

Caledonian Railway. The Caledonian Railway is a private heritage group which has restored a section of railway between the town of Brechin and

Bridge of Dun Station set in attractive countryside and close to the Montrose Basin nature reserve walks. The line today offers the opportunity on selected weekends throughout the year to travel behind steam engines or vintage diesels. The station at Brechin is worth visiting itself for its architecture including the decorative restored iron canopy along the front of the building. On running days there are usually four or five trains during the day to choose from and you can break your journey at either end of the line to visit the reserve or Brechin town.

The Caledonian Railway can actually be combined with a visit to Montrose Basin and the House of Dun. By taking the train back from Brechin to the Bridge of Dun Station you may alight here and within a short walk is the Montrose Basin or the House of Dun. Spend some time at either attraction and then take the train back to Brechin or a bus directly back to Montrose. This end of Montrose Basin is on the River South Esk and is quite scenic and rural. You can find out more about the railway, and check opening times at www.caledonianrailway.co.uk, or by calling the booking office on 01356 622992.

Return to Montrose to continue your journey. The train now heads inland through typical Aberdeenshire countryside with its rolling hills and farmland. Some services will stop at the reopened Laurencekirk Station which was originally closed in September 1967 and survived as almost a time capsule until its recent reopening. The railway passes through a narrow valley just before Stonehaven. Look out for Fetteresso Castle on the left. This 17th century mansion was abandoned in the 20th century but has now been converted into apartments.

Stonehaven

Situated on the cliffs overlooking Stonehaven Bay, the town was originally a fishing village. Its harbour is one of the most picturesque in the country and is surrounded by small pubs and restaurants. The town is also home to UK's only art deco heated Olympic-sized open air swimming pool. It's a tourist board four-star visitor attraction open from first Sunday in June to September each year (see www.stonehavenopenairpool.co.uk). If visiting New Year around look out for the unique Stonehaven Fireballs Festival. At midnight on Hogmanay every year these real fireballs and taken through the streets of Stonehaven. This festival attracts 10 – 12,000 visitors each year, and offers a unique way to see in the New Year (see www.stonehavenfireballs.co.uk). There are many fine traditional buildings including the market buildings and Town House.

Practicalities

Stonehaven railway station (Station Road, AB39 2NE) is an attractive red sandstone building with traditional slate roof dating from 1849. The platform has a full length wooden canopy to shelter passengers and is complete with traditional signal box. Facilities for passengers include a ticket office, waiting room, ticket vending machine, toilets and pay phone.

Tourist Information Centre. The Centre is located at 66 Allardice Street, AB39 2AA and is a 17 minute walk from the Station.

Places of Interest

Dunnottar Castle is situated on a rock in the sea just south of Stonehaven. The site must make it one of the best defended castles possible. Surrounded by sea and sheer 160 foot cliffs it is easy to see why a castle would be built here. It is thought that there has been a castle on this site for 5000 years. In 1650 Charles II asked for his Honours to be kept safe in the Castle. Seventy men held out for eight months inside before they were finally captured by Cromwell's troops, but not before the Honours had been smuggled out. Only a few years later in 1685 the Castle's darkest hour came. One hundred and twenty two men and forty five women were imprisoned in the airless Whig's Vault. Their crime was to refuse to acknowledge that the King rather than God was the ultimate authority on spiritual matters. Today the history of the Castle can easily be imagined. One of the nicest features of the Castle is that you can still walk there down quiet country roads as people have done for centuries. The walk is about 50 minutes in each direction from Stonehaven station. Due to the very steep steps to gain entry to this Castle, if you feel you could not walk out, it is unlikely you would enjoy scrambling about whilst inside either. The Castle is open from Easter till October and is privately owned. There is an admission charge. See www.dunnottarcastle.co.uk or call 01330 860223 for details.

On departure from Stonehaven Station the train crosses the Cowie Water River on the Glenury Viaduct which is also a good location for train watching or photography in Stonehaven with local passenger, InterCity, freight and sleeper trains crossing. **Portlethen Station** is soon reached serving the new settlement and the old fishing community of Old Portlethen. The train continues on a fast curving cliff top journey to Aberdeen with views out to the North Sea. On the approach to Aberdeen look out for Girdleness Lighthouse which was designed by Robert Louis Stevenson (grandfather to the author of the same name who wrote Treasure Island, Kidnapped and other novels) and built by James Gibb in 1833. The train arrives at the terminus of Aberdeen.

Aberdeen

Aberdeen is one of Scotland's oldest cities, the earliest known municipal charter having been granted by William the Lion in 1178. The city lies 150 miles north of Edinburgh on the east coast and has the distinction of being Scotland's third largest city. The city is situated between the Rivers Dee and Don and the sea has been important throughout its history. The docks remain in the heart of the city and today serve the North Sea oil industry and ferries to the Northern Isles rather than trading. The city is known as the 'Granite City' being principally constructed of the attractive grey stone. The city has been home to a university for five hundred years and in addition to its status as 'capital' of the north east it has been a major oil centre since the early 1970's. Many oil companies have their UK offices here and the port area is always busy with North Sea oil activity.

In the centre of Aberdeen are several buildings of interest including Aberdeen Art Gallery; the Music Hall (1822); James Dun's House (18th century); Provost Skene's House, built in the 16th century and the city's oldest surviving building; Tolbooth Museum, built between 1616 and 1629 as a prison; the Gordon Highlanders Museum; and Provost Ross's House (1593). The main shopping area is Union Street, just outside the Station.

Practicalities

The railway station (Guild Street) is located just off the main Union Street at the heart of the city, right beside the bus station and close to the ferry terminal. Guild Street station is an attractive original stone building dating from the railways opening with large central glass roof housing a huge waiting area for passengers. Unfortunately the best features of the building are now hidden inside a shopping centre with the passenger facilities moved out and into smaller, less adequate spaces. Platforms lead off the central area to the north and south, although the southern platforms see most of the activity now. The station is well kept and always staffed with ticket office, waiting areas, shops and toilets. There is also a first class lounge for first class and sleeper passengers.

Local Transport. Local buses are operated by First Bus and Stagecoach Bluebird buses. Both offer frequent, clean and reliable services. First operate most services within the city while Bluebird operate to the surrounding areas. City buses may be included in Plusbus fares to Aberdeen. The city centre can easily be explored on foot as a pedestrian. The Bus Station is situated next to the railway station for buses to outlying areas, while the port and ferry terminal are a short walk away.

Tourist Information Centre. Aberdeen Tourist Information Centre is located on Union Street opposite the Town Hall. Telephone 01224 632727.

On arrival visitors need only step outside of the Guild Street main station to see the 'Granite City' at its best. Right outside the station is the Union Square shopping centre, while a short walk up to Union Street leaves the visitor in the heart of the city.

Places of Interest

Union Street is the main street in Aberdeen and could be considered one of the finest streets in Europe. It is three quarters of a mile in length and seventy foot wide, and is constructed almost entirely from granite.

Shoppers will be pleased to note that its entire length is lined in shops and department stores of every description. Towards the north end is the Town Hall, with its impressive 210 foot tall tower.

Marischal College. A little to the north of the Municipal offices is Marischal College, part of the University of Aberdeen. The College was founded in 1593 by George Keith, Fourth Earl Marischal of Scotland. It is claimed to be the second largest granite building in the world, exceeded only by Spain's Escorial, once the home of the Spanish monarchy. The frontage is over 400 feet long, with an average height of 80 feet. The University has moved out to King's College with the building now leased to the local council. It is worth going inside to visit the Marischal Museum (although it is currently closed while building work takes place). The museum was founded in 1786, with material that has been donated by generations of friends and graduates of the University. This has resulted in collections of high quality material, most notably Egyptian and Classical antiquities, non-western ethnography, Scottish prehistory and numismatics that rank alongside the largest in Scotland. Today, the care of these collections is enhanced by a purpose-built conservation laboratory. Also contained in the building is the Picture Gallery and Mitchell Hall – the venue for University graduations.

King's College. In the heart of Old Aberdeen is King's College. Founded in 1494 the focal point of the campus is the Chapel, completed in 1509. This is the only remaining part of the original College and contains beautiful wood carving. Today this is the main campus of the University of Aberdeen, while the oldest buildings have been restored and are used as a conference venue. Use either bus service 1 or 2 from Union Street or 20 from Marischal College to get here.

Maritime Museum. The City's award-winning Maritime Museum brings the history of the North Sea to life. View displays and exhibitions on the offshore oil industry, shipbuilding, fishing and clipper ships then visit the museum shop and licensed Leading Lights café. Built in 1593, the building was Provost Ross's House and is now the third oldest dwelling in Aberdeen. The Museum is located on Shiprow (AB11 5BY) at the Harbour, close to the city centre and Station.

Aberdeen Art Gallery. Also in the city centre is Aberdeen Art Gallery. As one of the City's most popular tourist attractions the splendid 1885 Art Gallery houses an important fine art collection with particularly good examples of 19th, 20th and 21st century works. There is also a rich diverse applied art collection, an exciting programme of special exhibitions, a gallery shop and a café, all housed in an impressive marble lined building. To find the Gallery go to Schoolhill (AB10 1FQ). It is a ten minute walk from the station.

Nearby Places of Interest

Braemar. The village of Braemar can be reached by bus from Aberdeen Bus Station (next to the rail station) with Bluebird buses. Braemar is a pleasant village on the River Dee, and surrounded by mountains. The village is more famous for the nearby Balmoral Castle (the bus stops here on the way to Braemar Village). The Castle was purchased by Queen Victoria in 1848 and the Estate has been the Scottish home of the British Royal Family ever since. The grounds and exhibitions are open at certain times of the year. Check the web site at www.balmoralcastle.com.

On the way to Braemar, the bus will also make a stop at Crathes. The National Trust owned, **Crathes Castle**, Garden and Estate is one of Scotland's finest castles. The riverside setting in spectacular Deeside scenery makes the trip worthwhile in itself. While visiting look out for the original 16th century painted ceilings in the Castle, and the yew hedges in the gardens. There are also six woodland walks around the Estate to choose from. The Castle and grounds are open year round and have an admission charge. See the National Trust website for details.

Before entering the Castle, there is yet another visitor attraction at this location (use the same bus stop as for the Castle), in the form of the Royal Deeside Railway. The railway once ran all the way from Aberdeen. However a short section has now been restored. There is a visitor centre, gift shop, and train trips are offered. It is hoped that a steam train will be introduced in the near future. The railway is also home to a unique battery operated railcar that originally ran on the line. See www.deeside-railway.co.uk for opening times, fares and details.

8. Orkney and Shetland by Sea

NorthLink Ferries to Orkney and Shetland

Aberdeen is the starting point for the scenic sea crossings to Orkney and Shetland. It might be tempting to think that these Northern Isles are too far away. However the ferry journeys are mini cruises in their own right, while Orkney and Shetland have unique identities quite different to mainland Scotland. If you would like a Scottish holiday with a difference they might just be what you are looking for. On arrival at Aberdeen station simply walk through the shopping centre and bus station to the next door docks to reach the ferry terminal. It is about a ten minute walk or a short taxi ride. The Northlink Ferry terminal has a ticket office, pay phones, drinks vending machines, toilets, a waiting lounge and left luggage facilities. The left luggage office may be used by ferry passengers catching a sailing later that day who wish to leave their bags and explore Aberdeen before the early evening departure time.

Tickets and bookings

You may book tickets, obtain fares, and schedule information by visiting www.northlinkferries.co.uk or calling Northlink on 0845 6000449. The Freedom of Scotland Travelpass (for rail travel) will entitle you to a 20% discount off seated ferry fares on Northlink.

Sailing times

Ships depart from Aberdeen every evening and arrive in Shetland (Lerwick) early the following morning. Four days per week the same ferry calls at Orkney (Kirkwall) on its journey to Shetland. On these days it departs Aberdeen two hours earlier and arrives in Orkney late in the evening. Return sailings depart Shetland daily in the early evening, Orkney late evening (three days per week) and arrive into Aberdeen early the following morning.

Luggage and boarding

Remember to only take an overnight bag onboard with you with everything you will need for the voyage. Pack any toiletries, pyjamas, money, camera, medication or other items you might like during the crossing. It is a good idea to take some warm clothing and jacket if you wish to enjoy the sea air from the open decks as it can be cold outside even on summer evenings. All other luggage is checked in upon boarding and then collected on arrival at your destination. Also remember that all passengers over 16 require being in possession of photographic ID to board. Bikes are carried free of charge and are taken onboard the car deck and not as hand luggage.

Onboard

The Northlink Ferries are the largest and best appointed ferries in Scotland as they cover the longest distances. There is so much to do on board that you might be wishing you had a little longer to enjoy the crossing. On board food is one of the highlights of Northlink with high quality meals prepared onboard by the ship's chefs. On departure from Aberdeen there is a self service restaurant serving good quality evening meals, while during the main summer season there is also the choice of dining later in the à la carte dining room. These options are also available when returning from Shetland, but not from Orkney as the ship does not leave until very late in the evening. On arrival (07.30) in Lerwick or Aberdeen on the return there is no need to rush as a foot passenger as the breakfast room stays open until 09.00 and you don't have to disembark until 09.30, making for a leisurely journey.

Accommodation and Facilities

When travelling north to Orkney most passengers opt for a reserved reclining chair which is included in the ticket price. For the overnight crossings (Shetland and returning from Orkney) a chair reservation is included in the ticket price and you can hire a blanket and pillow (or take these with you) for a comfortable night's sleep. You can also upgrade for an extra charge to a cabin. All cabins come with ensuite toilet, washbasin and shower. They also have telephones linked to the ship's office. There is a choice of exclusive use of a cabin either for one or for your group, or to share with other passengers of the same gender. The last option is particularly cost effective for single travellers. Cabins come in a choice of two berth outside with window or four berth inside without a window. Some have TV and video for an extra charge and all have UK power sockets for personal electrical appliances. For those wishing to work there are executive cabins with desks for working and for the ultimate luxury, premium cabins with TV and other little extras. Both the premium and executive cabins are outside with a window and are twin berth. If you can afford the extra money, any of the cabins give extra comfort, although the reclining seats are spacious enough to get some rest on.

While on board there is plenty to keep you entertained. The coastal voyage has enjoyable views of the Scottish coast together with wonderful sunsets and sunrises over the northern North Sea. Inside there is a cinema which shows the latest films, a shop, lounge area and bar. Some lounges are designated 'quiet areas' without televisions or music for relaxation.

The Orkney Isles

The Orkney Islands are comprised of over seventy islands of which around twenty are inhabited. People have lived there for five and a half thousand years and today the islands are home to some of the best Neolithic sites in Europe. The Islands were owned by Norway until 1468 and even today many Orcadians view their heritage as quite distinct from that of the Scottish mainland. These islands are remote, beautiful and quite different from any other of the Scottish islands. They are an ideal destination for anyone interested in the history and historic sites, or who just wishes to enjoy their beautiful scenery and quiet pace of life. Kirkwall is the main town and is located on the 'mainland', the name given to the largest island. There are lots of other islands to explore and it is worth spending a bit of time here to get to know them.

Practicalities

The Northlink Ferries Terminal in Orkney is at Kirkwall, the Islands' capital. Northlink runs a complementary bus service from the pier head to the town centre including some of the hotels and the bus station. It also links with the Scrabster – Stromness ferry for passengers using the rail and ferry route via Thurso.

Getting around Orkney

Although a rural series of islands, Orkney is very well provided with bus services on the mainland. You can get around all the sites of interest using the network of regular bus services and all day rover tickets mean you have unlimited travel without worrying about taking change for bus fares or how much it is going to cost. Using the bus on Orkney could not be easier. Outside the towns simply ask the driver to stop at any point of interest or get on wherever you are with a signal to the driver – no need to look out for bus stops! With quieter roads and small size, the Orkney Islands are also a great place to explore by bike. The smaller islands are often ideal for cycling and walking with limited or no bus services. Taking the bike to Orkney by ferry and rail is free for the bike although you should remember to make reservations for the train as the rail sections have limited bike space. To find out more about the bus network see the website www.orkneypublictransport.com or phone 01856 870555.

There are also internal ferries to the smaller Orkney Islands. These are operated by Orkney Ferries and you can find out about times and fares from www.orkneyferries.co.uk or by telephoning the office on 01856 872044. Orkney Ferries have an enquiry office on Shore Street in Kirkwall.

Describing each bus service would be beyond the scope of this book so instead refer to the Orkney public transport website or pick up a timetable. A timetable of all transport on Orkney is available for download or to pick up from Tourist Centres. Traveline will also provide details of how to reach each place or attraction. As most bus and internal ferry services have their hub in Kirkwall it is probably the best place to be located during your stay. Make your way to Kirkwall Travel Centre which is the hub of the Orkney bus network. The Travel Centre also houses the Tourist Information Centre (West Castle Street, Kirkwall, KW15 1GU, Telephone (01856) 872856). The

Orkney Tourist Board also has an excellent website with accommodation details at www.visitorkney.com.

Places of Interest

Kirkwall Basin. In the centre of Kirkwall is the Basin. Everything that can't be grown or caught must come in by sea or air, and the harbour has been the focal point of activity on the Island for hundreds of years. Today this is also the location for local ferries to the smaller Orkney Isles, many of which are ideal for day trips from the mainland for walking, cycling or exploring. Visit www.orkneyferrries.co.uk or telephone 01856 872044 for fares and timetable information. The ferries leave from central Kirkwall to six local islands. During the summer a special excursion program is operated. There is a small charge for bikes carried on these ferries, but not the Northlink Ferries to Orkney from the mainland which is a different company.

St Magnus Cathedral. St Magnus Cathedral, known as the 'Light in the North', was founded in 1137 by the Viking, Earl Rognvald, in order of his uncle St Magnus and is the most northerly cathedral in Britain. It is also one of only three Scottish pre Reformation cathedrals still intact. Between 1154 and 1472 the Cathedral was under the care of the Norwegian archbishops and it was not until 1486 that King James III assigned the Cathedral to the people of Kirkwall. The Cathedral came through the Reformation unscathed although by the 20th century the condition of the building had deteriorated and restoration work was commenced. The building is constructed of red sandstone and the original builders are thought to have been trained at Durham Cathedral. It is an amazing landmark and literally towers above the Kirkwall skyline. For first-time visitors unaware of its existence the building comes as quite a surprise when discovered for the first time. The Cathedral is located in the centre of Kirkwall. It is open most days and services are held on Sundays. There are also guided tours of the upper levels held on Tuesdays and Thursdays. There is a charge for these and they should be booked with the custodian on 01856 874894.

The Bishop and Earl's Palaces. Kirkwall was the capital of Orkney under the Norse held Northern Isles. However in 1469 when Christian I of Norway failed to pay the dowry promised to his son-in-law, James III of Scotland, the islands were returned to Scotland. There were two seats of power in Norse Orkney, the Castle (demolished 1615) and the Palace. The Bishop's Palace was built around the same time as the Cathedral in the 12th century. In 1263 King Hakon IV of Norway passed away in the Palace while on a visit to Scotland. The Earl' Palace is much later having been constructed in 1606 by Earl Patrick of Orkney. It is another spectacular building with great detail in its construction. Both are now ruined but open to the public (admission charge) with a visitor centre operated by Historic Scotland. See www.historic-scotland.gov.uk or telephone 01856 871918 for details. It is five minute walk from the bus and local ferry terminals and located opposite the Cathedral.

The Orkney Museum. Also in Kirkwall is the Orkney Museum. The Museum was built as a house for the Cathedral clergy in 1574 and is well preserved. Entry is through the arched gateway that bears the coat of arms of Gilbert Foulzie who built the house. Exhibits are of international importance and trace 5000 years of Orkney history. The Museum is located at Tankerness House (opposite the Cathedral), Broad Street, KW15 1DH. Admission is free and it is open all year from Monday to Saturday. Call 01856 873191 for details.

Deerness Nature Reserve. On the east end of the mainland lies 95 hectares of heath and grassland on a cliff top setting. The sandstone cliffs are home to nesting birds such as kittiwakes, guillemots, razorbills and fulmars. Other birds, including gulls and skuas, prefer to nest on the open heathland. There is also interesting plant life and some historic buildings including the remains of a Norse Chapel. The site is a 25 minute bus journey from Kirkwall Travel Centre on the bus to Deerness and then a 20 minute walk from the bus stop. There are many pleasent cliff top walks once at the location. It is also possible to cycle out on relatively quiet roads from Kirkwall.

The Old Man of Hoy (Ordnance Survey map 7, grid reference 175009). This is the most famous sea stack in the Orkney Islands and is located on the Island of Hoy. To get there take a bus from Kirkwall Travel Centre (30 minute bus journey from Kirkwall) before taking the Orkney Ferries crossing to North Hoy. The Stack is a six mile walk through the glen between the Ward Hill and Cuilags to Rackwick Bay. There are places to camp or a bothy if staying overnight. The Stack is also viewable from the Northlink ferry route from Scrabster.

Skara Brae Prehistoric Village (KW16 3LR). In 1850 a huge storm unearthed a prehistoric village on the shores of the Bay of Skaill. This village was built over 5000 years ago and is remarkably well preserved. To put that time in context, the Great Pyramid of Giza was not built until 1300 BC. The houses are remarkably well preserved with even the stone made furniture still intact. The people who lived here were fishermen, hunters and farmers. However they found time beyond survival to produce objects of beauty including carved stones. Many of these artefacts have been found and are preserved and on display in the on site museum. If travelling from Kirkwall, change bus at Swanney or Stromness. Some direct buses run from Kirkwall and most journeys take one and half hours. There is an admission charge and the site is open all year. Telephone 01856 841815 or see Historic Scotland for details.

Westray Island and Noltland Castle. Take the ferry from Kirkwall town centre to reach Westray Island. The Island is only 4 miles long by 1 mile wide so there is no need to pay to even take a bike with you if you don't want to! Westray has a nice sandy beach on its south end and a pleasant small harbour. It is mostly farmland and a small community which lives scattered over the Island. Take some time to visit Noltland Castle, about a mile west of the ferry pier. The castle is not ruined but rather was never completed. It is a fine, Z-plan tower, built between 1560 and 1573 and is remarkable for its large number of gun loops and impressive staircase. It is open all year with free admission.

Rousay, Egilsay and Wyre Islands. These Islands are remote and tranquil. They are reached by Orkney Ferries from Tingwall on the west of the Orkney Mainland. Reach the ferry terminal by bus or bike from Kirkwall. Bus and ferry times in the summer allow a visit to each island in one day, although it is quite rushed and you may prefer to relax in the isolation of just one of the islands. Egilsay is noted for the ruins of a 12th century church (St Magnus Church) with its unusual round tower. The Church is half a mile from the ferry pier at grid reference HY 466 304. Rousay Island has a Neolithic chambered cairn with unusual arrangement of two burial chambers, one above the other. It is known as Taversöe Tuick Chambered Cairn and is located half a mile west of the ferry pier (grid reference HY 426 276). Also on Rousay is Midhowe Broch. This is a well-preserved broch, with remains of later buildings round it. A Broch is a large dry-stone, round structure only found in Scotland. It is about an hour's walk from the ferry pier and has very steep access, following the black and white poles to gain entry. All these places of interest have free admission.

Maeshowe Chambered Cairn. On the bus route between Stromness and Kirkwall is Maeshowe Cairn. It is the finest chambered cairn in northwest Europe and the finest Neolithic building in Europe. Thought to be around 5000 years old the tomb itself is quite small, only 4.7 metres across but it is housed in a much larger mounded building covered in earth to resemble a small hill. The passage into the tomb itself is 10 metres long. This site has been included in the Neolithic Orkney World Heritage Site. There is an admission charge to the site. Telephone 01856 761606 for details. Please note that due to the space constraints there is a ticketed entry system in operation so call to check details of travel and availability before visiting.

Italian Chapel (near St Mary's). The Chapel is located on the tiny island of Lamb Holm (connected to the Mainland by the first of the Churchill Barriers). It is a unique memorial to 550 Italian Prisoners of War who were interned there in the 1940s. This beautiful little chapel was converted internally from two corrugated iron nissen huts and has amazing paintings throughout the interior. Considering that the craftsmen had little or no materials it is all the more remarkable for the quality of the workmanship. It is open during daylight hours and is free to visit.

Shetland Isles

Return to Kirkwall Harbour for the overnight sailing to Lerwick on the Shetland Isles. Or if starting from Aberdeen, you may take a ferry direct to Shetland with or without calling at Orkney along the way. See the Orkney section for details of the ferry journey.

Practicalities

Arrival on Shetland is at the Lerwick Ferry Terminal (ZE1 oPR). The Terminal has tourist information, a staffed enquiry office and toilets. There is a bus stand outside from which buses to the centre of Lerwick and the main bus station depart. Buses on Shetland are coordinated by ZetTrans (a department of Shetland Islands Council) and you can find out about the bus network by visiting www.zettrans.org.uk or by phoning 01595 744868. A timetable of all services is available for download from that site or to pick up on arrival. The Islands are larger and more spread out than Orkney and it may be that you might wish to hire a car on the islands. However, if you are fit and able to walk or cycle, then getting about on foot and bus is possible and rewarding.

Shetland is quite unique from the rest of the British Isles with its own culture and heritage. There is a specific tourist information resource for the islands at www.visitshetland.com. Most people enjoy to tour, walk, cycle and find quiet places to relax and enjoy the atmosphere of these islands.

Places of Interest

Fort Charlotte. This five-sided artillery fort with bastions projecting from each corner dominates the centre of Lerwick. It was built in 1665 to protect the Sound of Bressay from the Dutch, but taken by them and burned in 1673 and then rebuilt in 1781. The current fort dates from that time. At the time Britain was at war with France and Spain which was linked to the American war of independence. The fort housed 270 men and has 12 guns overlooking the sea facing side. It was named after the wife of George III. To view the interior, request the keys by phoning 01856 841815.

Shetland Museum and Archives (ZE1 oWP). From geological beginnings to the present day, the Museum tells the story of Shetland. Being famous for textiles, there are specific displays on this particular aspect of the Island's past. The Museum is located in Lerwick at Hay's Dock. See www.shetlandmuseumandarchives.org.uk or telephone 01595 695057 for details of opening times.

9. The Fife Circle – Edinburgh to Dunfermline

The Fife Circle is a circular rail journey making its way from Edinburgh and across the famous Forth Railway Bridge to make a circular tour through Fife before returning to the Capital. Although often overlooked from the tourist itinerary this line gives access to some beautiful coastal towns and first class attractions which are all excellent day trips from Edinburgh.

Journey Summary

Route: Edinburgh – South Queensferry – Inverkeithing – Aberdour – Kinghorn – Kirkcaldy – Dunfermline – Edinburgh.

Operator: Scotrail.

Trains: Standard class accommodation only.

Trip Length: Various depending on destination and train direction.

Frequency: Hourly or more frequent to most stations.

Departing Edinburgh's Waverley or Haymarket stations the train heads through the suburbs and past the airport before heading towards the Firth of Forth and the first stop at Dalmeny.

Dalmeny / South Queenferry

Dalmeny / South Queensferry is perhaps one of the most overlooked and beautiful villages within easy reach of Edinburgh. However for those stopping to spend a little time in the village there is plenty of interest. The village High Street is unusual in that it borders the Firth of Forth. With attractive buildings on one side of the street and the water's edge on the other, there can be few more attractive village centres. The main building of interest in the area is the former administrative building, 'The Tollbooth'. This attractive building with its white clock tower dominates the centre of the village.

Practicalities

The station at Dalmeny serves the villages of Dalmeny and South Queensferry and is situated on the shores of the Firth of Forth, a natural bay leading out into the North Sea. The station is convenient for the village and is staffed part time in the mornings, although ticket machines are available at all times.

Places of Interest

Dalmeny Kirk, located in the centre of the village, is one of the finest remaining Romanesque parish churches and the best preserved Norman church in the country. Dating mainly from the 12th century the church retains many of its original features and you may even view some of the tool marks from its construction. The only modern feature is the tower which is a 1937 rebuild of what the original is thought to have looked like. Inside its arches, vaulting and doorways are particularly finely carved. In particular look out for the stone vaulting of the ceiling and the detailed stonework on the many arches. The church is a short walk from the railway station, and is still in use as a parish church.

The station at Dalmeny is at the south end of the **Forth Bridge**, sometimes known as the Forth Railway Bridge to distinguish it from the Forth Road Bridge. The world famous cantilevered bridge (opened in 1890) must be one of the most over engineered, and as such impressive, in the world. The bridge is made up of three huge four-tower cantilever structures which are each 104 m (340 feet) tall and 21 m (70 feet) diameter resting on a separate foundation. It is 1.5 miles in length and its double track mainline railway is held 46 m (150 feet) above tide level. Even today the bridge is considered an engineering marvel unequalled in the world. The reason for its extreme construction was the collapse of an earlier bridge across the Tay outside Dundee. With this tragedy in mind the Forth Bridge was constructed to such a high standard. South Queensferry is the most popular location for people to get off the train and view the bridge. There is a long promenade along the water's edge right up to and underneath the bridge and lighting is usually good for photographs from this angle rather than from the north side. Both bridges are overlooked by the **Queensferry Museum** (EH30 9HP) which tells the story of the Burgh. It is open year round with free admission.

While admiring the bridge it may be that you would also wish to see a much older Scottish landmark, **Inchcolm Abbey,** located on Inchcolm Island in the Firth of Forth. A tour boat runs from the pier underneath the Forth Bridge. The tour and bridge are both located about an eight minute walk from the station. The boat is named 'The Maid of the Forth' and runs regularly throughout the summer to the Abbey (see www.maidof theforth.co.uk for details). The Abbey is known as the 'Iona of the East' and was established in the 12th century during the episcopate of Gregoir, Bishop of Dunkeld. In 1235 it became a full Abbey and remained in use until the Reformation in 1560 when it was abandoned. However its ruins are amongst the most complete of any Scottish monastic house. The cloisters, chapter house, warming house, and refectory are all complete, and most of the remaining cloistral buildings survive in a largely complete state although the church itself is mostly ruined. The site is now cared for by Historic Scotland. With the significance of the site, the beauty of the island and the Forth and the boat trip to get there this could be one of the less well known gems of Scotland. There is an entrance charge, plus the boat fee to reach the island. See www.historic-scotland.gov.uk for opening times and details.

Also of interest near Dalmeny is **Dalmeny House**. Although only two miles from the Station, it is located along a fairly busy road, so you are best to take a very short bus journey along to the start of the driveway or a taxi from the station to the house. If taking the bus option, the driveway is about a 25 minute walk in total. Dalmeny House is a Gothic revival mansion, completed in 1817. It is still the home of the Earl and Countess of Rosebery and was the first house in Scotland to be designed in the 'Tudor Revival' style. It is open during the summer and there is an admission charge for entry. See www.dalmeny.co.uk for details.

North Queenferry

Departing Dalmeny, the next station on the line is at the north end of the Forth Bridge and named **North Queensferry**. This is not such a good location for viewing the bridge as the previous Dalmeny station. North Queensferry Station retains its original station building which was opened shortly after the Bridge in 1890. The station is most often used today by visitors making the journey to the popular **Deep Sea World** (KY11 1JR), Scotland's National Aquarium, just a few minutes walk from the station. Deep Sea World has a 112 metre - long underwater tunnel (one of the world's largest) allowing visitors to actually walk amongst the fish and marine life. In fact if you are a qualified diver, you can even swim with the residents of the tank! However all visitors may enjoy watching creatures that few of us actually ever see hidden under the waves. The Aquarium has an active shark breeding program and these are some of the most popular attractions as you walk through the glass tunnel with views of many other rare species of fish and amphibians. Outside, there is another very special exhibit, the seal rescue pools. Abandoned or orphaned seals are taken back to health at the centre and they are always popular with visitors, especially children. Deep Sea World is open all year and has an admission charge. Through rail and admission tickets are available from any station in Scotland – buy at the ticket office or on the train. For details of the Aquarium, see www.deepseaworld.com.

The **Fife Coastal Path** begins in North Queensferry with a series of walks all the way to Tayport. It is possible to take short walks between North Queensferry and the stations at Inverkeithing, Aberdour, Burnisland and Kirkcaldy. There is also a longer walk between Kirkcaldy and St Andrews. Find out more at: www.fifecoastalpath.co.uk.

Departing North Queensferry the train makes a short coastal journey to the next station at Inverkeithing.

Inverkeithing

Inverkeithing as a human settlement goes back a long time. In medieval times it was a walled town with four gates, although the town walls were pulled down sometime in the 1500s. However a number of buildings survive from this period. The Inverkeithing Parish Church, located on the main street near the station, is a comparatively modern building dating from 1837; however the tower goes back to the 1300s. Also of interest in the town centre is Greyfriars Convent which was the boarding house for the nearby Convent (maybe viewed externally only). While there, look out for the Mercat Cross (1400s) and the Tollbooth from the 1770s. Although located on the coast, Inverkeithing is an industrial waterfront and became famous in the 1920s for its ship breaking activities.

Practicalities

Inverkeithing railway station is fully staffed with a ticket hall open for most train departures, an indoor waiting room and public toilets. The town is small and the areas of interest to the visitor are easily explored on foot and close to the Station.

After Inverkeithing the train heads inland and makes its way through the dormitory settlement of **Dalgety Bay**. The town has fine views of the Firth of Forth and the Forth Bridge.

Aberdour

Aberdour is a hidden gem in Fife. Most people hurry through on the train to somewhere else, but for those taking the time to get out there are some amazing places to enjoy. Aberdour has two Blue Flag quality beaches in the village with beautiful views out over the Firth of Forth. They are ideal for picnics, lazy days relaxing or perhaps some more energetic beach games with friends or family. Also in the town is Aberdour Castle and Gardens. The Castle is perhaps the oldest standing castle in Scotland and is now under the care of Historic Scotland. There is also a beautiful natural harbour and the village itself is filled with attractive old buildings. Look out for the old clock tower and red phone box when making your way to the beaches from the station.

Practicalities

Aberdour railway station is located in the heart of the village, close to the beaches and opposite the castle. The station was built by the North British Railway and is an attractive stone building in a 'cottage' style with an old canopy over the entrance to shelter waiting passengers. It is a regular winner of the 'best kept station' awards and is perhaps amongst the nearest thing you will find to a classic station on the national network. There is a staffed ticket office (a.m. only) enclosed waiting room, ticket vending machine and public toilets. It is practical to walk everywhere from the station as the village is very small.

Places of Interest

Aberdour Castle and Garden. The Castle is perhaps the oldest in Scotland. The building comprises three main sections. The tower is the oldest part first built around 1200 and then rebuilt in the 15th century.

Although now a ruin, the basement area is still intact along with the southeast wall giving visitors a good idea of how the building would have looked when complete. The extremely thick walls show that this castle was purely about defence. The next section is called the Central Range and is again a ruin although in much better condition than the tower. The area included the great hall and many bedrooms, kitchens and other areas. It was built in the 15th century and greatly increased the area of the castle. At around the same time a defensive wall was constructed around the entire buildings. The final part of the Castle to be built was the East Range in 1635 and which remains in excellent condition and is roofed. Outside, visitors are able to enjoy the castle gardens. These also have the distinction of being the oldest gardens in Scotland and date from 1540. There is a formal walled garden and also terraced L - shaped garden leading down to an orchard laid out in 1690 and recently replanted. All of the gardens have wonderful views over the Firth of Forth towards Edinburgh. Also of interest in the gardens is a unique bee hive shaped doocot (pigeon house). All the buildings are grade A listed, the highest level of protection and significance given to historic buildings in Scotland. The Castle and gardens are now under the care of Historic Scotland and are open all year. They are located opposite the railway station. For opening times and details of entry fees check www.historic-scotland.gov.uk.

Aberdour Church. Named St Fillian's, the church is likely to have been constructed before 1123, which is the earliest record of its existence. The Church is a very fine example of early Norman architecture and contains a pre-reformation church bell, a Bible dated 1628 and beautiful stained glass. It is said that Robert the Bruce gave thanks for his victory at Bannockburn in 1314 here. Unfortunately the church fell into disuse in 1790 but was restored and re-dedicated in 1926 after the efforts of villagers to restore their church. It is still in use as a place of worship today. Sunday services are at the time of writing held on the first Sunday of each month (except January) however you can check these details by phone or email by checking the Church's website at: www.dunfermlinepresbytery.org.uk.

Aberdour's Harbour. The Harbour is not a harsh industrial landscape but rather a small natural harbour and bay surrounded by small rocky tree - covered cliffs. Located at the mouth of the Dour Burn (stream), the Harbour is separated from the Blacksands Beach by the Hawkcraig Point, another beautiful natural feature. The area is a nice place to explore or just relax with a picnic on a sunny summer's day. The Harbour originally gave the village its existence as ships would regularly come in to load coal here. For this reason a strong stone pier was constructed in the 1700s and not only still stands but is in use by the local boat club. The Harbour is about a ten minute walk through the village from the railway station.

Aberdour Beach. There are two beaches in Aberdour. Aberdour Blacksands Beach is a small secluded stretch of sand on the south side of the village. It has attractive natural features including rocky outcrops and is ideal for swimming or fishing. The beach is also good for watching wildlife including oystercatchers, redshank and occasionally seals and whales further out at sea. There are toilets and a shop near the beach. It is also on the Fife Coastal Path. To get to the beach just follow the signs through the village from the station which is about a ten minute walk away. The village's other beach is the Silver Sands Beach. Located on the north side of the village, this beach is also a ten minute walk from the railway station. It has a more countryside feel than the Harbour beach and is surrounded by trees and grass and has views out to the islands of Inchmickery and Inchcolm – with its famous Abbey. However it has perhaps got better facilities as lifeguards are on duty during the summer. There is also a café, toilets and a first aid station. For hygiene reasons dog access is restricted to this beach. Again it is a great location for wildlife watching (with similar species to the Harbour Beach), relaxing or something more active such as swimming or surfing. Both beaches are cleaned regularly by the local authority.

Finally, the **Aberdour Festival** is now in its 25th year. Featuring sports, art, crafts, song, dance and more the Festival is a ten day event usually held in the last week of July and first week of August. There are usually local and international events to watch and even take part in. Musicians, food, cooking displays, sports, comedy, environmental awareness events and usually a race you can join in make up the Festival. See www.aberdour-festival.org for details of this year's event.

Burntisland

Burntisland railway station is located in the Forth Place area of the town. This was once a major transport hub as the railway terminated here and passengers transferred to ferries operating from the adjacent dock. The present station dates from the opening of the Forth Bridge in 1890 when it was decided to build a new station on the town side of the railway line. Prior to this, the attractive symmetrical stone station dating from 1847 was used. For those who like to explore some long forgotten history, the 1847 station is still in existence. Head over the bridge to the south side of the line and you will be able to view the building. It is now owned by the Port Authority but is unfortunately disused and boarded up. However you can still view how it is located opposite the docks for easy transfer to the ferries.

The present day station is staffed in the mornings only, has an enclosed waiting room and ticket vending machine.

Behind the town are some attractive hills and near the centre, 'the links' are a large grassy area popular for recreation. Near to the station is **Rossend Castle** that is unfortunately not open to the public, however you may view it from the exterior. The Castle is a white tower constructed in 1119 which was once captured by Oliver Cromwell in 1651. However despite surviving for nearly 900 years it was nearly demolished in the 1970s by the local council who owned it and let it fall into disrepair. Thankfully after a public campaign to save the Castle, it was restored by an architectural firm who still use it as their offices today.

In 1611 King James VI of Scotland attended the General Assembly of the Church of Scotland being held in St Columba's Church in Burntisland. It was at this Assembly that a proposal was put forward to translate the Bible into a new English version and in 1611 the resulting publication, 'The King James Version' was published. For this reason the Church, still in use, is known as the 'Kirk of the Bible'. It is now most commonly referred to as the Parish Church. It is located to the south of the High Street and close to the railway station. The building is one of the oldest post Reformation churches in existence, construction starting in 1592 and being completed in 1595. Today it is popular with people coming from all over the world to see this historic building. The building has an unusual tower coming from the middle of its roof and is also notable for an external staircase to 'the sailors' loft'. This allowed sailors to leave according to tidal conditions without disturbing the others. The church is still a worshiping community today and you can find out more at www.burntislandkirk.org.uk.

Return to the train for the short journey to Kinghorn and Kirkcaldy.

Kinghorn

Clinging to the cliffs is the village of Kinghorn. The station is in the heart of the village overlooking the cliffs. There is a staffed ticket office, waiting room and public toilets. This attractive village has few formal attractions but is popular for its beach. For those who have been to the major tourist attractions already, it is a relaxing place to spend the day with the family or a friend.

Kinghorn Pettycur Beach is an open sandy beach which is sheltered and popular for enjoying the sun, swimming, beach games and picnics. It is located just five minutes walk from the railway station through the village. As well as the pretty backdrop of the village, beach users may enjoy fine views across the Firth of Forth to Edinburgh. There are shops and toilets located nearby. Those following the beach round the headland find themselves in the **Harbour Beach**, another sheltered sandy beach which is also home to the Kinghorn Lifeboat Station. The Lifeboat Station has existed here since 1965 and is open to the public many weekends during the summer when the beach is busiest. Another popular recreation area is **Kinghorn Loch**, located about a 15 minute walk from the station, behind the village. As well as being a haven for wildlife, birds and bird watching, the Loch is also surrounded by many countryside walks, including the one from the village to the Loch.

The train departs Kinghorn and continues its coastal journey to the largest town so far on the route, Kirkcaldy. Look out the carriage window for a collection of abandoned industrial steam engines located in a scrap yard in the town. They have rested here for years and although their future is probably unlikely to involve restoration, they seem to be secure for now and provide travellers with an interesting talking point.

Kirkcaldy

Kirkcaldy was originally formed as a Burgh under the control of Dunfermline Abbey. It grew during the industrial revolution as an industrial centre and today remains the most significant town in south east Fife.

Practicalities

Kirkcaldy railway station is located in the centre of the town, although it is known as one of the longest towns in Scotland with a four mile long High Street! For this reason you may wish to take a local bus around town which can be added on to your railway ticket with Plusbus. A sign at the station will tell you where to go to connect to local town buses. The station is staffed for all departures, has luggage trolleys, toilets, ticket vending machines, an enclosed waiting room and ticket office.

Places of Interest

Located only a few minutes walk from the station is **Beveridge Park**, a Victorian pleasure park with a lake, formal gardens and areas for families to relax and play. The park is free to enter and has toilet facilities. Just remember to take some bread for the ducks and swans!

There are two museums in Kirkcaldy. The **John McDouall Stuart Museum** recounts the story of this remarkable explorer who with his companions in 1862, completed the first European crossing of Australia from Adelaide to Van Diemen Gulf. The journey involved passing through the hot and hostile centre of the continent and returning safely along the same route. Even today this is one of the most inhospitable places on earth. To attempt a similar journey can often result in death from dehydration and other dangers. The Museum is located opposite the station. Also only 100 metres from the station is **Kirkcaldy Museum and Art Gallery**, housed in a large 1925 building. The Gallery has a stunning collection of work by a number of well-known artists, ranging from the Scottish Colourists to Jack Vettriano. Four permanent galleries are dedicated to showing these works. E-Mail: kirkcaldy.museum@fife.gov.uk to find out more about both museums and for opening times. Both offer free admission.

Ravenscraig Castle was constructed in 1460 by James II. The Castle is situated in a location which in some respects is attractive, by the sea and in a park, but in others is very ordinary as the Park is surrounded by a modern housing estate. Unfortunately the Castle's location makes it a little off the tourist trail so it is not staffed and most of the remaining rooms are not open to the public. However it is an interesting building, and the main landmark in Kirkcaldy. To get there take a bus heading towards the town of Leslie and ask the driver to let you off near Ravenscraig Castle. It is about a five minute walk towards the sea from the bus stop. Alternatively it is about a half an hour walk through the town or along the shoreline, which is quite attractive for most of the walk, to reach the Castle. Look out for signs to 'Ravenscraig Park' to direct you there.

The train now heads west and inland, stopping at Glenrothes with Thornton. This is the stop for Glenrothes town. This new town was established in 1948 to provide accommodation for workers at the nearby coal mine. The town was not long built when the mine closed and shortly afterwards a development corporation was set up and the town eventually became the heart of Scotland's electronics industry. The train continues through the rolling hills and farmland of Fife, making stops at Cardenden, Lochgelly, Cowdenbeath (Plusbus is available in Cowndenbeath) and Dunfermline Queen Margaret, a new station built to serve the hospital on the site.

Dunfermline

This historic town should be on the tourist map to a much greater extent than it is. Dunfermline was a city until 1970 but of much greater significance was its status as Scottish capital from the mid 11th century until 1437 when King James I was assassinated in Perth and the Royal Family moved to the safety of Edinburgh Castle. Edinburgh has remained Scotland's capital ever since but visitors to Dunfermline today will find a rich history. In more modern times, the town was the birth place of the Scottish-American industrialist, businessman, and philanthropist, Andrew Carnegie who left his mark on the town building the world's first Carnegie library there. The town has been a centre of textiles and engineering, and more recently of electronics.

Practicalities

There are two railway stations in the town, Dunferline Queen Margaret (for the hospital) and Dunfermline Town, which is ideal for visiting the historic heart of the town. The Town Station has a staffed ticket office, waiting room, ticket vending machine, public phones, toilets and customer information monitors.

Local Transport. Buses in Dunfermline are operated by Stagecoach. For bus information see www.stagecoachbus.com or telephone Traveline on 0871 2002233. Local buses are included in Plusbus rail tickets to Dunfermline.

Places of Interest

Dunfermline Town Centre. Right outside the railway station, the town centre, offers a good place to shop, eat and explore some fine architecture.

Most of the historic buildings are located here including the Town Hall with its clock tower, the Mercat Cross, pleasant Margaret's Street and Priory Lane.

Dunfermline Palace and Abbey. The Priory was established in the 11th century by King Malcolm III and Queen Margaret. In 1128 their son David I promoted the then Priory to Abbey status. The Abbey is still one of the most stunning pieces of Romanesque architecture in Scotland. Much of the great Nave, which dates from this time, is still complete. Over the years the Abbey became a mausoleum to many of the Kings and Queens of Scotland and their tombs may still be seen today. In 1303 the Abbey was badly damaged by Edward I, however the rebuilding by King Robert Bruce also resulted in the construction of the impressive monks' refectory. Many people though are curious as to how the building came to be ruined. After the Reformation of 1560 the Nave was converted into the local parish church which secured its survival. The Choir on the other hand was allowed to collapse. In 1818 a new Parish Church was constructed on the site of the Choir and the Nave was taken into state care. The Parish Church continues the tradition of worship on this site and is the direct descendent of the original Abbey. For this reason it is still known as Dunfermline Abbey. Also on the site was a Royal Palace built by King James VI after the Reformation and home to the King and Queen Anne of Denmark. After the King's death the Palace fell into disrepair but the ruins still survive to give visitors an idea of its original state. The present site is under split ownership with the Parish Church section being owned by the Church of Scotland. Services are held regularly and the buildings are open freely to the public. See www.dunfermlineabbey.co.uk for details. The rest of the site is under the care of Historic Scotland. There is an admission charge and the site is open all year round. See www.historic-scotland.gov.uk for details. The Abbey is located on St Margaret's Street, a ten minute walk from the Station.

Abbot House Heritage Centre. The unique Abbot House was built in the mid 15th century and is one of the few buildings to have survived the great fire of 1624. Although built as an Abbot's house, the building has also been a mansion house, art school, iron foundry and witness to some of the most significant history in Dunfermline and Scotland. Today the Centre has displays on 1000 years of Scottish history and that of Dunfermline, a café, shop and garden. The Centre is open all year and there is an admission charge. See www.abbothouse.co.uk for information. Located at 11 Maygate Street, the Centre is an 11 minute walk from the Station.

Andrew Carnegie Birthplace Museum. Perhaps Dunfermline's most famous resident, Andrew Carnegie was the son of a weaver who emigrated to America and amassed a huge fortune as an industrialist, after starting out humbly as a telegraph operator. Although he had many business interests, it is steel where he made the majority of his fortune. He gave away most of his wealth to educational causes which he was particularly interested in, building libraries, schools and universities. Today's museum tells his story and is situated inside the cottage where he was born and brought up. The Museum is located on Moodie Street, an eight minute walk from the Station. It is open from Easter until October and is free to enter. See www.carnegiebirthplace.com for details.

The Carnegie Library. Dunfermline is understandably proud of Carnegie and you will find all kinds of buildings named after him, and gifted to the town by him wherever you go. Of perhaps special significance though is the town's Carnegie Library. Still in use today as the public library, it holds the distinction of being the first Carnegie Library to be built, in 1883. It was the first of two and a half thousand to be built and even today if you live in the UK, USA, Ireland, Australia, New Zealand, Serbia, the Caribbean or Fiji you are probably not far from one. Most were constructed in the United States and they come in many different architectural styles.

Pittencrieff Park is probably the best public park in Scotland. Gifted to Dunfermline by Andrew Carnegie in 1904, the Park uses a natural glen and the surrounding former estate to provide an area of natural beauty and recreation in the heart of the town. The Park offers a children's play area, animal centre, greenhouses, woodland walks, skating area and toilets. Inside the Park is Pittencrieff House Museum which opened inside a former mansion house at the same time as the Park's opening. Both the Park and Museum offer free entry and are located ten minutes walk from Dunfermline Town Railway Station.

On leaving Dunfermline the railway heads south a few miles towards the Firth of Forth completing its circular journey through Fife.

Rosyth Station. Rosyth is another commuter town for Edinburgh and effectively linked to Inverkeithing. The train has come full circle and will shortly head back across the Forth Bridge. The town of Rosyth is most famous for its Dockyard. In 1994 it closed as a Royal Navy Dockyard but was soon purchased by a private company to continue contract work for the Royal Navy. Rosyth Dockyard is the planned location for the assembly of the new Queen Elizabeth aircraft carriers. The dock was also the terminal for the ferry service to Europe, although this service was discontinued in December 2010. One notable feature of the Dockyard is Rosyth Castle. Now a ruin on a small area of grass at the entrance to the Dockyard, the Castle dates from the 15th century. The tower is almost complete but in poor condition. Old photographs show that the Castle was on a small island in the sea but land reclamation for the docks has resulted in its new and very unattractive shore based industrial landscape.

Returning to the train the railway joins the mainline and once again crosses the Forth Railway Bridge, this time returning to Edinburgh.

10. The Highlands – Edinburgh to Inverness

The Edinburgh to Inverness rail line takes visitors over the famous Forth Rail Bridge and on to the Highland Mainline from Perth to Inverness. The journey starts in Scotland's capital city, Edinburgh and ends in the capital of the Highlands, Inverness. In between the train stops at top tourist destinations such as Perth, Pitlochry, and Aviemore. It is one of the country's most scenic railways as well as the highest, as the train crosses the Grampian Mountains between the sea level towns of Perth and Inverness. Along the way you will pass through Fife coastal scenery, the forests of Perthshire, the remote mountain ranges of the central Highlands and pass right through the Cairngorm National Park. It's a journey that takes the passenger thorough some of the most natural landscapes left in Scotland.

Journey Summary:

Route:	Edinburgh – Perth – Dunkeld and Birnam – Pitlochry – Blair Athol – Kingussie – Aviemore – Inverness.
Operator:	Scotrail with one East Coast service daily.
Trains:	Scotrail with standard and first class. Most have a trolley service. East Coast trains have standard and first class, café car and luggage van.
Trip Length:	3 hours 25 minutes.
Frequency:	Nine trains in each direction daily over entire route with five on Sundays. Additional trains over parts of route.
Links:	In Edinburgh East Coast and Cross Country trains to England. Air services from USA and Europe to Edinburgh. Local bus services at all towns along the route. Edinburgh, Perth and Inverness offer Plusbus tickets.

Falkirk

Trains follow the same route from Edinburgh as trains to Glasgow until they reach Falkirk (see the Chapter 11 for details of Falkirk). At Falkirk, Inverness trains branch off and call at the **Falkirk Grahamston Station**. The Station is fully serviced with a ticket office, ticket vending machine, waiting room, toilets, shops, luggage trolleys, pay phones and a taxi rank. Sleeper trains and the daily InterCity 'Highland Chieftain' service from London, both use Falkirk Grahamston, while Edinburgh to Glasgow trains call at Falkirk High station. On departure from Falkirk the train will go through Camelon Station (used by local services only). The **Falkirk Wheel** is clearly visible to the left of the train. At this point the train passes the site of a Roman fort and crosses the junction with the railway from Glasgow. If you started your journey at Glasgow Queen Street this is where the railway from Edinburgh joins and both continue the journey north from Edinburgh here together with passengers from Glasgow changing at Stirling, or more commonly Perth. Announcements on board will let you know which location to change at. Just before Larbert Station the train crosses the River Carron and the railway enters the most scenic part of the route which will continue until journey's end at Inverness. The line curves slightly to the west bringing the Ochil hills into view on the right. If travelling north on a summer's evening these hills are particularly beautiful with the sunset warming the steep rocks. The highest of these hills is **Ben Cleuch** (721 m) and it is an easy half day's hill walk starting in Tillicoultry village. To get there take a bus from either Stirling bus station or Alloa from a stance close to the railway station. See Traveline for details. In front of the hills is the River Forth which flows into the Firth of Forth just slightly to the east of the train.

Stirling

It has long been said 'He who holds Stirling holds Scotland'. With its strategic position between the Scottish Lowlands and Highlands, the crossing of the River Forth and highly defendable hill on which Stirling Castle sits, it has long been one of the key centres of power and influence in Scotland. Today it is a beautiful old town with a magnificent castle on the hill overlooking the town, a river and medieval old town. As one of the key towns in the Kingdom of Scotland, it was created a Royal Burgh by King David I in 1130, a position which was retained until 1975 when local government was reorganised. City status was granted in 2002 in celebration of Queen Elizabeth II's Golden Jubilee.

Although surrounded by hills, to the west, the Carse of Stirling flatlands are some of the most agriculturally productive in Scotland. In contrast are the Ochil Hills which end near the town centre at Abbey Craig, easily recognised by the tall stone Wallace Monument.

For today's visitor there is everything to keep you entertained from theatres, cinemas, restaurants and cafés to one of the most diverse range of attractions in Scotland. The town centre is easily explored on foot and has many pleasant places to stay, eat and shop. When walking through the town look out for several places of interest. On Castle Wynd (on the route to the Castle) the façade of **Mar's Wark** is visible. This remarkable Renaissance mansion was built by The Earl of Mar, Regent for James VI in 1570. In the town centre, next to the branch of WH Smith is the Bastion. This easy to miss underground cell is were criminals where housed as a punishment and has only recently been rediscovered. On Broad Street is the **Tolbooth**. This was once the hub of civic life and justice but has now been reinvented as a 21st century arts and performance space.

Practicalities

Stirling railway station (Goosecroft Road, FK8 1PF) is a large and busy station conveniently located in the town centre. The station is constructed of fine stone with glass canopies over the platforms to the rear. At the time of writing Stirling is still controlled by the old semaphore signalling system. Look out for the Stirling Middle signal box, one of the largest still in existence. The railway reached Stirling in 1848 while the current buildings date from 1916 and are Grade A listed. The station is fully serviced with a travel centre, ticket machines, waiting room, cash machine, telephones, toilets, newsagent, café, luggage trolleys and taxi rank. The station is busy with local trains to Glasgow, Edinburgh and Alloa, in addition to the long distance services.

Tourist Information. Stirling Tourist Information Centre is located at 41 Dumbarton Road, FK8 2QQ (eight minute walk from the Station) or telephone 08707 200620.

Local Transportation. Stirling town centre is small enough to explore on foot. Some attractions are better visited by using a local bus. Buses are operated by First Group, call Traveline for information on 0871 2002233. Local buses fares are included in Plusbus rail tickets to Stirling.

Places of Interest

Stirling Castle. Situated on the hill above the town, the Castle resembles Edinburgh's in style and with its imposing size and architecture is one of Scotland's most impressive. It has played a prominent role in Scottish history and the lives of every Scottish monarch up to the time of union with England in 1603. In 1304 it was taken by Edward I of England after a three month siege, but it was retaken ten years later by Bruce, after the Battle of Bannockburn. James II (1430) and James V (1512) were both born in the Castle. Highlights of the Castle include James IV's Great Hall (the largest medieval banqueting hall ever built in Scotland), James V's Palace, The Chapel Royal (1633), the Great Kitchens (recreating the banquets of James IV's time), and the regimental museum of the Argyll & Sutherland Highlanders. With its high position on the castle hill there are also amazing views across the countryside in all directions from the battlements. The Castle is open all year, there is an admission charge and it is a 14 minute walk from the railway station. See the Historic Scotland website or call 01786 450000 for details.

Argyll's Lodging is Scotland's finest surviving 17th century townhouse. The restored interiors reflect the opulent taste and lifestyle of its owners from William Alexander 'the father of Nova Scotia' to the powerful Argyll family. Painted ceilings, tapestries, four poster beds and period furnishings are the setting for the story of the house, told by costumed performers in summer. The House is open all year and there is an admission charge. However entry is free if you purchase a ticket to Stirling Castle. See the Historic Scotland website or call 01786 450000. It is located on the approach to Stirling Castle.

The Old Town. Located between the station and the Castle is the Old Town. This is history stretching back to the small community that grew up at the foot of the Castle rock. Look out for the Renaissance façade of Mar's

Wark, the unicorn on the Mercat Cross outside the Tolbooth and the 16th and 17th century merchants' houses as you stroll up Spittal Street and back down Broad Street. This is one of the few locations where you can experience Scottish architecture at its most traditional. Explore the closes and vennels between the buildings for unexpected views of the city and look out for the purple plaques which tell the story of individual buildings.

Wallace Monument. This is the national monument to one of Scotland's national heroes who led the Scots into battle against the army of King Edward I in 1297 and his harsh rule over Scotland. It stands on the Abbey Craig, a volcanic crag above Cambuskenneth Abbey, from which Wallace was said to have watched the gathering of the army of English king Edward I, just before the Battle of Stirling Bridge. Admission to the exhibition area and steps to climb to the top is charged. It is open all year. See www.nationalwallacemonument.com for details. The Monument is a short bus journey from the city centre, and is included in Plusbus fares to Stirling.

Church of the Holy Rude. Often overshadowed by the nearby Stirling Castle, the church is of almost equal significance and architectural interest as its more famous neighbour. Although established in 1129, the original building burnt during a fire in 1405 which destroyed most of the town. Rebuilding started slowly and the building gradually came together for completion in 1414. A second building phase between 1500 and 1555 completed the church as we now see it. The Church is unique in Britain as being the only active church other than Westminster Abbey to have hosted a coronation. This occurred on the 29th of July 1567 when King James VI as an infant became King of Scotland here. The name of the Church 'Holy Rude' means Holy Cross. It is open daily between 10.00 and 16.00 and is located on St John Street (FK8 1ED), a ten minute walk from the station on the way to the Castle.

Albert Halls. Since its opening over a hundred years ago the Albert Halls have been at the heart of Stirling's artistic and civic life, attracting many high-profile concerts and conferences and acting as a focus for the local community. Telephone 01786 473544 or alberthalls@stirling.gov.uk to find out what is on.

Cambuskenneth Abbey. The Abbey was established as long ago as 1140. However, it was destroyed and ruined by 1560 along with many others during the Reformation. All that remains today is the bell tower which is a wonderful example of 13th century architecture. The Abbey was very important to the life of the Castle, along with the Church of the Holy Rude. To get there follow Shore Road and then Abbey Road to the east of the station and cross the river on the footbridge to reach the opposite bank and the Abbey. It has free entry and is open all year. See the Historic Scotland website for details.

Old Bridge. This handsome bridge was built in the 15th or early 16th century and is located in the town centre just north of the station. The southern arch was rebuilt in 1749 after it had been blown up during the rebellion of 1745, to prevent the Jacobite army entering the town. For the first 400 years of its existence it was the lowest crossing over the River.

Nearby Places of Interest

Return to Stirling station for a trip to **Alloa**. Alloa is the largest town in the historic county of Clackmannanshire in central Scotland. It is situated on the north bank of the River Forth, with the Ochil Hills forming a glorious background. The railway between Stirling and Alloa opened in 1853 but was closed by British Railways in 1968. In 2008 after an effort to reopen the line, the rail link was restored. The short 12 minute journey between Stirling and Alloa is along the foot of the Ochil Hills and under the Wallace Monument. Trains run directly from Glasgow via Stirling to Alloa or you may change at Stirling if travelling from any other destination. Alloa Station (Station Road, FK10 1BA) is in the town centre and is a modern building with a waiting room and self service ticket machine. There is no ticket office, toilets or other facilities at this station.

Although Alloa is not a tourist destination, it is worth making the journey to view the National Trust property of **Alloa Tower** (Alloa Park, FK10 1PP). This 14th century building is the largest remaining medieval tower house in Scotland and is set in an attractive park. Once owned by Earls of Mar, there are now excellent displays of the family's art, furniture and belongings. The Tower is located in the town centre, about a 12 minute walk from the station. It is open from April until October and there is an admission charge. See the National Trust website or telephone 0844 4932129 for information.

Return to Stirling station to continue your journey. Shortly after departure the train passes through **Bridge of Allan station** (local trains stop here). The station has a ticket machine, waiting shelters and pay phone. Bridge of Allan was once a spa town and still has an attractive town centre with local shops. It is also possible to get there by using the Stirling Plusbus ticket, taking a bus from Stirling via the Wallace Monument. From Bridge of Allan it is only a few miles through a small wooded valley before arrival in Dunblane.

Dunblane

Dunblane is an attractive small town with the Allan Water River flowing through the town centre. The High Street and Cathedral are on the east bank of the river and the whole town is surrounded by pleasant wooded hills. The town centre is compact and retains many of its older buildings. The **Leighton Library** is the oldest private library in Scotland and is open to visitors on selected days during the summer. It contains around 4,000 volumes and 78 manuscripts, dating from the 16th century to the 19th century. The collection is founded on the personal library of Archbishop Robert Leighton (1611 – 1684) and is now owned by the nearby University of Stirling. Close by is the medieval **Dean's House,** which now houses the local history museum. It is open during the summer with free admission. Also look out for the Dunblane Hydro. This impressive Victorian Italianate hotel was constructed in 1878 as a resort and became popular with people coming to 'take the waters'. For those wishing to take a longer walk it is possible to walk either to or from the nearby Bridge of Allan along a river walk known as the Darn Walk. It is only about a mile and a half walk but if you don't feel like walking back you can always take the train.

Practicalities

Dunblane railway station (Station Road, FK15 9ET) has a ticket office, ticket vending machine, waiting room, toilets and pay phone. The station was once a junction at the start of the Callander and Oban railway, which closed in 1965. Today local rail services terminate here from the south and several long distance services from Inverness and Aberdeen also call here.

Places of Interest

The main attraction in Dunblane is the **Cathedral** (FK15 0AQ) which may be seen from the train. Construction was started in the 11th century and it is still in use today as the local Church of Scotland. The base of the Bell Tower dates from that time, having been extended in the 15th century, while the nave dates from the 13th century. The entire building was refurbished between 1889 and 1893 by Sir Rowand Anderson. It is remarkable in having retained more of its medieval choir stalls than any other Scottish church, and for its grand Gothic west front entrance. Today it is under the care of Historic Scotland and is open year round with free admission. See www.dunblanecathedral.org.uk or the Historic Scotland website for information. It is only a five minute walk from the station.

The train departs Dunblane and makes its way along the side of the hills which lead up to Sheriff Muir. This is a popular area for walking and is reached from a path at the back of Dunblane. On the left of the train is Cromlet Hill (406 metres) while the river is the Allan Water. After the small village of Blackford (no station) look out for the Glen Eagle valley stretching up to the right. The valley gives its name to the next stop for the luxury Gleneagles Hotel.

Gleneagles Railway Station still displays some of its grand past, but although now unstaffed still has a daily InterCity service. There is a seating area, information point and pay phone. The station was built in 1919 by the Caledonian Railway to serve the nearby **Gleneagles Hotel** which was opened a few years later in 1924, also by the Caledonian Railway. The station also serves the community of Auchterarder which with its 1.5 mile long High Street is known as the 'Lang Toon'. The Hotel is a 16 minute walk from the station while the town of Auchterarder is best reached by taxi or bus from Perth.

From Gleneagles the train makes its way through a wide and attractive valley following the course of the River Earn on the left of the train. Kirkton Hill is on the left of the train as the line joins with the alternative route from Edinburgh via Kirkaldy. Most Scotrail services run via this other route through Fife (described in Chapter 7, Edinburgh to Aberdeen) and both now meet to head through the Kirkton Hill tunnel and into Perth.

Perth

This is an ancient town claiming to go back to Roman times and has a long association with the Scottish Kings. Many Scottish monarchs where crowned on the Stone of Destiny at Scone Palace. Little now remains of the old town, however this does mean visitors today are greeted by a well preserved and exceptionally laid out Victorian town centre. The town is picturesquely situated on the banks of the River Tay, which is Scotland's longest river at 119 miles in length. There is a pleasant river walk and many places to enjoy the view. The town centre is clean and well laid out, while compact enough to explore on foot. There are lots of shops, including many locally owned, places to eat and hotels.

Practicalities

Perth railway station is in the city centre on Leonard Street (PH2 8RT). The station was built by the Scottish Central Railway and designed by Sir William Tite, who won an award for this building. It is still an impressive building, while several old large platform clocks and architectural details to keep waiting passengers amused. When using Perth Station make sure to check what part of the station your train is leaving from. The curved platforms on the east side serve trains to and from Aberdeen and Glasgow, while the main part of the station has trains for Inverness, Edinburgh and occasionally Glasgow. The station is fully serviced with ticket office, ticket vending machine, luggage trolleys, toilets, waiting rooms, information, a café, bookstore and a taxi rank outside. The bus station is located nearby, opposite the Station Hotel.

Tourist Information. Perth Tourist Information provides a full range of services including an accommodation booking service. It is located at: Lower City Mills, West Mill Street, Perth, Perthshire, PH1 5QP. Tel: 01738 450600. E-Mail: perthtic@perthshire.co.uk

Local Transport. Local buses are operated by Stagecoach. See www.stagecoachbus.com or telephone Traveline on 0871 2002233 for information. Buses in Perth are included in Plusbus rail tickets to Perth.

Places of Interest

Huntingtower Castle. Consisting of two towers built in the 15th and 16th centuries, the Castle was known as the House of Ruthven. It is set in attractive Perthshire countryside on the edge of the ever expanding town of Perth. Highlights of a visit today include a 16th century painted ceiling, the now resident owls and the maiden's leap. The leap is a gap between the top of the two towers which is named after a daughter of the Ruthvens, Dorothea, who jumped over it while fleeing from her mother after being discovered visiting her fiancé in the other tower. The gap is just over 9 feet wide. The Castle has had many famous visitors including Mary Queen of Scot's who took her honeymoon here in 1565. It was a residence for 300 years until it was abandoned in the 18th century. See the Historic Scotland website or tel. 01738 627231 for details of opening times and charges. It is open all year. To reach the Castle, take Stagecoach bus number 14 from Perth to Pitcairngreen. Stay on the bus for eight minutes and get off at the end of the Castle driveway from where it is a six minute walk. This bus journey is included in Plusbus rail tickets to Perth.

Kinnoull Hill Woodland Park. This woodland hillside part is close to the city centre on the east side of the river. The view from the top is spectacular looking along the River Tay and is famous due to its extensive use in tourism publications. The woodland park was Scotland's first, opening in 1924. It actually consists of five hills – Corsiehill, Deuchny Hill, Barn Hill, Binn Hill and Kinnoull Hill. Although near the centre of the city, there are miles of grassy paths and way-marked nature trails through fine mixed woodland of Scots pine, larch, oak, birch and Norway spruce, with the added benefit of some excellent open viewpoints. The summit is 222 metres above sea level. Look out for the spectacular cliffs on the south of the hill and Kinnoull Tower, a 19th century folly said to be inspired by the castles of the German Rhineland. As well as walking, cyclists are welcomed on specific trails. The start point is a pleasant 19 minute walk through Perth city centre and across the river. To get there either walk up Bowerswell Road or Lochie Brae to the Park entrance. Alternatively bus number 11, the Kinnoull Hill circular, from the city centre, passes close to the entrance.

Branklyn Garden. Close to Kinnoull Hill is Branklyn Garden (PH2 7BB) which is owned by the National Trust for Scotland. It is said to be the finest two acres of garden in the country. It was the work of the original owners, who started to transform this former orchard in 1922. Seasonal highlights include the renowned collection of primulas, alpines and rhododendrons in May and June, while in the autumn the garden comes to life with the fiery red acers. The Garden is predominantly a collection of plants from China, Tibet, Bhutan and the Himalayas. It is easily reached on foot from the centre of Perth. Follow the signs at the south end of Tay Street near the Fergusson Gallery. The walk takes about 25 minutes. See www.branklyngarden.org.uk or telephone 01738 625535. It is open Easter until October and there is an admission charge.

Perth Museum and Art Gallery (George Street, PH1 5LB). Perth's museum is housed in one of Scotland's oldest museum buildings, having opened in 1824. The attractive building with its white columned entrance hall is everything one would hope to find at a traditional museum. The exhibits are of an equally high standard and include silver, glass, art, human history, archaeology, geology and natural history. It is open all year with free admission and is a 14 minute walk from the station.

The Fergusson Gallery (PH2 8NU). Housed under the round dome of the former Perth Water Works (constructed 1832) is the Fergusson Gallery. The Gallery is home to a collection of John Duncan Fergusson's work. Fergusson was one of the most influential Scottish artists of the 20th century and one of the few British artists who took part in the Impressionist revolution of Paris prior to the First World War. To reach the Gallery from Perth station head east along Marshall Place towards the river for 400 metres. Entry is free. Telephone 01738 441944 for opening times.

Scone Palace (PH2 6BD). Known as the Palace of Kings, the site was the crowning place (the location – not the Palace, which is much later!) of Scottish Kings prior to the present Palace's construction. This is the location where Macbeth, Robert the Bruce and Charles II, amongst others, were crowned. There is a replica of Stone of Scone or Destiny on display. The original is on display at Edinburgh Castle. The present day building dates from 1808. The interior of the Palace is open together with the formal gardens and woodland walks. To get there either walk (50 minutes through town and along river) or take bus number 58 or 3 which drops you off at the end of the Palace driveway. The journey is included in Plusbus railway tickets to Perth. It is open from Easter until October and has an admission charge. See www.scone-palace.co.uk or telephone 01738 552300 for details.

Return to the Station for the journey north. On leaving Perth the train begins what is possibly one of the most beautiful stretches of line in the country, the Highland Mainline. About two miles out of Perth, the observant may catch a glimpse of Stanley Junction. This former junction was once the start point of the Highland Railway which used the tracks of the rival Caledonian Railway to reach Perth, and is the official start of the mainline.

The line now runs through beautiful Perthshire countryside. A mixture of farmland and forest with rolling hills, it has been a popular tourist destination since the railway arrived. The River Tay is on the right of the train until Stanley. When the River comes back into view a few miles north the train enters a narrow valley with Birnam Hill and Wood on the left and Crieff Hill on the right. This beautiful valley is the location of Dunkeld and Birnam, our next stop.

Dunkeld and Birnam

Birnam is linked to its twin village, Dunkeld, by a seven-arched bridge built by Thomas Telford. The village is surrounded by wooded and hilly Perthshire countryside, and in particular 'The Hermitage', a beautiful wooded gorge. The area inspired Beatrix Potter, who spent her childhood holidays here. She is celebrated in the Birnam Institute and the Beatrix Potter Garden.

Dunkeld was proclaimed the first ecclesiastical capital of Scotland by Scotland's first King, Kenneth MacAlpin. The majestic and partly ruined cathedral dominates the town from its idyllic river side setting. The **Cathedral** was constructed between 1260 and 1501. Unfortunately, it was soon badly damaged by unrest. After rebuilding in 1600 it again suffered during the 1689 Jacobite uprising when it was burnt down. Today the tower and chapter house are complete and have a small museum on the history of the Cathedral. The east end is still a local church while the west end is now ruined, having never been rebuilt. On the way to the Cathedral look out for the Atholl Memorial fountain which was erected in 1866 by public subscription in memory of the 6th Duke of Atholl.

The brightly coloured 'little houses' of Dunkeld were built in the early 1700s. Restored to provide homes for local people, they are now in the care of The National Trust For Scotland (NTS). Another NTS property is the Ell Shop featuring the original 'ell' measure, just over a metre long, used for measuring cloth.

Atholl Street still provides variety with its specialist and locally owned shops while a riverside path provides excellent views of Thomas Telford's Dunkeld Bridge. The surrounding area is excellent for walking and cycling, with forest walks, cycle trails and standing stones all nearby.

Practicalities

The impressive stone built station building at Dunkeld (PH8 0DP) is no longer staffed, although there is a telephone help-point and information for passengers. Waiting shelters are also provided, and there is a public pay phone. The towns of Dunkeld and Birnam are both located a very short walk from the station. Make sure to use the underpass to cross the busy road outside the station. The area is easily, and best explored by foot or bike but taxis are on call from the rail station if required.

Tourist Information. Dunkeld Tourist Information Centre is located at The Cross, Dunkeld (PH8 OAN). Tel. 01350 727688. E-Mail: dunkeldtic @perthshire.co.uk. The Centre is a short walk from the railway station.

Places of Interest

Forest Walks. There are a number of forest walks in the area: Atholl Woods, Craigvinean Forest, Fungarth Hill, Niel Gows Oak, The Birnam Oak, The Dunkeld Larches and Rumbling Bridge Falls are all either within easy walking or cycling distance of the village. Leaflets on all of these are available from the Tourist Information Centre or are marked on Ordnance Survey maps of the area.

Rumbling Bridge Falls. An old stone bridge spans the gorge high above the deep, rocky narrows and takes its name from the furious rumbling of the River Braan below. Queen Victoria visited this spot in 1865 and was much impressed by the dramatic watery scene. In her diary for 11th October she wrote that the flow was "most splendid" and that "swollen by rain, it came down with an immense volume of water, with a deafening noise". Landscape painter Sir John Millais stayed in nearby Rumbling Bridge Cottage when he worked on his well known landscape paintings "The Sound of Many Waters" (1876) and "St Martin's Summer" (1877). The River Braan was the inspiration for both these works.

Both the waterfall and old bridge may be seen as part of the Braan Walk, a way-marked route that forms part of the Dunkeld and Birnam walks network. An information leaflet is available from Dunkeld Tourist Information Centre.

Birnam Hill. Standing on the edge of the Highland boundary fault line, Birnam Hill is a wonderful viewpoint; eastwards across Loch of the Lowes and on to the fertile farmland of Strathmore; westwards to the hills of Perthshire. The hill rises steeply to 1300 feet and can be climbed by a well signposted circular route that forms part of the Dunkeld and Birnam walks network. Lower slopes are gentle and covered in deciduous woodland, while the path to the summit (also known as The Kings Seat) is heathery and rougher as it leads onto high open ground. On the way round look out for The Stair Bridge viewpoint, a high bridge that looks out onto some small lochs, and Rohallion Castle, a ruined old tower. Both these points of interest are signposted and worth the small detour. Birnam Hill is a naturalist's delight. By treading softly it is often possible to watch small groups of roe deer in the shady glades. These deer have short, vertical antlers and red brown coats in summer. Black grouse and the large capercaillie bird also live on the hill and feed on pine needles and blueberries found at the summit. Capercaillies are noisy birds and make a horse-like 'clop clop' call – befitting the translation of their name which means 'Horse of the Woods'!

The Birnam Institute (Station Road, PH8 0DS). The Birnam Arts & Conference Centre has its origins in the scheme initiated by John Kinnaird, the local stationmaster, in 1880 to create a community facility for 'education and entertainment'. Today the Centre has rapidly established itself as a hugely successful new multi-arts and conference centre right in the heart of Scotland. There is a year round programme of high quality exhibitions, music, theatre, dance and comedy performances, as well as the chance to participate in a wide range of workshop activities for children and adults alike. Further information can be obtained from the Institute's website at www.birnaminstitute.com.

The Hermitage (PH8 0AN). This conifer and deciduous wooded gorge through which the River Braan plunges is one of the highlights of the area. Also to be observed is the picturesque folly 'Ossian's Hall', built in 1758. It is located a short walk from the station.

Loch of the Lowes. A short cycle ride or taxi from the towns is the Loch of the Lowes which is managed by The Scottish Wildlife Trust. The star attraction from early April to late August is a pair of breeding ospreys. Their usual location is situated within 200 metres of the hides, allowing the ospreys to be observed both through telescopes and on a monitor in the Visitor Centre. If you are lucky you may even see them catch a fish in the loch! Other wildlife is also present at the site including otters, fallow and roe deer. Other birds which may be seen include redstart, spotted and pied flycatcher, crossbill and kingfisher. See the Scottish Wildlife Trust website for details – www.swt.org.uk.

Returning to the station, the train continues north alongside the River Tay. The large woodland on the left of the train is the Tay Forest Park and Craigvinean Forest. The paths through this forest start in Dunkeld. First head to the Hermitage and then simply continue through the Forest as far as you wish. The train however is now heading to the right, across the river Tay on a bridge and up through the valley, which has now widened into a large valley floor with the railway, river and road sharing the space between the mountains on either side of the train. The scenery is changing too with fewer trees and more heather as the ancient forest on this higher ground has been destroyed in favour of sheep grazing and deer. A fast sprint up the track brings Athol Palace Hotel (in Pitlochry) with its four spires into view on the right before arrival at the station.

Pitlochry

This town has a wonderful setting on the River Tummel and backed by Ben Vrackie. It is perhaps at its best in the changing colours of autumn. There are wonderful walks along the River Tummel and through the woods around Loch Faskally, and there is the new beauty of the Scottish Plant Collectors' Garden, opened in 2003. An unusual attraction at Pitlochry Power Station and Dam is a salmon ladder, which helps the fish by-pass the dam and get into Loch Faskally. The ladder is open to the public to watch the fish leaping upstream. Downstream is the nationally renowned Pitlochry Festival Theatre.

Practicalities

Pitlochry railway station (Station Road, PH16 5AN) is an attractive stone built building originally constructed by the Highland Railway Company. On the island platform the decorative wooden structure houses a second waiting room for that platform. There is also a more modern ornamental 'porter' sculpture which is popular with children and photographers. The station is staffed and has a ticket office, public telephone, toilets and luggage trolleys. There is a taxi rank outside and buses depart from nearby on the town's main street. There is also a bookstall in the station.

Tourist Information. Pitlochry Tourist Information Centre is located at 22 Atholl Road (PH16 5BX). Tel. 01796 472215.

Places of Interest

Pitlochry Festival Theatre. With over 60,000 visits a year from theatre-goers throughout the UK and abroad, the Theatre is probably the most special of Scotland's theatres, and loved by audiences far and wide for the outstanding quality of its productions, and its Highland setting. See www.pitlochry.org.uk or Tel. 01796 484626 for information.

Pitlochry Dam and Fish Ladder. The Pitlochry dam and power station has a built in fish ladder. This is accessible via a short walk from the car parks at the south side of Pitlochry. Viewing panels allow close observation of the wild salmon as they use the fish pass to move up and over the 86.5 metre high dam to get upstream to Loch Faskally and their spawning beds in the river beyond. On average 5000 wild salmon pass through each year, between April and late September.

Explorers Garden tells the stories of some of the men who risked their lives travelling the globe to find new plants and trees for cultivation, commerce and conservation. The Garden is separated into glades, representing the areas of the world from where plants originated. One minute you can be strolling through a North American glade, the next you're trekking through Nepal. Various sculptures, artworks, specially commissioned buildings and stunning views appear around every corner. The Fish Ladder, Theatre and Explorers Garden are all located on Port-Na-Craig Road (PH16 5DR), about ten minutes walk from the station.

Black Spout Wood is situated to the south of Pitlochry and takes its name from the impressive Black Spout waterfall, some 60 metres high on the Edradour Burn. A series of way-marked paths meanders through the wood, with linking footbridges constructed over the burns. Close to the waterfall, a carefully positioned viewing platform offers dramatic views. The route to the waterfall takes the walker through a delightful variety of quiet mixed woodlands. The walk to the Black Spout waterfall is easily accessible, on foot, from the centre of Pitlochry.

Blair Athol Distillery is one of the oldest working distilleries in Scotland. After enjoying a leisurely conducted tour, you can mull over the distinctive character of the finished article as you sip your dram of Blair Athol 12 Year Old. Please note that the distillery is in Pitlochry and not Blair Athol as the name might suggest! It is located a short walk from Pitlochry station on Perth Road (PH16 5LY).

On departing Pitlochry look out of the left side of the train for one of the most interesting sections of the line. The train climbs along a ledge on the side of the Killiecrankie Pass. This very narrow ravine with the River Garry at the bottom is forested and is one of the scenic highlights of the journey. The train slows and the wheels squeal as it makes its way through the tight curves. After leaving the Pass, the valley widens and the train travels amongst the hills to Blair Athol station.

Blair Athol

Blair Athol station (on the main street, PH18 5SL) is unstaffed as the stone building has been converted into a house. However the station remains open and most trains make a stop here. There is an information point and waiting shelters on both platforms. The station is situated amongst the hills and is right on the main street of the small village. The village itself is small but very attractive with a hotel, post office, shop, church and some attractive stone houses. The surroundings take the rail passenger back to another time. Additionally with the help of a highway bypass, motor traffic is kept to a minimum. On leaving the station take a walk through the village. On the opposite side of the road to the station, and a little down the street, are the gates of the driveway leading to Blair Castle. If you choose to visit the Castle late in the day, these gates will be closed when you leave. However it is still possible to get out that way through them as a pedestrian, don't follow the cars leaving the long way!

Blair Castle is the seat of the Dukes of Athol and home to Europe's only private army, the Athol Highlanders. This is a beautiful white castle which was started in 1269 and progressively developed since then. Visitors can choose to visit the grounds only or the castle and grounds. There is plenty to see so allow the whole day for a visit. The gardens include a recently restored walled garden and Britain's highest tree at 67.8 metres tall. The castle itself is entered through the main hallway. From there a self guided tour will take you on a visit to over 30 different rooms through the entire building. There is also a shop and restaurant. Children will enjoy the suits of armour on display while adults will enjoy the many pieces of fine furniture and antiques to be found on the tour.

The train departs Blair Athol and makes its way through the most mountainous section of the line. Hills tower above the train on both sides of the line as Glen Garry, followed by Drumochter Pass are crossed on one of the few easy passages of the mountains. At the Summit of Drumochter there is a traditional sign marking the highest point on the British railway network at 1484 feet (452m). Considering that the line begins and ends at sea level it is easy to imagine why this line was quite a challenge to steam trains. The valley opens up as the train heads out of the Pass, while Loch Ericht provides an entirely different type of view on the left of the train. The loch is actually a seven miles long and all that is seen from the train is the end, most of the Loch being hidden behind the hills as the train is inside the Pass. Some trains now make a stop at Dalwhinnie Station.

Dalwhinnie Station. The station is located on the street in Dalwhinnie (PH19 1AD) and is now unstaffed, although several trains a day do make the stop here. There is an information point, waiting room and shelter and pay phone. In addition to serving the small community of Dalwhinnie, the stop is popular with walkers and those wishing to explore the surrounding countryside and hills. See an Ordnance Survey map for details of where to walk. You can also alight here to visit the Dalwhinnie Distillery. The distinctively shaped roof of the kiln (where the grain is dried) can be seen from the train as you pass shortly after leaving the station.

At this point the train enters the Cairngorm National Park (refer to the Aviemore entry for full details). The Park begins at Dalwhinnie and the train will make its way through the Park until just after Carrbridge Station. Glen Truim is the next section of line for the train to cross. This is one of Scotland's major glens stretching for nearly 18 miles from Drumochter Pass to Kingussie. The high heather covered hills on either side of the train are in contrast with the rich fertile valley floor with its attractive river meandering through.

Newtonmore

Newtonmore Station (PH20 1AL) has a traditional stone Highland station building now converted into a house. There is an information point and waiting shelter. Newtonmore is a traditional Highland village with idyllic streets, houses and atmosphere. All the services you would expect for the visitor are available here but without the modernisation that has changed nearby Aviemore.

Places of Interest

Walking and outdoor activities. Paths radiate from Newtonmore and are ideal for walking, cycling or mountain biking. Simply buy an Ordnance Survey map and pick your route. There are numerous surrounding hills for those interested in hill walking.

Highland Folk Museum (Kingussie Road, PH20 1AY). Hands on activities, demonstrations and recreations mark this 32 acre, one mile-long open air museum which traces Highland life from 1700 to the present day. The site includes farm areas, woodland and open areas, together with a huge selection of buildings which have been recreated on the site. There are many collections of smaller items including the domestic, sports, agricultural, crafts, trade and textiles collections. On a larger scale there is an impressive collection of Highland vernacular architecture through buildings which have been saved and re created in an authentic environment. As artefacts in their own right they include a smoke house, school, church, clockmaker's workshop, croft house, post office, railway halt and joiner's shop. The Museum contains one of the most important collections in the country. It is open from Easter until October. To find out more see www.highlandfolk.com or telephone 01540 673551. The museum is a 24 minute walk from the Station down Newtonmore Main Street or alongside the golf course. It is recommended you allow three to five hours for your visit.

Newtonmore Golf Club. This pleasant course is situated right beside the station, and set in attractive National Park scenery. See www.newton moregolf.com for information and to book a visit on the course.

Waltzing Waters. A unique attraction in Newtonmore is the Waltzing Waters show. This water and light show is performed to music each day at the attraction. See www.waltzingwaters.co.uk for information. It located a 16 minute walk from the station on Main Street (PH20 1DR).

The train departs Newtonmore and makes the short sprint along the valley floor and alongside the River Spey to Kingussie.

Kingussie

Kingussie is a pleasant small Highland town with restaurants, cafés, shops and a good selection of places to stay. As with Newtonmore many people prefer its quieter pace compared with nearby Aviemore. If considering a place to stay, Kingussie has the advantage over Newtonmore that more trains stop here. The architecture is traditional stone construction and the town is attractive, if lacking any buildings of particular note. Being in the heart of the National Park means that Kingussie's best feature is the surrounding countryside. There are many walks and cycle routes from the town.

Practicalities

Kingussie railway station (Ruthven Road, PH21 1EN) is an attractive single storey stone building built by the Highland Railway Company. It has a decorative iron, wood and glass canopy over the main platform and a traditional signal box which is still in use. It has a staffed ticket office, luggage trolleys, toilets, waiting room and waiting shelter.

Kingussie Tourist Information. This seasonal office is located at the Highland Folk Museum, Duke Street, Kingussie, PH21 1JG. Tel 0845 2255121.

Places of Interest

Kingussie Museum. Although not open to the public except on special occasions, you may view the buildings of the Museum from near the main street. It is part of the Highland Folk Museum which has its main base and collections at the Newtonmore site.

From Kingussie Station follow Ruthven road south (walk or cycle). This is a National Cycle Network Route to Aviemore which starts in Newtonmore. The Newtonmore to Kingussie section is a traffic free route while the section from Kingussie follows a quiet road. About a 20 minute walk south of Kingussie is **Ruthven Barracks**. This now ruined building was constructed in 1719 following the 1715 Jacobite uprising. It was captured by Charles Edward Stuart's army in 1746 and burnt. All that remains are the walls of the accommodation block and stables. A further ten minute walk along the route (less by bike) takes you to the **Insh Marshes Nature Reserve**. This spectacular wetland is one of Europe's most important. It is best to visit in springtime for nesting lapwings, redshanks and curlews, or visit in the winter when the marsh floods. It is owned by the RSPB – see www.rspb.org.uk.

Departing from Kingussie, the journey continues along the valley. On the right side of the train enjoy views of the Insh Marsh Nature Reserve. Behind the reserve is Inshriach Forrest. There are miles of cycle or walking trails in this area which may be reached by local bus from Aviemore or Kingussie. If travelling by bike, Kingussie Station is a good starting point for exploring these. Behind the Forest the Cairngorm Mountain Range comes into view, which is the heart of the Park. The train then makes its way alongside Loch Insh with the mountains in the background. Have your camera ready at this point especially if travelling north as the sun sets in the evening. Beyond the Loch another smaller loch comes into view on the left, Loch Alvie and on the right is the Duke of Gordon's Monument.

Aviemore & Cairngorm National Park

Aviemore was once an important junction on the Highland Railway network. This small railway town grew and later became an important Highland tourist resort. In the 1970s in an effort to boost this industry which was going through hard times, the Aviemore Centre was built. This was designed to be an all year tourist destination. The focus was skiing in the winter and all year attractions at the Centre. Unfortunately with unreliable snow conditions and poor architecture, it soon fell into disrepair and always lacked the charm of competing resorts in Europe. More recently the area was incorporated into the new Cairngorms National Park. An effort is underway to promote Aviemore as a destination again, this time more sensibly focusing on the area's greatest asset – its natural scenery. The old Centre has been demolished and new hotels and accommodation constructed in its place. The village has also been much improved. Today it offers a convenient and pleasant location from which to explore the Cairngorm National Park.

Practicalities

The station (Grampian Road, PH22 1PD) is a very attractive wooden building with three platforms and numerous buildings. It was the largest on the former Highland Railway network and has large canopies spanning the platforms. There is a staffed ticket office, waiting room, luggage trolleys, toilets, payphone, newsagents and café. Please note that the steam railway ticket office is on Platform 3 rather than at the main ticket office. Taxis and buses leave from outside the main building. The station is in the middle of the village on the main street.

Local Transportation. The best way to explore the Park area is on foot and by bike. Bike hire is readily available or take your own on the train. For the less energetic there are good bus links through the entire Park area departing from outside the railway station. A particularly useful bus link for visitors is the bus to the Cairngorm Mountain itself which also takes in lochs and forests along the way. It serves a number of attractions and departs from the station. Not to be forgotten, there is also a steam railway departing from the station to the nearby Boat of Garten and Broomhill. Between the rail, bus, walking and cycling there is no need for a car to enjoy the Park.

Tourist Information. Aviemore Tourist Information Centre is located in the shopping centre at Unit 7, Grampian Road (PH22 1RH). Tel: 0845 2255121. The office is located close to the rail station on the main street. For accommodation information, a good place to start is Aviemore's own official tourist site – www.visitaviemore.com.

Places of Interest

Craigellachie National Nature Reserve. Behind the village is the reserve on a hill, simply follow the signs from the centre. It is about an hour's walk and is renowned for its birch trees and peregrine falcons which often nest high on the rocky crags.

The **Strathspey Railway** takes visitors on a scenic journey to Boat of Garten and Broomhill by steam train. The line starts in Aviemore and travels through the heart of the National Park. The railway's existence is the result of a group of volunteers who wished to save the railway from Aviemore to Grantown on Spey and see steam run in the Highlands. Their hard work paid off in 1978 when the first train ran. Ever since steam trains have delighted the public each year. While there are many steam railways all over the country, this line must possess some of the finest scenery of them all. From Aviemore passengers are treated to a pine forest and heather filled view of the Cairngorm Mountain range, while after Boat of Garten the scenery changes to farmland, while running alongside the River Spey. The line presently terminates at Broomhill, useful for walkers and cyclists to reach the village of Nethy Bridge. However there are plans to reinstate the line as far as the attractive Speyside town of Grantown on Spey. At the moment an alternative bus service runs between Aviemore, Boat of Garten and Grantown on Spey for days when the train is not running, or for those who wish to travel the full route. Rail enthusiasts will be pleased to find a good selection of locomotives and rolling stock, together with three authentically restored railway stations. While at Boat of Garten, take time to visit the nearby **RSPB Loch Garten** nature reserve where ospreys may be viewed between April and August. It is a three mile walk from the station through nice scenery, or take your bike as it is on the National Cycle Network (on road route). Alternatively there are numerous **forest walks** starting from the station and some good places to eat. Both Boat of Garden and Broomhill Stations provide access to the **Abernethy Forest** trails and Speyside Way long distance walk. See www.strathspeyrailway.com or telephone the railway's office at Aviemore for information (01479 810725). When travelling on the Strathspey Railway, remember to buy your ticket before boarding. All of the stations have staffed ticket offices and gift shops. First and third class tickets are available and you may take your bike or canoe in the guards van. Trains are able to accommodate wheelchair using passengers in a specially converted coach.

Scenic Bus Journey to Cairngorm Mountain. The bus (number 34) departs from Aviemore station and makes its way through the Glenmore Forest Park before climbing the Cairngorm Mountain. There are lots of places of interest along the way, so ask about an unlimited travel ticket as you will probably want the flexibility to get on and off the bus to visit the various attractions. For the more energetic there is a footpath all the way from Aviemore to the top of Cairngorm Mountain.

On leaving Aviemore the bus winds its way through the **Rothiemurchus Estate Forest**. This is one of the few places in Scotland where the original Caledonian Pine Forest still exists. The area is abundant in local wildlife including the native red squirrel, deer and ospreys. Most visitors start at the Rothiemurchus Centre which is the main office for the Estate and also has an on site restaurant. It is the first stop for the bus, or you can walk from the station in about 30 minutes as a footpath is provided. There are many activities available at the Estate including archery, astronomy, canoeing, walking, climbing, safaris and wildlife watching. See the website at www.rothiemurchus.net or telephone 01479 812345 for information or to make a booking.

The bus then makes its way to **Loch Morlich** and travels alongside the Loch for its full length. This area is filled with footpaths so alight anywhere in the area for walking. It is also a popular location for picnics.

At the end of the Loch is the **Glenmore Forest Park**. Owned by the Forestry Commission it is a continuation of the Caledonian Pine Forrest of Rothiemuchus. The Glenmore Visitor Centre provides a café, shop and toilets, together with a Ranger post to supply information on the walking and cycling opportunities around the Park. It is open everyday except Christmas from 09.00 until 17.00. Telephone 01463 791575 or see the Forestry Commission website for information about the Park. There are numerous walks from a half hour to all day around the area with a choice of both low and high level walks. **Loch Morlich** is next to the Park and with its Cairngorm Mountain backdrop is one of Scotland's most popular leisure lochs. Unusually it has a pleasant sandy beach which is ideal for picnics. It also offers a range of water sports – kayaking, wind surfing and sailing – with tuition and equipment hire available. See www.lochmorlich.com or telephone 01479 861221 for prices, opening times and to make bookings.

Return to the bus for the final leg of the journey to the top of the Mountain. **Cairngorm Mountain** at 1245 metres (4084 feet) is the sixth highest peak in Britain. The mountain is often confused with the Cairngorm Mountain ski and activities resort of the same name. However the mountain is also popular with hill walkers and a look at a map will show the large number of high level walks and climbs around the summit and on to surrounding peeks. The resort itself provides everything you would need for winter sports and is Scotland's premier ski centre. To find out about winter sports and equipment hire see www.cairngormmountain.co.uk. There is also a funicular railway to take walkers, skiers and view finders to the summit. It is open year round and departs from the bus arrival point.

Nearby Places of Interest

Highland Wildlife Park. The Park was established in 1972 by the Royal Zoological Society of Scotland, the owners of Edinburgh Zoo. It provides a natural environment for Scottish wildlife and a more spacious place for some of the larger animals from Edinburgh to live. Species collections are divided into Scottish, European, Mountain and Tundra. Many people do not realise that much of Scotland's wildlife is now extinct in the wild and only remains in the Park. Bison, wolf, elk and wild boar are amongst some of the more unusual species on display. Also new to the Park are a family of Amur tigers. These are the largest of all big cats. In the autumn of 2009, Britain's only polar bear arrived at the Park and is proving to be very popular. Tours start at the main gate where foot visitors are driven around the open display areas before entering the enclosures to walk around at your own pace. There is an interpretation centre, shop and café on site. There is also the opportunity to be 'Warden for the Day', where you may actually join with a keeper to help look after the animals. The Park is one of Scotland's best attractions and not to be missed. To get there, buses leave from the Aviemore railway station. It is a 13 minute bus journey to the Park and the stop is marked as 'Kincraig Highland Wildlife Park' in timetables. Rail and bus users, walkers and cyclists are met at the main gate of the park and taken for a tour of the open areas (that is the parts with dangerous animals that you can't walk through!). There is an admission charge and it is open all year, although call first in the winter months as weather conditions may close the Park. Visit www.highlandwildlifepark.org or telephone 01540 651270 for details.

Close to the Wildlife Park (take the same bus) is the **Loch Insh Watersports Centre**. The Centre provides a safe place to try out all kinds of water sports including canoeing, river trips, sailing and windsurfing. There are also land based activities including a cycle hire facility for mountain biking, climbing, abseiling and archery. See www.lochinsh.com for information.

Returning to the train at Aviemore, the line makes its way through the forest and shortly arrives at Carrbridge. The area marks the limit the National Park and is again abundant in paths and trails for exploring.

Carrbridge.

Carrbridge station (Station Road, PH23 3AJ) is down a side road from the main part of the town. Choose the road or the forest track to reach the village. The station has an information point, waiting shelters and seating.

The village takes its name from the **old packhorse bridge** which crosses the river here. You can still see the bridge, although due to its age and condition, it is no longer possible to cross. The bridge, erected in 1717 by General Grant, has extremely steep approaches from either side and almost defies gravity in staying up. It is in the village centre and is best viewed from the main street. While in Carrbridge the most popular attraction is the **Landmark Forest Theme Park**. The theme park is based around the ancient Caledonian Pine Forest. The park is different to most theme parks in that it aims to bring knowledge of nature to children while having fun. This excellent family day out features a tower to climb, tree top trail, maze, red squirrel trail, microworld, steam powered sawmill and Clydesdale horses. See www.landmark-centre.co.uk or telephone 01479 841613. The Park is at the south end of the village and is a pleasant 25 minute walk from the station. It is also possible to cycle there on the National Cycle Network from Aviemore or to take a bus from Aviemore station.

On departure from Carrbridge the train takes a scenic route through the heather covered hills. Look out for the River Findon, crossed on an impressive viaduct. Also watch out for Slochd Summit, the second highest part of the line. Further north the train crosses another of the line's highlights – Culloden Viaduct. This impressive stone arched structure carries the line across the valley at Culloden. Culloden was the site of the Battle of Culloden in 1745. The site is now owned by the National Trust for Scotland. It is easy to reach by local bus from Inverness town centre, but be careful not to take the service to Culloden housing area of the same name as it's a significant walk from the site of the battle! The train curves to face Inverness and on this last downhill section passengers are treated to a wonderful view of the Moray Firth. On a summer's evening when arriving on the 'Highland Chieftain' from London the sight of the sun setting over the Firth is a spectacular end to a wonderful journey. Soon the train is passing through the Inverness rail yards and arrives into the station.

Inverness

Inverness is known as the capital of the Highlands and is situated at the mouth of the River Ness and on the Moray Firth. While there has been a settlement here for centuries, the present town dates largely from the arrival of the railway. For the visitor, the city's most pleasant feature is its river flowing though the city centre. There are riverside walks leading from the High Street past the Castle, Cathedral, and Theatre and on to what is locally known as 'the islands' – a park, set on a series of small wooded islands in the river. Also in the city centre are the Victorian markets. The Market Arcade is restored to its original appeal and features a large number of independent retailers. Inverness is most useful as a base for exploring the Highlands, being located at the start of four rail lines.

Practicalities

Inverness retains its original, although much modernised, railway station situated next door to the former Highland Railway hotel. The station has an unusual shape with lines going north, east and south from this terminus. There are all the facilities one would expect of a large station including an enclosed waiting area, Caledonian Sleeper lounge, cash machine, ticket office, ticket vending machines, newsagent, café, left luggage, luggage trolleys, British Transport Police office and customer service staff.

Local Transport. Stagecoach Inverness operates buses in the area. Regional buses leave from the nearby bus station and there is a walking route signposted between the two. City buses leave from Union Street and Queensgate, both opposite the station, while there is a taxi rank outside. Car hire can be arranged and several companies have offices beside or near the station.

Inverness Tourist Information Centre (Castle Wynd, IV2 3BJ) is open all year and has a Caledonian MacBrayane booking office in addition to the usual facilities. It is located next door to the Museum.

Places of Interest

Inverness Museum and Art Gallery. The Inverness Museum and Art Gallery is located on Bridge Street, at the bottom end of the High Street. As with all city centre attractions it is within easy walking distance of the station. The Museum is housed in the 1960s Bridge Street development, an ugly scar on the Inverness cityscape. However inside the museum has done a wonderful job in representing the history and culture of the area. There are displays on local silverware, wildlife and early human history. Gallery exhibits are regularly changed.

Inverness Castle. A castle was originally built on the site in the 11th century and was destroyed by the Jacobite Army in 1746. Today the site consists of a mock castle built in 1835 to house the Sheriff's court and police station. The police station has since moved to new premises but the building is still used as the court. On days when the Union Flag flies from the tower, the High Court is in session. The Castle's prominent position on a hill overlooking the river, together with its attractive appearance, has made it one of the city's most famous landmarks.

Cathedral. The Cathedral is located opposite the Castle on the banks of the river. Built between 1866 and 1869 in the Gothic style to the design of Alexander Ross, the Cathedral features twin towers with a ring of ten bells. The Cathedral was the first to be built in the UK after the Reformation and was originally planned to have two huge steeples on top of the towers. This plan was never implemented but you can see a painting of how it might have looked inside. To the rear, an octagonal Chapter House is now occupied as the café. Inside, visitors can view pillars of polished Peterhead granite, stained glass, sculptures, an angel font after Thorvaldsen (Copenhagen) and icons presented by the Tsar of Russia. The Cathedral has is open on most days to visitors.

Town House. Formally the seat of the Inverness Town Council, this splendid Victorian mock gothic building dominates the High Street. In 1921 it hosted a historic meeting of the British Government (known as the Cabinet) – the only Cabinet meeting ever held outside London. Although not open to the public it can be viewed from the outside and is located next door to the Museum.

Nearby places of interest

Urquhart Castle. Situated on the shores of Loch Ness, the Castle is almost entirely ruined, and yet remins one of Scotland's top visitor attractions. The Castle is owned by Historic Scotland, has an admission charge and is open year round. Visitors can use a frequent bus service from Inverness (see Traveline) or continue by Citylink coach all the way to Fort William. It is also possible to visit Loch Ness and the Castle using a boat tour down the Caledonian Canal and Loch, which may be booked at the Tourist Information Centre.

Inverness is the end of this particular journey, but there are further places to explore. The Far North line to Thurso and on to Orkney begins here, as does the route to Kyle of Lochalsh and Skye, and the coach link to Ullapool for the Isle of Lewis ferry. It is possible to return south via Aberdeen or by taking the coach link to Fort William and then travel south on the scenic West Highland Railway.

11. Central Scotland – Edinburgh to Glasgow

There are four separate routes between the two major Scottish cities. Most passengers choose the Scotrail route via Falkirk as it has the most frequent service and the fastest journey times, however there are three other alternative routes:

Route Option 1: Edinburgh to Glasgow via Falkirk High. This is the most popular route with its short 50 minute journey time and departures every 15 minutes throughout the day. It also has the most interest for the visitor along the way as the other lines tend to just call at suburban residential areas with little for the tourist.

Route Option 2: Edinburgh to Glasgow via Airdrie and Bathgate. This line was reopened in 2010. Trains continue through Queen Street Station and onto the north Clyde route to Helensburgh Central so for people visiting the north Clyde coast it will eliminate the need to change trains in Glasgow.

Route Option 3: Edinburgh to Glasgow via Shotts. This is a suburban rail line between the two cities.

Route Option 4: Edinburgh to Glasgow via Carstairs. This is the 'mainline' railway and makes use of the West and East coast mainlines, connecting at Carstairs Junction.

Edinburgh – Glasgow, via Falkirk

The Edinburgh to Glasgow railway line is Scotland's busiest railway with trains running in each direction every 15 minutes throughout the day. The line opened in 1842 as the Edinburgh and Glasgow Railway linking Haymarket Station in Edinburgh with Glasgow's Queen Street. It later became a key part of the North British Railway which was headquartered in Edinburgh. Today all trains call at both Edinburgh stations (Waverley and Haymarket) and Falkirk High. Selected trains also call at Croy, Polmont and Linlithgow.

Journey Summary:

Route:	Edinburgh Waverley – Edinburgh Haymarket – Linlithgow – Polmont –Falkirk High – Croy – Glasgow Queen Street.
Operator:	Scotrail.
Trains:	Standard and first class. Most have a trolley service.
Trip Length:	50 minutes.
Frequency:	Up to every 15 minutes during most of the day.

Links: Connections to rail routes for travel throughout Scotland and the rest of Britain from Edinburgh and Glasgow. Connections with the Glasgow Subway and Plusbus services in Glasgow, Edinburgh, Falkirk and Linlithgow.

For Edinburgh information see Chapter 7, the East Coast.

On departure from Edinburgh's Waverley and Haymarket stations, the train passes Edinburgh Airport with its distinctive cone-shaped 57 metre tall control tower which opened in 2005. The train passes through typical lowland farms with some small hills to the south of the train, adding interest to the horizon. Just out of view to the north is the Firth of Forth. The sharp eyed, however, may catch a glimpse of the Forth Rail and Road bridges. The train arrives at Linlithgow (not all services call here, so check before boarding).

Linlithgow

Linlithgow with its old town centre, loch and palace is an ideal place to spend an afternoon. Being so close to both Edinburgh and Glasgow, it is also very popular as a day trip destination. Arrival in Linlithgow is on the High Street with everything of interest to the visitor being only a few hundred metres from the Station's front door.

With the town's origins going back to the 1100s, it has long been an administrative centre and a favourite residence of Scottish royalty. Linlithgow Palace was the birthplace of James V and Mary Queen of Scots. The Palace now dominates the town centre along with the surrounding Linlithgow Loch and Park. In more recent times it became important as a centre along the Union Canal linking Edinburgh and Glasgow. Linlithgow is also surrounded by interesting local villages including Bo'ness (home of the Scottish Railway Preservation Society) and Blackness which has long been Linlithgow's port on the shores of the Forth and has the added attraction of Blackness Castle, now restored and open to the public. Both these villages are included in Plusbus rail fares to Linlithgow with regular departures from near the station.

Many visitors head to the Information Centre to pick up a leaflet for a walking tour of the town centre which takes in the Palace, lake, Canal, museums and some local buildings of interest. One such building is the Linlithgow Town House, constructed in 1668 by John Smith. It is one of the most sophisticated burgh buildings of its period in Scotland, with its three-storeys, regular pedimented windows and the six-stage balustraded tower to the rear, which once carried a belfry. St Michael's Kirk (www.stmichaelsparish.org.uk) is an equally famous Linlithgow landmark as the next door Palace. It has been a place of worship for over 750 years. Other buildings in the Kirkgate area beside the Palace and Church also add to the period feel of the area.

Practicalities

Linlithgow station (Station Road, EH49 7DH) is one of the best preserved of the original Glasgow and Edinburgh Railway Company stations, and dates from 1842. It is well presented with flower displays arranged by the local community. There is a ticket office, ticket vending machine, waiting room, toilets, pay phone, cash machine and customer help point.

Tourist Information. The Tourist Information Office is located in the County Buildings on the High Street (EH49 7EZ) and is open seasonally.

Local Transport. First Group operates buses in the Linlithgow area – see the First Group website or call Traveline on 0871 2002233 for details. Linlithgow is a Plusbus town so you can add unlimited local bus travel in the Linlithgow area to your train ticket for a small supplement.

Places of Interest

Linlithgow Palace (EH49 7AL). Without a doubt Linlithgow's main attraction (which may also be seen from the railway line) is the Palace and Loch. Few palaces have such a tranquil setting in a town environment. Most of the Stuart Kings and Queens of Scotland lived here at the Palace, while James V and Mary Queen of Scots were born here. Begun in 1424 by James I, the Palace became the ultimate pleasure palace on the road between Stirling and Edinburgh Castles. The life of the Palace though came to an abrupt end in 1745 when it was burnt down. Today the ruins still display its once amazing grandeur. In particular look out for the magnificent great hall, the 'oriels' – elegant projecting windows off the king's and queen's bedchambers and the beautiful three tiered fountain in the centre of the courtyard. The fountain is switched on every Sunday in July and August. There are also a number of sculptures to look out for including angel musicians in the chapel. Outside the Palace is the **Loch and Peel** (the name of the park). A ranger service (office located outside the Palace) provides information on the varied birdlife to be found around the lochside and there is a pleasant walk around the Loch which takes around an hour to complete. The Palace and Park are open all year round and there is an admission charge to the Palace while Park entry is free. See the Historic Scotland website or call 01506 842896 for details. The property is two minutes walk from the Station.

Linlithgow Heritage Trust – the Linlithgow Story. The Heritage Trust is located 200 metres along the High Street from the station and has a good small museum on the history of the town from 1400 to the present day.

Linlithgow Canal Centre (Manse Road Basin, EH49 6AJ). Before the railway reached Linlithgow, the fastest and easiest form of transport was the Edinburgh & Glasgow Union Canal. This 31½ mile [50 km] long canal runs from Edinburgh to Falkirk, where it is linked to the Forth & Clyde Canal at Falkirk by the new Falkirk Wheel to continue the journey to Glasgow. The Centre tells the history of the canal and also operates boat trips on authentic replica canal boats to the Avon Aqueduct every Saturday and Sunday afternoon from Easter until October. The Centre is 5 minutes walk south of the station. See www.lucs.org.uk for opening times and admission charges.

Nearby Places of Interest – using Plusbus connections

Blackness Castle. Described as 'the ship that never sailed' (it resembles a ship and is situated beside the sea) this 15th century castle was built by the Crichton family and was soon converted into a formidable artillery fortification by James V in 1537 in expectation of war with England. The Castle withstood many sieges until it finally fell to Oliver Cromwell's troops in 1650. The Castle later served as a state prison and amongst the people to be held there were many Covenanters including some from St Andrews. Today the Castle has been restored and has a very attractive position alongside the Firth of Forth. It is open all year and there is an admission charge. See the Historic Scotland website or call 01506 834807 for details. To get to Blackness either take a bus travelling to Bo'ness bus station (20 minutes) or the service to Edinburgh (15 minutes) from Linlithgow. It is a nine minute walk from the bus stop to the castle.

Bo'ness is a small town on the shores of the Forth has been the site of a port from 1707 until its closure in 1959. The town is only just over two miles north from Linlithgow making it accessible for days out. It is also attractively situated on the shores of the Forth. **Kinneil Estate** is just west of the town centre and about a ten minute walk from the bus stop. The Estate consists of beautiful parkland and a number of places of interest within the grounds. At the heart of the Estate is Kinneil House, a traditional Scottish mansion. The oldest part of the house is a 15th century tower remodelled by the Earl of Arran between 1546 and 1550 and transformed into a stately home for the Dukes of Hamilton in the 1660s. It can always be viewed externally but is also open to the public on selected days throughout the year. Check the Historic Scotland website for information. Beside the house is Kinneil Museum which is managed by Falkirk Council. The Museum is located in the 17th century stable block of Kinneil House. The main feature is the exhibition '2000 years of history' which tells the story of the park from Roman times to the present day. Telephone 01506 778530 for information. Behind the House is a small roofless building – James Watt's Cottage. This small building is where inventor James Watt worked on his development of the steam engine. The site also has excavations and remains of a Roman Fortlet which was in 140 AD part of the Antonine Wall, the Empire's most northerly frontier.

Staying in Bo'ness head back into the town and towards the shore (about five minutes walk from the bus stop) to get to the railway station of the **Bo'ness & Kinneil Railway and Scottish Railway Preservation Society**. The Society operates this restored steam railway which runs from Bo'ness and along the shores of the Firth of Forth before heading south to the mine at Birkhill. On days the railway is operating, guides take visitors underground to find out about the Fireclay miners and fossils which may be seen in the rock. Alternatively visitors may enjoy the Avon Gorge or take a picnic in the dedicated area. The line is only three and a half miles long but there is actually another station mid way, Kinneil, which allows visits to the Kinneil Kerse nature reserve. The railway has the most extensive collection of preserved steam and diesel locomotives together with old carriages in Scotland and is recognised as a collection of national significance. As well as the operating collection of trains there is also an extensive railway museum of Scottish railways known as the Scottish Railway Exhibition. See www.srps.org.uk or telephone 01506 825855 for details of operating days and fares. The Scottish Railway Preservation Society also has a regular tour programme of sightseeing trains which explore all areas of Scotland, usually starting in Edinburgh. See their website for details of tours.

Also in the town centre is **the Hippodrome**. This is an A-listed building, brainchild of film-maker Louis Dickson and designed by local architect Matthew Steele. It was completed in 1911 and is a rare example of pre-Art Deco cinema architecture and Scotland's oldest purpose-built picture house. After years of disuse and vandalism it was restored by Falkirk Council and reopened in 2009. See www.falkirk.gov.uk for information and movie times.

Return to the Linlithgow railway station and the journey west to Glasgow. Some trains make a stop at Polmont Station before arrival at Falkirk High Station.

Falkirk

Falkirk and the surrounding area became an industrial centre with many mines, foundries and mills benefiting from its location on the canal, and later railway, network. In the latter part of the 20th century the decline of heavy industry was offset by new industries such as the huge oil refinery at nearby Grangemouth.

Practicalities

Falkirk has three railway stations – Falkirk Grahamston, Falkirk High and Camelon. Edinburgh to Glasgow trains stop at Falkirk High (High Station Road, FK1 5QX). The station has a ticket office, ticket vending machine, waiting room, toilets, pay phone and taxi rank.

Tourist Information Centre. The Tourist Information Centre is located at the Falkirk Wheel (FK1 4RS) – see below for details.

Local Transport. Buses are operated by First Group, see their website or call Traveline on 0871 2002233 for bus information. Local buses are included in Plusbus rail tickets to Falkirk.

Places of Interest

Falkirk Wheel (Lime Road, FK1 4RS). The Forth & Clyde Canal was opened in 1773 and extended from Grangemouth on the River Forth, to Bowling on the River Clyde. The Union Canal (or Edinburgh & Glasgow Union to give it its full name) was opened much later in 1822 and operated from Edinburgh to Falkirk with a series of locks connecting the two canals at Port Downie in Camelon. The locks at Camelon were demolished decades ago when the canals fell into disuse. The site was then cleared to make way for housing. Happily in 1992 the new Falkirk Wheel was opened to once again connect the two canals. Measuring 115 feet it is the world's only rotating boat lift and has quickly become a modern day engineering masterpiece and national landmark. There is a visitor centre and open areas where people may freely watch the wheel in operation or you can go for a short one hour boat ride which will take you through the wheel and along the canal a little way. To find out about opening hours see www.thefalkirkwheel.co.uk or telephone British Waterways on 08700 500208. The best station if walking to the Wheel is Camelon which is a 20 to 30 minute walk. Or by using Falkirk High there are regular buses to the Wheel which are included in Plusbus railway tickets to Falkirk.

Callendar House. The imposing Callendar House has a 600 year history and has hosted many historical figures including Mary Queen of Scots, Oliver Cromwell, Bonnie Prince Charlie and Queen Victoria. Externally its French château style makes it a most attractive building set in beautifully landscaped grounds making it an ideal place for photography and painting. The house has been purchased by the local council who have an excellent museum inside the House together with having restored much of the interior to its condition in Georgian times. Callendar House is a 23 minute walk from Falkirk High station, while the entrance to the Park is about a five minute walk. The Museum and Park are open all year round and have free admission. Telephone 01324 503770 for information. Callendar Park offers a beautiful parkland surrounding to the House and also has woodland walks, boating pond and other activities such as a bouncy castle, crazy golf and go-karts. The Park is also the location for a section of the remaining Antonine Wall. This Roman wall dating from 140 AD once ran all the way from the Firths of Forth and Clyde. It has recently been designated a UN World Heritage Site and a permanent exhibition has been arranged at Callendar House.

Returning to the train, the journey continues with a short stop sometimes made at the town of Croy, which is now effectively part of the new town of Cumbernauld. The modern and uninspiring station buildings replaced the original station on this site. It is then only a few more minutes before arrival at Glasgow Queen Street station.

Glasgow

Glasgow is the largest city in Scotland, lying on the River Clyde in the west central lowlands. It is famous for its shipbuilding and industrial heritage. It was once a rival to Liverpool for its ocean trade and to Manchester for its industry. Today most of the industry has gone and the river, once busy with trade, is quiet and much cleaner. Many of the former quays and shipbuilding yards have been converted into modern apartment developments. Some of Glasgow's most famous products were those of the North British Locomotive works whose locomotives powered trains across Africa, Asia and Australasia – some of them until recently. Equally famous were the ships of the Clyde including Cunard's former RMS Queen Elizabeth II. In 1898 alone Glasgow produced over 250 large steel ships. Other chief industries were cotton, iron, chemicals, tubes, boilers, sewing machines, weaving, printing and pottery. Today the city has changed and although these industries have almost disappeared, it is still a thriving business centre. Commerce now consists of offices, insurance, media and banking amongst others.

The visitor to Glasgow will enjoy its rich heritage and many museums. It sometimes surprises people to find that the city rivals Edinburgh for its museums, galleries and parks. Visitors will also be pleasantly surprised that almost all the top quality attractions in Glasgow offer free admission (see www.glasgowmuseums.com). Glasgow has also worked hard to rival Edinburgh as a shopping destination with the Sauchiehall Street, near Queen Street Station, and the Merchant City between, Queen Street and Central Stations, being two of the most popular shopping areas in the Scotland. If walking around the city centre, look out for several remaining police boxes. These were used as mini police stations until the arrival of radio in the 1970s and were painted red rather than the blue associated with the Dr Who television series box. Many have now been painted blue and become coffee outlets.

Practicalities

Glasgow has two main railway stations together with numerous suburban stations within the greater Glasgow area. The main station for services to the north is **Queen Street Station** on George Square. This station has services north to Fort William, Oban, Inverness, Perth and Aberdeen. It also serves the East with trains to Falkirk and Edinburgh. Queen Street is a full service station. It has platform staff, travel centre, waiting room, shops, cafés, toilets, left luggage, cash machine and taxi rank. A few minutes walk from the Station is the Buchanan Street Bus Station which is the hub of the Strathclyde bus network and long distance coach network in Scotland. Located at Queen Street Station is Buchanan Street Underground Station for easy transfers to the Glasgow Subway line.

The other main station is **Central Station** on Hope Street. It handles most trains of the Strathclyde suburban network together with services to the south and west including the Clyde coast, Ayrshire, Stranraer and Carlisle. There are also long distance InterCity services to Edinburgh and all parts of England including Manchester, Bristol, Bath, Birmingham and London. This is a full service station operated by Network Rail. It has platform staff, a travel centre, waiting room, shops, cafés, toilets, left luggage, cash machines and taxi rank. A bus link to Glasgow Airport operates from Buchanan Street Bus Station, stopping at both Queen Street and Central Stations. A free bus operates between Central and Queen Street stations throughout the day. Simply show your rail ticket to use the service.

Local Transportation. There are easy connections to the entire Strathclyde area and Glasgow city itself. The Strathclyde area has one of the best transport networks in the country, organised by Strathclyde Partnership for Transport. It comprises a comprehensive rail and bus network, together with some ferries and an underground railway. There are value unlimited travel tickets for both rail and bus journeys. Find out more from www.spt.co.uk or visit a SPT Travel Centre. The travel centres offer advice on all modes of transport within the Strathclyde area. Offices in Glasgow are located at Buchanan Bus Station, St Enoch Subway Station (near Central Station), Hillhead Subway Station and Glasgow International Airport (in the domestic arrivals area).

Tourist Information. The main tourist information centre is located at 11 George Square, opposite Queen Street Station. It is also a short distance by foot from Central Station.

Places of Interest – City Centre

Cathedral. Glasgow Cathedral (Castle Street) is a wonderful medieval building and the best preserved pre-Reformation church in the country, dating from the 12th to 15th centuries. The building is 320 feet long by 70 feet wide and 90 feet high, while the tower stands at 220 feet and still dominates its local skyline. Notable features of the structure include the 14th century Nave, stained glass windows from Munich, and the Crypt with its fine vaulted ceiling, supported by 65 pillars. The Cathedral is within easy walking distance (12 minutes) of the city centre and Queen Street Station. It is open daily and has free admission. See the Historic Scotland website for further details. Across the street from the Cathedral is the 'Provand's Lordship'. This is the oldest building in Glasgow and the only surviving building from the medieval city, dating from 1471 when it was built as part of the St Nicholas Hospital. There is a display Cuthbert Simpson, the priest who lived here in the 16th century, together with a large collection of 17th century furniture donated by Sir William Burrel. Admission is free and it is open year round.

On the west side of Queen Street Station is **Sauchiehall Street**. This famous shopping street is still one of the best places to go shopping in Glasgow. It has now been added to by the presence of a shopping centre along its length, known as the Buchanan Galleries. Those interested in shopping should also seek out the **Merchant City** area, between Queen Street and Central stations.

George Square outside Queen Street station is probably the finest open space in Glasgow. It was named in honour of King George III. The Square is surrounded by fine buildings including the former Post Office, Bank of Scotland and hotels. It is dominated however by the splendid Municipal Buildings of Glasgow City Council. Tours are sometimes offered at 10.30 and 14.30 on weekdays (call 0141 2874018 to check availability). The Square is dominated by a column raising 80 feet high and surmounted by a statue of Sir Walter Scott. Alongside are statues by Marochetti of Queen Victoria and Prince Albert. There are also others of James Watt, Robert Burns and Dr Livingston. There are numerous benches and it is a popular place to spend some time. Just off George Square is the Royal Exchange Square (G1 3AH) which is home to the **Gallery of Modern Art,** which is the largest British modern art gallery outside of London.

Tenement House (145 Buccleuch Street, G3 6QN). More than any city, Glasgow is associated with the tenement flat. This restored Victorian tenement flat is located in the city centre and represents the life of Miss Agnes Toward who lived here for 50 years. It is typical of the type of housing of many Glasgow people in the early 20th century. The flat is now owned by the National Trust for Scotland and is open from March until October. Travel to Cowcaddens Subway station, which is a seven-minute walk from the house.

Places of Interest – Kelvinhall Area and West End

Glasgow University. Located on the hill to the west of the Kelvin Park is the University (travel to Hillhead or Kelvinhall stations on the Subway, both are a five minute walk away). The University was founded as early as 1450 and moved to its present location in 1870. The magnificent buildings were designed by Sir G. G. Scott and form a rectangle some 503 feet long by 295 feet wide making them the world's second largest gothic style buildings. It is divided in two by the Common Hall. The Central Tower is some 200 feet tall and is surmounted by a 100 feet high spire. The fine 17th century gateway cottage to the University was re-errected in a modified form at the entrance to the University grounds. A little to the north of the University are the **Botanical Gardens**. The Gardens are internationally famous for their collections of rare plants including many tropical species. Founded in 1817, the Park covers some 50 acres. Various theme gardens are situated around the site, together with parkland with specimen trees. Perhaps the Garden's highlight is the Kibble Palace Glasshouse, an 'A' listed beautiful glasshouse containing many of the Garden's most important collections and the Main Range of glasshouses, built in the 1880s and recently restored. The Gardens are open year round, usually from 07.00 till dusk and unlike the similar Kew Gardens of London, offer free admission. Call 0141 2761614 for information. The nearest station is Hillhead subway station, a five minute walk away.

Charles Rennie MacKintosh was one of the most significant designers of the late 19th and early 20th century, and Glasgow is filled with his creations. Places you may wish to visit include the Glasgow School of Art, the Willow Tea Rooms and The MacKintosh Church. The MacKintosh Society (www.crmsociety.com) offers an all inclusive ticket to venues which includes bus and rail travel to the venues. It is available from Tourist Information Centres and SPT Travel Centres.

Victoria Park & Fossil Grove. The Park is one of Glasgow's most popular, with formal gardens, an arboretum, a boating pond, bowling greens and tennis courts. There is also a display of tree fern fossils. The Park is open year round and has free admission. Jordanhill mainline station is a ten minute walk from the Park.

Places of Interest – Riverside

The Tall Ship. The Glenlee is a traditional 1896 three masted barque. The ship having originally been built on the Clyde is appropriately back at Glasgow Harbour as a museum ship. It is typical of the type of ship that connected the world prior to steam powered ships in the 20th century. As well as being a beautiful sailing ship, its history is fully displayed in exhibitions on board. Alongside the Glenlee is the Kelvinhaugh Ferry, a typical former Clyde passenger ferry which is also open to the public. There is an admission charge and the ship is open all year. Travel to Exhibition Centre station from where the ship is a ten minute walk. The Tall Ship is due to move to the same location as the Glasgow Transport Museum after opening in 2011 so check before visiting. See www.glenlee.co.uk.

PS Waverley. The world's last ocean going paddle steamer makes Glasgow its home when not touring around the country. During the summer months there are regular excursions from Glasgow, and other Clyde ports. The ship was built in 1946 for the London & North Eastern Railway and is a real steam ship which is pleased to let visitors view the engine room. However as in past times the main attraction is the pleasure of slowly steaming through Scotland's most spectacular coastal scenery. To find out about excursions telephone 0141 2218152 or visit the company's website. Waverley has an extensive UK tour schedule each year and for times when the ship is away another historic motor vessel, Balmoral, provides Clyde sailings. See www.waverleyexcursions.co.uk.

Scottish Exhibition and Conference Centre (SECC). The SECC is Scotland's purpose built exhibition and conference venue. In addition to trade events there are many public events and concerts. Visit www.secc.co.uk to find out what's on. Travel to Exhibition Centre Station from Glasgow Central. While there look out for the **Finnieston Crane**, a 1926 landmark still existing from the River's industrial past.

Transport Museum. The Transport Museum details the history of Glasgow and Scottish transport including road, sea and rail and is Scotland's second most popular free attraction. Exhibits are of international importance together with local significance. The first and last (and many other) of Glasgow's trams are on display together with the only remaining Highland Railway locomotive in existence – number 103. The Clyde room is packed with wonderfully detailed scale models of all types of ships built on the River Clyde. Included are famous ocean liners such as Empress of Canada, the former Royal Yacht Britannia and many more humble yet equally impressive ships. Admission is free and it is open year round (from Spring 2011. The museum has moved from Kelvinhall and is now located on the Riverside at Glasgow Harbour. Travel to either Partick Interchange mainline or Subway stations from where the museum is a five to ten minute walk away.

Places of Interest – South

Travel to Pollokshaws West Station for three amazing attractions. Situated beside the Station is **Pollok Country Park** (Pollok Country Park, G43 1AT). The Park is a huge area of countryside and hidden gardens which is all the more amazing for being situated in the heart of the city. There is a herd of Highland Cattle and plenty to amuse the whole family. The Park is free and open all year. Within the Park are two other attractions. **Pollok House** is a 1747 country house in the city. Set in parkland and formal gardens it has displays of Edwardian furniture and interiors. The site has been the home of the Maxwell family for over 700 years. There is also a well preserved range of servants' quarters. The House is owned by the National Trust, has an admission charge and is open year round. The other attraction at the Park is the **Burrell Collection**. Sir William Burrell donated this world class collection of over 9000 pieces of art in 1944. As well as modern European art there are Medieval pieces and a huge collection of artefacts from the ancient civilisations of China, Greece, Rome and Egypt. Pollokshaws West station is on the edge of the Park by the river. Follow the paths into the Park to find the House, Burrell Collection and the Park itself.

Places of Interest – Nearby

Titan Crane. The Titan is a 150 foot high crane built in 1907 for the John Brown Shipyard and used in the construction of battleships and liners. The yard is gone but the crane is now open to visitors. The nearest station is Clydebank, a ten minute walk away. See www.titanclydebank.com for opening times and admission prices.

12. The West Highlands – Glasgow to Oban (for Mull), Fort William, Mallaig, the Small Isles and Southern Hebrides

The West Highland Line has a character of its own, quite unlike any other. It was voted the world's most scenic railway by readers of Wanderlust magazine in 2009 and 2010, although passengers have long since held it in such high regard! Trains take a leisurely journey through the rural west Highlands, connecting many small communities along the way. Compared to the commuter and InterCity lines of Scotland this railway has a much more relaxed feel. There are stations where the train only stops on request, i.e. if someone wants to use it, and to a greater extent the railway retains the atmosphere of the perhaps more simple days in which it was first constructed. For most of the route, the line passes through rugged hill scapes with lochs and moors appearing almost constantly. For those wishing to 'get away from it all' there can be no better escape within Britain. As well as the communities along the line there are several connections to Scottish islands from stations at the end of the routes. Scotrail operate four trains daily (on weekdays) in each direction to Oban and Fort William.

Journey Summary:

Route:	Glasgow – Crianlarich – Oban or Glasgow – Crianlarich – Spean Bridge – Fort William – Mallaig.
Operator:	Scotrail.
Trains:	Standard class only. Most have a trolley service.
Trip Length:	3 hours 50 minutes to Fort William, 5 hours to Mallaig and 3 hours to Oban.
Frequency:	Four trains daily in each direction, with two on Sundays.
Links:	There is a coach link from Oban and Fort William to Inverness, while ferries run to Skye, Mull and the Hebrides. Local buses around Fort William are included in Plusbus tickets to Fort William. The Caledonian Sleeper to London calls at most stations on the route to Fort William.

Glasgow

See Chapter 11, Central Scotland, for information about the city.

Trains depart from the attractive Queen Street Station on George Square. This large terminus was constructed in 1877 and has a wonderful glazed roof which spans the entire station including all the platforms. While regular commuters may have got used to its splendour, the visitor can still take time to enjoy the station's atmosphere, little changed from the days of steam, except perhaps for the glass being cleaner these days! The station is located at the bottom of a steep bank which is climbed by all departing trains. In the days of steam, many trains had to have a helper locomotive on the rear to get out. Today's trains make light work of the same incline. The station has many shops and food outlets.

Departure from Queen Street Station takes the train through the northern suburbs of Glasgow. Urban Scotland is not the most attractive part of this journey, but there are some notable features along the way. The train crosses the River Kelvin on a viaduct in Dawsholm Park and then passes under the Forth & Clyde Canal in a short tunnel. Although the Canal passes through these Glasgow suburbs it is more convenient and interesting to visit it at Falkirk or Linlithgow.

Many stations are passed without stopping as the longer distance trains will only call at the major ones. The first stop is at Westerton. This suburban station is the Glasgow stop for the Caledonian Sleeper service from Fort William to London, as it does not use Queen Street Station due to the track layout. It is mostly used by passengers wanting a very early train north from Glasgow to Fort William. All other West Highland train services use Queen Street as their Glasgow terminus.

The railway joins the Glasgow suburban 'blue train' line at this point and is electrified. There is a branch line to Milngavie Station. This, or Balloch, are both starting points for the West Highland Way walking route. You can catch a train to either from Queen Street or Central Stations.

Look out for the station named **Singer** (suburban trains stop here). It is indeed named after the Singer Company of New York who built a huge sewing machine factory here in 1883. The station was provided for the factory so employees could easily get to work.

The train has now left the Glasgow suburbs and has reached the Clyde coast, travelling alongside the River Clyde on the left and the hills on the right.

Dumbarton. The train makes a brief stop at the ornate Dumbarton Central Station. Look out for the River Leven at this point, flowing from Loch Lomond. Dumbarton was the home of William Denny's shipbuilder's yard. This was the construction site of the famous Cutty Sark tall ship which is now preserved and on display in London. It was also instrumental in the development of the hovercraft before the yard's closure in 1963. The branch line to Balloch and Loch Lomond leaves our line at this point (see the Balloch Branch section of Chapter 21 for details). The town is also the location of **Dumbarton Castle**, which is a remarkable attraction on the twin peaks of White Tower Crag and the Beak, two volcanic rocks overlooking the Clyde shoreline. There has been a military presence on this rock for 1500 years since 500 AD when it was the capital of the Kingdom of Strathclyde. Later in the middle ages it was strengthened against Norway, who ruled the Hebrides and Islands in the Clyde only ten miles away. In the 17th and 18th centuries it was redeveloped as a garrison fortress, destroying most of the medieval and Dark Age castle. These are the attractive buildings that visitors will find today. The Castle is open year round, although has restricted opening times in the winter and there is an admission charge. See the Historic Scotland website or call 01389 732167 for details. It should also be noted that the Castle is closest (15 minutes walk) to Dumbarton East Station, and not the Central Station. Take a local train to Helensburgh Central from Glasgow Central to get there. There are also a large number of steps to reach the Castle so it is not suitable for wheelchair users or those with limited mobility.

Helensburgh Upper Station.

Ben Bowie hill is passed on the right while the electrified tracks to Helensburgh Central Station branch off to the left. Helensburgh was a pleasant Victorian resort town and still has a fine promenade, tree lined streets, parks and Victorian villas overlooking the Clyde. Our own train swings round to the rear of the town and makes a stop at the Helensburgh Upper station. Alight here for **Hill House** (Upper Colquhoun Street, G84 9AJ) or alternatively travel to Helensburgh Central Station which is a slightly longer walk but has a much more frequent service. Hill House is the most famous of designer Charles Rennie MacKintosh's creations after the Glasgow School of Art. The amazing house is sited on a spectacular position overlooking the Clyde. The House is complete with its original interiors and furniture making it highly interesting to anyone with an interest in MacKintosh or design in general. It is open from March till October and is owned by the National Trust for Scotland. See the NTS website or call 01436 673900 for details.

The departure from Helensburgh is the start of the real West Highland Line and the spectacular scenery that continues until journey's end. The line starts to head north along the banks of Gare Loch. Below the line to the left are numerous settlements of large Victorian villas all along the shoreline. This was a popular place for wealthy Glasgow residents to live. Also look out for the HM Clyde Naval Base near the village of Faslane. This is the base of the Trident submarines. The base was opened in 1943 and had a rail connection. One of the first users was Prime Minister Winston Churchill who boarded a ship across the Atlantic for a meeting with President Roosevelt.

Garelochhead is a pleasant village at the top of the Loch. The station at Garelochhead is typical of those found along the route. Unlike most British railway stations with two platforms linked by a footbridge, the West Highland stations have a central platform with a track on each side and a building in the middle. The stations are built in a 'Swiss Chalet' style which is unique to the West Highland Railway. On leaving Garelochhead the train now continues north and crosses the peninsula to travel up and alongside the spectacular Loch Long. For those travelling up from London on the overnight sleeper this will probably be your first view of Scotland when you awake in the morning. On a summer's morning the stillness of the water and calm peace of the valley are very special having gone to sleep in the capital the night before. On the shore below the line there is a jetty. It is used by oil tankers which offload crude oil here to be pumped through a pipeline to Grangemouth on the east coast, some 60 miles away.

The line descends steeply as it clings to the hillside and crosses Manse Viaduct to reach the twin villages of **Arrochar and Tarbet**. The station here is useful for those wishing to climb the mountains surrounding the villages which include Cruach Tairbeirt (1364 feet) and Ben Reoch (2168 feet), but there are many others. There are also miles of low level forest walks which can easily be completed in a few hours. Both the walks and hills have great views of both Loch Long and Loch Lomond. The station is unstaffed (in common with most on the line) but there are waiting rooms to shelter from the elements.

A few minutes beyond the station, the banks of Loch Lomond come into view. On the opposite shore, the dominant hill is Ben Lomond. The Loch itself is described in detail in chapter 21 of this book as the most popular station for the Loch is at Balloch on a different line. However people who prefer to get into some of the more remote parts of the Loch Lomond and the Trossachs National Park use these stations on the West Highland Line. The train now passes through the Park, which became Scotland's first national park in 2001. It sometimes surprises visitors to know that Scotland with its spectacular scenery has been so slow in creating parks. The Loch itself has been popular with railway passengers for years having been heavily promoted by the London & North Eastern and British Railways in artist-commissioned paintings which perhaps depict the Loch as a model of perfection which it cannot quite live up to.

The train continues alongside the Loch until the station at **Ardlui** is reached. Walkers sometimes find this station useful for exploring the surrounding hills. Train passengers leave the lochside behind as the line now heads cross country towards Crianlarich. On the right Ben Glas mountain comes into view closely followed by the Falls of Falloch and then Ben Chabair (1523 feet). The railway closely follows the route of the West Highland Way walk and walkers can often be seen from the train. For those opting to walk to Fort William, good views and photography of the railway may be enjoyed.

Crianlarich. This location has developed as a junction for the railway and a small settlement now exists. The station no longer has railway staff but has been opened as a very nice refreshment room. The former stone engine shed still exists and is now used for track maintenance vehicles. Prior to the closure of the line going east towards Stirling in 1965, this was where the West Highland Railway and Oban railway crossed (although there was a connection). When the line east was closed, due to a rockslide, the Oban trains were rerouted by the West Highland line from Glasgow to Crianlarich. Trains now divide here with one portion going to Oban and the other to Fort William. Make sure you are on the correct portion of the train for the destination you intend to reach. We will describe the Oban section and connections first before returning to Crianlarich to describe the journey to Fort William.

The Oban Route

On departure from Crianlarich Station the first stop is at **Tyndrum Lower Station**. Not to be confused with the tiny village's other station, Upper Tyndrum – which is on the Fort William section of this line! The railways to Fort William and Oban travel together towards Tyndrum where they split and you may often see the other portion of the train across the river on the opposite line.

The train now makes its way west through Glen Lochy. The Glen is steep with hills on either side and is nicely wooded. Have your camera ready when passing Lochan ni Bi, just after Tyndrum. There are many other scenic locations along this stretch of line as it follows the course of the River Lochy through the narrow valley. The next stop is at **Dalmally**. There are pleasant woodland walks in this area. The station has an attractive stone building, although it is now disused.

The railway suddenly emerges to cross the Orchy Viaduct and share the banks of Loch Awe. On the left look out for views of Kilchurn Castle. This is one of the most famous views in Scotland and an ideal photo opportunity from the carriage window.

Loch Awe Station. The small halt at Loch Awe serves the village of the same name. There are no station buildings but there is a refreshment room in a converted railway carriage. Also alight here if you wish to visit Kilchurn Castle. Kilchurn has a four-storey tower built in the mid 15th century by Sir Colin Campbell. Much enlarged in 1693 it incorporates the first purpose built barracks in Scotland. The substantial ruins are some of the most picturesque in the country with spectacular views down Loch Awe. It is open in the summer only. The castle is now under the care of Historic Scotland (see their website) who should be consulted for details of boat times and admission prices.

The train continues along the banks of Loch Awe to Falls of Cruachan. The tiny request stop station at **Falls of Cruachan** is open during the summer only as there is no station lighting. Also be aware that there are steep steps up to the single platform. This station is in a ravine with steep sides and on the opposite side of the tracks is the River Awe. The station opened as long ago as 1893 and is purely a tourist destination, there being no settlement here. It allows access to the Falls of Cruachan, which are easily explored from the station. More recently it has also provided access to Ben Cruachan and the Cruachan Power Station Visitor Centre. The mountain is known as the hollow mountain on account of the hydro power station inside. The power station is open to the public with daily tours and many people enjoy stopping here for what must be one of the world's few hydro stations which allow visitors. See www.visitcruachan.co.uk for details. The power station is 200 metres from the railway station. On departure from the station, enjoy the views of the River Awe as the train makes its way up the ravine.

Taynuilt (PA35 1JH) lies near to the south shore of Loch Etive. There is a small unstaffed station here. The main street runs north and includes a selection of local shops and a Post Office. It also has an antiques shop that attracts visitors from far and wide with its excellent selection of dolls' houses, fixtures and fittings. Much of the village is built in an attractive grey stone that blends well with the surrounding mountains. The more adventurous will come across Taynuilt while following the route of the Coast to Coast Walk from Oban to St Andrews.

The line now follows the scenic south shore of Loch Etive with views across the entire length of the Loch. You pass the site of Ach-na-Cloich station which once served steamers on the Loch, although nothing now remains.

Connel Ferry (at PA37 1PA). A small halt serves this village. You can still see the bridge which once carried a branch line north to Ballachullish. Although the line closed, pedestrians may still use the bridge to reach North Connel village. Nearby is **Dunstaffnage Castle & Chapel**. Built before 1275 on a huge rock overlooking the Firth of Lorn, Dunstaffnage was the mighty stronghold of the MacDougalls. The castle, with its huge curtain wall, was captured by Robert the Bruce in 1309 and remained in royal possession for some years. Dunstaffnage became the temporary prison of Flora MacDonald in 1746. The castle is well preserved and intact. To reach the castle cycle either from Connel Ferry or Oban. Alternatively take a bus from Oban to Dunbeg (only five km from Oban) which is a short walk from the castle. It is also possible to walk from Connel Ferry station along the road which is only three km away. The Castle is under the care of Historic Scotland, check their website for opening times and admission charges.

The line now heads down across Glencruitten Summit (301 feet) and then steeply down into Oban through rock cuttings which allow the line to descend so quickly into the seaside town.

Oban

Oban is a wonderful resort town situated on an attractive and sheltered bay and overlooking the nearby islands. The bay is calm and a popular place for yachts to stop. Overlooking the town is Oban Hill with 'McCraig's Folly' as its crown. This is an unfinished version of Rome's Colosseum. Its building was instituted by John Steward McCaig in a period of unemployment amongst local stonemasons.

Practicalities

Oban railway station (Railway Pier, PA34 4LW) is located at the harbour and right next to the Caledonian MacBrayne Ferry Terminal. Sadly the attractive original station with glazed platform canopies and clock tower was allowed to fall into disrepair and was demolished in the 1980s. The new station is staffed and has a booking office, waiting room, telephones, toilets, luggage trolleys and a newsagent's shop.

Places of Interest

Oban Open Top Bus Tour. Oban is a small town but the open top bus tour takes visitors to some of the nearby scenic locations also. The tour runs on Easter weekend and then from May until September. The tours depart at 11.00 and 14.00 from the railway station and head north to the Falls of Lora then return to Oban for a short trip through the town before heading to the scenic Ellenabeich, taking in the spectacular views of Loch Feochan, the Bridge over the Atlantic and Easdale Island. After a short break with an opportunity for refreshments and a visit to the local art gallery the bus returns to Oban. A full commentary is provided throughout the tour which lasts approximately two and a half hours. Contact West Coast Motors by telephone 01586 552319 or see the company website at www.westcoastmotors.co.uk

Oban Distillery Visitor Centre in Stafford Street (near the North Pier) is open Monday to Friday all year round (and Saturdays from Easter to October) for guided tours. There's an audio-visual exhibition and gift shop. Telephone 01631 572 004 for information.

St John's Cathedral (George Street). Work finished when funds were exhausted in August 1910, and by then only the sanctuary, chancel, one transept and one bay of the nave were completed. This was knitted in to the existing building, albeit that the latter was twelve foot lower than the Sanctuary, and orientated at right angles to the new structure, which had to be buttressed by remarkable riveted girders. Two major campaigns to rebuild or complete the building have not been successful. One, the famous Oban Cathedral Fund Appeal run from Staten Island, New York, foundered in the Crash on Wall Street. The other, led by two Highland Chiefs from the Diocese, Maclean of Duart and Cameron of Lochiel, only raised funds sufficient for Ian G Lindsay in 1968 to improve the existing structure, including the creation of the narthex. The Cathedral is located on The Esplanade and is open most days.

Nearby is the **Oban War & Peace Exhibition**, housed in the Old Waiting Room on North Pier.

McCaig's Tower is a replica of the Colosseum of Rome. A banker called John McCaig had it built between 1897 and 1900 as a memorial to his family and to provide employment for the townsmen. It's quite a steep climb to the top of the hill, but there are a couple of benches where you can sit and get your breath back. On a clear day you can see over to Mull. Some books refer to it as McCaig's Folly. He was born on the nearby island of Lismore.

Nearby Places of Interest

There are a number of other destinations easily accessible from Oban by Caledonian MacBrayne ferries. In fact a visit without one of these added trips would be a missed opportunity. Mull is the largest island, with its famous neighbour, Iona. There are also many other islands where you can go to escape the crowds and experience nature, peace and quiet. All ferries depart from the pier alongside the railway station and are operated by Caledonian MacBrayne. There is a modern terminal building with ticket facilities, waiting area and toilets for ferry passengers. All the ferries listed in this section and operated by Caledonian MacBrayne are included in the Travelpass railway tickets of Scotland.

Isle of Mull

From the pier at Oban railway station, catch the Caledonian MacBrayne ferry for the short 45 minute journey to the Isle of Mull. In addition to the ferry fare, bus travel on the Isle of Mull with Bowmans Coaches is included in the Travelpass ticket. Buses connect with ferries arriving from Oban. This short crossing has one of the largest and best appointed ships in the CalMac fleet. The MV Isle of Mull carries up to 960 passengers and has plenty of open deck space, a passenger lounge, restaurant, bar, toilets and offers packed lunches. There are up to six sailings daily in each direction of which two or three are rail connected, although the others may also be useful to rail passengers if staying in Oban. During the peak season discounted tickets are restricted on many sailings, but not for rail or foot passengers.

Close to the ferry terminal is the tourist information centre, and the island's most popular attraction, Torosay Castle Estate. The Castle and gardens are popular with visitors making a day trip to Mull, and can be reached by the unique Mull miniature railway, which departs from close to the ferry terminal. Unfortunately in autumn 2010 the Castle was sold and it is unclear whether the castle and railway will remain open as visitor attractions.

When on Mull, take time to explore the island. The mountains that stretch across the middle of the island rise to over 900 metres and are particularly popular with hillwalkers. Mountain ranges in the south and the east are pierced by glens and waterfalls.

The island's main town of **Tobermory** is the setting of the CBeebie's series, 'Balamory'. As a result, Tobermory has become the top holiday destination for kids desperate to see the colourful houses where PC Plum and Suzie Sweet live.

Mull is home to a wide range of wildlife and is one of best places in Europe to see the Golden Eagle and White Tailed Sea Eagle. It also offers a home to the elusive European Otter. Organised whale and dolphin watching trips, on which Minke Whales and dolphins among others can be seen, are available on the Island. Isle of Mull Wildlife Expeditions, founded by David Woodhouse, is at the forefront of eco-tourism initiatives in Scotland and has been operating for over 25 years. This has recently been recognized with the Caledonian MacBrayne sponsored 'Excellence in Tourism' Award, and has been mentioned on BBC 'Springwatch' series which described Mull as one of Britain's Top 10 Wildlife Destinations. Full details of Isle of Mull Wildlife Expeditions can be found on the website www.scotlandwildlife.com

Continue across Mull by bus to the **Island of Iona**. Iona is often referred to as 'The Cradle of Christianity in Scotland' as it was here that Columba first landed after being banished from Ireland in 563AD. Once settled on the island, Columba and his followers built a wooden monastery. This was later replaced with stone when the monastery was turned into a Benedictine Abbey around 1200. Today the abbey has been fully restored. It is owned by Historic Scotland and open to the public. The highest point of the island is Dun I at 323 feet and commands wonderful panoramic views towards Mull, Staffa and beyond. The ferry to Iona is a non-reservable service. Tickets for this service can be purchased at the Caledonian MacBrayne office in Fionnphort or on board the ferry. As it is a small island it is best explored on foot.

Lismore Island

Ferries to Lismore use either the MV Eigg or MV Bruernish. These small ferries have an open deck, enclosed shelter and toilet facilities. The crossing time is fifty minutes and there are usually five sailings per day in each direction. Lismore has a tranquil, rolling landscape and is ideal for cyclists. The main village of Achnacroish lies halfway along the island's eastern coast. As well as having the shop and the school, the village is the terminal for the main ferry service from Oban. The highest point on the island is the hill at the southern end known as Barr Mòr – at just short of 130m high, the views from this low summit are unforgettable. There are several popular walks on Lismore from the ferry's arrival point. One popular walk is to Achadun Castle (also known as Achanduin Castle), which was once the residence of the Bishops of Argyll. There is very little remaining of the Castle but the views, as all parts of the Island are amazing. There is also a four hour walk to two of the Island's best known archaeological features, Tirefour Broch and Castle Coeffin. Find out more at the Island's own community website, www.isleoflismore.com. All parts of the island may be explored by foot or bike from the ferry terminal at Achnacroish.

Colonsay Island

Services to Colonsay are usually provided by either the MV Lord of the Isles or the MV Hebridean Isles. Both carry just over 500 passengers and offer a self-service restaurant, shop, lounge, open deck space, and toilet facilities. There is a departure most days from Oban, at various times, and the journey takes two hours twenty minutes. Colonsay is an ideal place for those with an interest in archaeology as artefacts dating back to the Stone Age have been found here. There are also many historical ruins and ecclesiastical relics on the island. It is however for the natural beauty that most people come here. There are numerous beaches throughout the island and impressive cliffs on the west coast. The island is also noted for the diversity of its wild flowers with more than 400 species recorded. The island is easily explored by foot or bike and has its own website at www.colonsay.org.uk.

Coll and Tiree Islands

Both Coll and Tiree are usually served by either the MV Clansman (630 passengers) or MV Lord of the Isles (500 passengers). Both vessels offer excellent passenger facilities with a choice of lounges, outside deck space, self-service restaurant, bar, shop, packed lunch service and toilets. The journey takes just under three hours from Oban to Coll and four hours to Tiree. The ship takes a route past Mull and then through the Sound of Mull, a long strip of sea between the Isle of Mull and the mainland which is particularly scenic. It then heads out into open waters for the main part of the crossing. Services go to both Islands, although not every day of the week.

The low-lying **Island of Coll** is characterised by its landscape of sandy beaches, sand dunes and freshwater lochs. The Island's only village is the quiet, fishing village of Arinagour. It's the perfect place for those wishing to escape modern life and do nothing more strenuous than walk the Island's beaches or discover the local flora and fauna. In summer particularly, the sound of skylarks, the fragrance of the flowers and the views of distant shimmering islands make this a very special place.

From May to August, Coll's Royal Society for the Protection of Birds (RSPB) reserve plays a crucial role in the protection of the corncrake, a bird that is globally endangered but one of the rarest and fastest declining in the UK due to intensive agricultural methods. On this reserve, and throughout the islands, the RSPB encourage corncrake-friendly farming methods. However, the corncrake is just one of many species found on the island –

the opportunity to see redshanks, lapwing, snipe and in winter, barnacle and Greenland white-fronted geese make this an ornithologist's paradise.

And it's not just a place for nature lovers. Those interested in the islands heritage will be fascinated by Coll's iron-age forts, crannogs (an ancient type of loch side house) and 'Na Sgeulachan' (Teller of Tales) standing stones. The Island is 13 miles long in total and may be explored by foot or bike.

Tiree Island. Scarinish, the main village on Tiree, houses shops and a hotel as well as providing the ferry terminal for the island. The coastline of Tiree is a mixture of rocky outcrops and long stretches of white sandy beach which, along with the uninterrupted Atlantic winds, makes Tiree a perfect place for windsurfing. It is southwest of Coll and is more populated, with 800 inhabitants.

Barra and South Uist Islands

Another route from Oban is that to the village of Castlebay on the Island of Barra or Lochboisdale on South Uist. Ferries usually sail to both on most journeys, although may not run every day. This route is usually served by the same ships as Coll and Tiree and in fact some services call there on the way. MV Clansman and MV Lord of the Isles both have excellent facilities with passenger lounges, bar, self-service restaurant, shop, open deck space and toilets. Both also offer a packed lunch service for people heading ashore. Journey times are five and a half hours to South Uist or Barra from Oban, and seven hours if sailing first to the other destination.

The Island of **Barra** is a paradise of hills, beaches and big open skies, with a surprising amount to do. Beyond the many opportunities for walking and cycling around the paths and roads (cycle hire is available) there is fishing, rock climbing, kayaking, kite buggying, surfing and more. The entire Island is only 23 square miles but if you don't feel like walking there are some local bus routes around the Island. The 'Overland' bus service also begins at Castlebay Ferry Terminal, and takes a route north through all the islands to Stornoway on the Island of Lewis in the north. It is worth taking the trip up to the north of the Island, or perhaps returning home by air, to see the unique Barra Airport. Situated on the beach at Tràigh Mhòr, which in English means the big beach, the sands are large enough to accommodate three runways. Barra is one of only two airports in the world which uses a beach for a runway, actually landing on the sands. There are daily flights from Barra to Glasgow and Benbecula. Find out more from Highlands & Islands Airports at www.hial.co.uk. Arriving at the small village of Castlebay passengers immediately see the Island's main formal attraction, **Kisimul Castle**. Known locally as 'the castle in the sea', Kisimul is situated on a tiny island off the shore from Castlebay which it literally covers the entire area of, rather like a lighthouse. The Castle consists of a central tower with is surrounded by a curtain wall inside which are various ancillary buildings. It dates mostly from the 15th century. Telephone 01871 810313 or visit the Historic Scotland website for details. The property is open from April until October, weather permitting due to the boat trip to reach it.

The Island has an excellent website, www.isleofbarra.com, giving details of things to do, transport, bus times, and accommodation. Also refer to the travel section of the Western Isles Council website at www.cne-siar.gov.uk for details of bus times throughout the Western Isles, including the 'Overland' bus route.

South Uist, to the north of Barra, may be reached by bus and ferry or by alighting from the ferry at Lochboisdale, which is the main village on the Island. For bus times on South Uist, refer to the travel section of the Western Isles Council website at www.cne-siar.gov.uk. Buses continue right through South Uist and onto the Island of Benbecula and North Uist. South Uist is one of the larger of the Western Isles, some 22 miles long by 7 wide. Its geography is interesting with the west coast being one continuous sandy beach, bordered by grasslands followed by lochs, while the east coast consists of a series of mountains. The lochs are so numerous that on a map those areas of the island appear to be made up more of water than land, which is probably true. The most notable mountains are Beinn Mhòr at 620 metres and Hecla at 606. **Lochboisdale** itself is a very small but attractive village with the main role being that of ferry terminal. Visitors most often come to South Uist for the excellent beaches and the two mountains. With the remote location you may even find the beach to yourself, even in summer!

This concludes the description of the line to Oban and its connections and we return to the train at Crianlarich for the journey north to Fort William and Mallaig.

To Fort William

Departing Crianlarich the train soon arrives at **Upper Tyndrum Station**. The other station in the village, Tyndrum Lower, is on the Oban line. So make sure you are in the correct station if travelling to Oban or north. When travelling south, you may use either as trains are heading in the same direction – to Glasgow. The train departs and makes its way around the hill Ben Odhar before traversing a unique horseshoe curve, where the line will double back on itself. Have your camera ready for this particularly scenic section of the railway. **Bridge of Orchy Station** is a popular stop with climbers and walkers. It has a hotel and is one of many points where the West Highland Way walk is crossed.

On departure from Bridge of Orchy the line travels alongside Loch Tulla while the West Highland Way makes takes a route behind the Loch and through the hills. Just after the Loch are the remains of Achallader Castle. This was a 16th century tower but only two walls now remain.

The train now begins its crossing of Rannoch Moor. To the railwayman this was known as 'the moor'. While diesel trains make light work of the route, this was a challenge to the crews of the steam powered trains which once made their way across this line (and still do on special occasions!). The West Highland Way walking route skirts the edge of the moor, but the railway crosses through its heart. To achieve this feat of engineering the line was 'floated' across using tree roots, bushes and thousands of tonnes of earth. The landscape is a treat for the visitor. Watch this expanse of peat bogs, lochans, streams and ancient forests slowly pass by. **Rannoch Station** is the stop for the moor. It is idea for walkers wishing to get out and explore this unique environment. With no road access and few creature comforts, this is a true wilderness experience. It is situated on the huge Rannoch plateau, 1000 feet above sea level and surrounded by hills. When the route of the line was being surveyed the party conducting the evaluation decided to walk across the moor in winter. Being ill prepared and in the most remote part of the UK they almost perished having got into trouble. When construction of the railway began, it was not the end of the challenges at this location. The moor not only swallowed materials but money and at one stage the whole scheme was in danger of financial collapse. One of the Directors, Mr J Renton, stepped in with his own money and saved the project. Afterwards grateful navvies (the people who manually built the line) rolled a huge boulder onto the platform at Rannoch Station and carved a image of Renton in his honour. It is still there today for passengers to view. Although there are no longer any railway staff at the station, there is a tearoom, which is open from Easter until October.

The line continues through the wetlands to **Corrour Station**. This is the highest point on the line being 1350 feet above sea level. While the station has been here since the line opened for railway workers and the local estate, it did not officially open to the public until 1934. It was also used by navvies working on the Kinlochleven hydro electric dam some ten miles to the west. Today it is well used by walkers. There is a bunkhouse and restaurant in the station buildings and a selection of walks from the Station. There are no public roads in this area, making this one of the few parts of Britain, if not the world, where you can travel as people have for thousands of years – by foot! The shortest walk is just one mile from the station to the east which will take you to Loch Ossian and if you feel like a longer walk it is possible to walk right round the Loch. If you have a good map with you, there are other paths that lead north and then west. It is still possible to follow the old path to Kinlochleven some ten miles away or to then join up with the West Highland Way and walk to Fort William. If walking to Kinlochleven, there are buses to take you the rest of the way to Fort William.

The railway travels alongside Loch Treig before descending from the moor into the relatively fertile and contrasting Glen Spean. **Tulloch** is the first station in this area. There was once a proposal to join the Highland Mainline to the west at Tulloch, providing a rail link from Inverness to Fort William. With the likely limited traffic levels this was never given serious consideration but it would have been a really useful transport link.

The train now heads through the woods and valley to **Roy Bridge Station**. Just before Roy Bridge station look out for the waters of Monessie Gorge. It is shortly followed by **Spean Bridge**. The station serves the small community here and there is a popular restaurant in the former station buildings. Just out of sight on the hill to the right is the monument to the commandos who trained here during the Second World War. It is easy to see why such a location was chosen as the terrain can be harsh even in summer. If you decide to take a coach from Fort William or Spean Bridge to Fort Augustus or Inverness, you will pass right by the memorial. The journey is now almost over as the train covers the last few miles into Fort William.

Fort William

Situated at the foot of Ben Nevis, Britain's highest mountain, and alongside Loch Linnhe, Fort William is an attractive small Highland town. Visitors are instantly aware of the peace, fresh air and beautiful views along the Loch. The town itself is relatively small and from practically any point the visitor can still view the surrounding countryside.

Opposite the station is the High Street where most of the shops and restaurants are to be found. About half way along, is Cameron Square where the West Highland Museum tells the story of the area. Also to be found in Cameron Square is the Tourist Information Centre. A short walk to the Loch side gives the opportunity to experience Seal Islands Cruises. The company takes visitors out into Loch Linnie to view the resident population of seals who make there home there.

Practicalities

The modern station at Fort William is unappealing, if functional. It replaced the original to make way for road improvements in the town. The structure is single story with two platforms. This is a staffed station with ticket office, waiting room, cash machine, luggage trolleys, information, toilets, showers, café and newsagent. The station is busy with trains to Glasgow, overnight to London and also as the start of the line to Mallaig.

Local Transportation. The bus and coach stop is located next door to the station with connections to the local area. Taxis leave from outside the station and are on call. Car hire is also available. Of significant interest to the visitor is the coach link to Inverness. This also takes in the Great Glen, Fort Augustus and Loch Ness. Local buses are operated by Stagecoach in the Highlands, see www.stagecoachbus.com or call Traveline on 0871 2002233 for information. Local buses are included in the Fort William Plusbus rail ticket which is exceptional value considering that buses as far as Spean Bridge, Corpach, Kinlochleven and Ballachulish are included.

Tourist Information. Fort William Tourist Information Centre is located on Cameron Square, Fort William, Lochaber, PH33 6AJ. Tel: 08452 255121.

Places of Interest

Ben Nevis. Dominating the town and providing a beautiful backdrop is Ben Nevis. This is Britain's highest mountain standing at over 4406 feet above sea level which is all the more amazing when one considers that it starts at sea level! It is also one of the largest being 24 miles around the base. This is a wonderful hill to climb. On a clear day there are views as far away as the Cairngorms, Western Isles and Wester Ross from the summit. Be sure to be properly equipped and prepared for this serious climb. It is recommended that people new to the hills don't attempt this mountain between November and May or in bad weather, and stick to the tourist path. The mountain may be reached by local bus from Fort William bus station. Close to the walking route is the Nevis Range resort. This is an all year round ski, mountain bike and gondola experience. See www.nevisrange.co.uk. It is also served by the bus route, but note the gondola does not go all the way to the summit. Those views are reserved for the walkers!

Ben Nevis Distillery. Established in 1825 this is one of Scotland's oldest distilleries. It is situated in the town at the base of Ben Nevis and offers tours of the whisky making process.

West Highland Museum. The museum holds significant collections of photographs, writing and artefacts depicting life in the West Highlands through the years from stone age to modern day. This independent museum has prided itself in being of the highest quality. It is open year round and is situated in Cameron Square, just off the High Street. There is a small admission charge. Find out more from the Museum website at www.westhighlandmuseum.org.uk

To get out onto the water and really appreciate the scenery of Fort William, take a **Crannog Cruise** from Fort William Town Pier. From March until October the boat takes passengers for a scenic cruise down Loch Linnhe enjoying the scenery and wildlife. During the summer there are evening sunset cruises on the same route. See www.crannog.net.

The railway continues beyond Fort William to Mallaig on what is often referred to as 'the extension', as it was opened later in 1901. The route today is a popular day trip, even by those on motoring holidays in the Fort William area.

Fort William to Mallaig

The West Highland Mallaig Extension, as this line is known, is one of the most scenic rail journeys in the world. Even if you don't have time for the entire West Highland line, make sure not to miss out on this section of the route. Scotrail operate four trains daily in each direction. The comfortable 'super sprinter' trains have large windows for you to enjoy the scenery and space to take your bike, or luggage. During the summer a scheduled steam train forms the fifth train of the day. Special tickets are required for this journey which is operated by the West Coast Railway Company in association with Scotrail. These are available from the booking office at Fort William. For those on motoring holidays, taking a day trip from Fort William to Malliag is a popular option, especially when the steam train is running.

Journey Summary:

Route:	Fort William – Glenfinnan – Arisaig – Morar – Mallaig.
Operator:	Scotrail and West Coast Railway Company (summer steam services).
Trains:	Scotrail trains have standard class accommodation and most have a trolley catering service. West Coast Railway trains are steam hauled and offer standard and first class accommodation, a luggage van, buffet car and souvenir shop.
Trip Length:	1 hour 22 minutes.
Frequency:	Four trains in each direction daily with five in summer.
Stations:	Intermediate stations are unstaffed but have waiting shelters and information boards. Some are request stops, at these make a clear signal to the driver if wishing to board or tell the conductor if you wish to alight.
Links:	Ferries from Mallaig to the Small Isles and Skye.

Upon leaving Fort William station the train passes Fort William signal box. The station area is still controlled by the traditional semaphore signalling system, although the rest of the entire West Highland route system has long since changed to a new radio signalling system. This signal box was once named Mallaig Junction (to mark the start of the Mallaig extension) but was renamed to avoid confusion. The train passes the Fort William rail yards which during the summer are busy servicing the steam locomotives of the West Coast Railway Company.

Banavie is the first stop on the extension as the train slows to cross the **Caledonian Canal** at its southernmost end. The canal was constructed by Thomas Telford. It was designed to cross Scotland and avoid the long and hazardous shipping route around the north coast. Today it is popular for leisure sailing and for cycling and walking along its length. Located at

Banavie is one of the highlights of the canal, Neptune's Staircase. This remarkable system of lock gates is now floodlit at night and looks spectacular. You can get here by train of course, but it is also only a short cycle journey or bus link from Fort William. On leaving Banavie, look out for the new signalling centre controlling the entire West Highland Lines. It is built in the style of a traditional signal box although it is actually packed with modern electronics. The Great Glen Way walk to Inverness starts in Fort William, or you can start it here at Banavie Station.

The train winds back towards the sea which is now starting to form the sea loch of Loch Eil. At this point it is known as 'the narrows' and the name is appropriate with the hills of the opposite shore being very close at this point.

Corpach Station is the site of a large paper pulp mill. There are rail sidings for the supply of raw materials by rail. Of greater interest is the beautiful sea loch of Loch Eil which is on the left side of the train. There are also wonderful views back towards Fort William and Ben Nevis. The train will make a request stop at **Loch Eil Outward Bound** if required. This new simple halt was constructed from old railway materials to serve the outdoor recreation centre located here. The train continues alongside Loch Eil for several miles on this particularly beautiful stretch of line. **Locheilside Station** serves this remote area before the train heads inland through the narrow pass which brings the line to Glenfinnan. The line heads around a long and tight curve which takes it over the famous Glenfinnan Viaduct.

Glenfinnan. The railway was built by Sir William MacAlpine who was nicknamed 'Concrete Bob' for his innovative use of the material on the line. The viaduct at Glenfinnan is constructed entirely of concrete and rises to a height of 100 feet as it crosses the valley. This was the first concrete viaduct in Britain. There are wonderful views down to Loch Sheil at this point. Beside the shore you will see the Glenfinnan Monument, constructed to mark the landing of Bonnie Prince Charlie and the spot he started his 1745 Jacobite uprising. The station at Glenfinnan provides access to the monument, now cared for by the National Trust for Scotland. There is also a small museum in the station building.

Between Glenfinnan and the next station at Lochailort, the train first makes its way between some of the highest mountains to surround any British train journey. At between 500 and 790 metres the hills tower above the train on either side and with their steep sides seem to come right up to the carriage windows. They get only slightly less dramatic and tall as the train clings to the hillside to negotiate the edges of Loch Eilt. Unsurprisingly the location, along with much of the West Highland Line, is a favourite with railway photographers. Another narrow pass is negotiated in the foot of Creag Bhàn mountain (510 metres) on the right of the train.

A stop is made at **Lochailort Station**. Another hotspot for railway photography with the nearby Lochailort Viaduct and surrounding hills, this is also a popular location with walkers. While less visible, the train traveller will encounter seven tunnels in the few miles surrounding this station. Look out on departure for amazing views on the left down Loch Ailort. Also at this point look out for the small white church of 'Our Lady of the Braes'. Although there has not been a service here since 1964, it has been made famous by photographers of the West Highland Railway. The train crosses the small peninsula before heading through a series of tunnels and alongside the incredibly rocky and rugged coastline which is crossed on Loch nan Uamh Viaduct. Although less famous than Glenfinnan Viaduct it is arguably the more scenic with its coastal setting. The small halt at **Beasdale** was once a private station for Arisaig House. It is passed just before another viaduct at Borrodale before Arisaig is reached.

Arisaig. The pleasant station at Arisaig has been unstaffed for many years, although it still provides a vital transport link to this remote community. After departure from the station look over Loch Nan Ceall for views of the islands of Rum and Eigg with its distinctive flat top. The view of the islands is short before the line heads inland and north for the final stretch before Mallaig. At the small station of **Morar** look to the right to see Loch Morar. This is Scotland's deepest Loch while it also has Scotland's shortest river running out and into the sea on the opposite side of Morar. The white sands of the beach were made famous by the 1983 film, 'Local Hero'. Along with their blue waters they are a popular place to spend the day. Although the village has only 200 inhabitants, it is a popular place for visitors to stop and has a restaurant and hotel.

The train heads through a few hills before returning to the sea for the short section into Mallaig station.

Mallaig

The seaside terminus at Mallaig has a special small town feel. For those who enjoy west coast scenery and life it does not get more authentic than this. Even today there is a working fishing port which visitors can view, a ferry terminal for some of the west coast islands and the life of a remote Scottish village.

Practicalities

The train terminates at the small Mallaig station. This is a simple two platform station with an attractive stone built station building. There is a staffed ticket office, toilets and waiting room.

Local Transportation. Close to the Station is the ferry terminal. There are year round regular sailings to Armadale on the Isle of Skye. From Armadale there are coach connections to the entire island, or the crossing may be taken as a scenic day trip to Armadale. You can also make a connection to Kyle of Lochalsh and return via the scenic Kyle railway and Inverness.

Passenger only ferries also make connections to the islands of Canna, Eigg, Muck and Rum.

Tourist Information. Mallaig Tourist Information Centre is located at East Bay, Mallaig, PH41 4QS. Tel: 01687 462170.

Places of Interest

Boat Trips. The are opportunities to see whales, seals and dolphins from boat trips. These depart during the summer from Mallaig harbour. See the local website, www.road-to-the-isles.org.uk for information about the tours and other attractions in the area.

Heritage Centre. Situated alongside the station, the Centre is filled with exhibits about the town, fishing and railways. The Heritage Centre is not linked to the former Marine World which closed after storm damage in 2007.

Nearby Places of Interest

Ferry from Mallaig to Armadale and Skye

The Mallaig to Armadale (on the Isle of Skye) ferry is operated by Caledonian MacBrayne. There are four rail connected sailings in each direction daily, and a choice of up to eight sailings for those staying in Mallaig. The route is usually operated by either the MV Coruisk or MV Lochnevis. Both carry around 200 passengers, provide a café, lounge, open deck space, and toilet facilities onboard. The journey takes around 30 minutes.

Departing Mallaig the ship turns to head into the Sound of Sleat with views down the Sound towards the Island of Rum. Looking in the opposite direction the isolated village of Inverie comes into view in Loch Nevis with its impressive hills. On this crossing of only 30 minutes, Skye soon comes close into view along with the destination of Armadale. The Sleat Peninsula which Armadale sits on is relatively low lying so the Cullin mountains some 15 miles behind the village dominate the skyline.

The tiny village of **Armadale** is most visited for the Castle and Museum of the Isles. If travelling here, the visitor has two options, either making this a day trip returning to Mallaig on a later sailing, or heading across Skye to visit more of the Island. It is then possible to return via the scenic Kyle of Lochalsh to Inverness railway. See chapter 20 if you are interested in this option.

Armadale Castle Gardens and Museum of the Isles (IV45 8RS) is actually two attractions in one. The site was taken over by the Clan Donald's Lands Trust in 1971, who have restored this 40 acre woodland garden beside the Castle. These beautiful gardens benefit from almost frost free conditions and have existed since the 17th century. There are also woodland walks and nature trails for those less interested in formal gardens. These are all set within the grounds of the Castle, which although at first glimpse looks complete, is actually now a ruin without any interior. The Museum of the Isles was opened in 2002 in a purpose built building and despite its small size has excellent displays. Also on the site is the Stable Block which now contains a gift shop and restaurant. The Trust also offers self catering accommodation and a conference centre. There is an admission charge which covers both the Gardens and Museum. Opening times are from April until October, although the Gardens and accommodation are open all year. Telephone 01471 844305 or visit www.clandonald.com for information.

Mallaig to the Small Isles

Mallaig is also the departure point for the 'Small Isles' consisting of Eigg, Muck, Rum and Canna. These passenger only sailings are provided by Caledonian MacBrayne with their vessel MV Lochnevis. This small 190 passenger vessel has excellent facilities with large open decks for viewing the passing scenery, a comfortable passenger lounge, coffee cabin serving light snacks and providing picnic bags, a bar service and toilets. Recently these islands have all had purpose built piers installed ending the practice of passengers (and cargo!) going ashore by 'flitboat'. These small boats came out to meet the ferry with passengers transferring at sea to get ashore. The ferry service runs from Mallaig to a selection of these islands daily except Sundays so for overnight stays a calendar will be as useful as a watch to known when to catch the ferry home! Day trips are also offered either from Mallaig or by coach and ferry from Fort William. Consult the CalMac office at Fort William Railway station for details of these tours.

The Islands themselves are remote and sparsely inhabited. Each offers something quite unique to the visitor. **Rum** is by far the largest island and with its jagged volcanic mountains, is a distinctive feature of the west coast. The Island is an important nature reserve with otter, sea eagle and a unique mountaintop colony of Manx shearwaters. Also on the Island is the remarkable Kinloch Castle. The Castle has appeared on the BBC 'Restoration' television show and you can find out more at www.kin lochcastlefriends.org. It is located close to the ferry terminal. The Island is covered in tracks and small trails making it ideal for exploring on foot or bike. **Eigg** is a community island which is now owned by the inhabitants of the Island. The main geological feature is a huge basalt plateau 1000 feet above sea level, and a great stump of columnar pitchstone lava, known as An Sgurr, rising out of the plateau another 290 feet. This gives the Island its distinct shape. **Muck** is the smallest of the isles and is famous for its sandy beaches, rocky shores and the 452 feet Beinn Airein, with its panoramic view of the surrounding islands. Finally **Canna** is the small five miles long island which is owned by the National Trust for Scotland and has a population of just 20. For total escapism to just enjoy the views and walk, this is the ideal location. Look out for the high basalt cliffs and compass hill, which has such a high metal content that it will distort a compass. The Island is home to large colonies of seabirds, including shags, puffins, razorbills and black guillemots. See the National Trust website for details.

All of these islands are tranquil with no roads or busyness. They are ideal for people wishing to relax and walk. For those not wishing to spend so long there a day trip round them by ferry just viewing the scenery from the ship is an enjoyable if less intense way to enjoy these locations.

This concludes the tour of the West Highland Railway. It is possible to take a Citylink coach to Inverness and return via the railway south to Perth.

13. Northern Clyde Coast to Weymss Bay (for Rothesay) and Gourock (for Dunoon)

This railway hugs the south side of the River Clyde taking you to the coastal towns of Weymss Bay and Gourock. The journey begins at Glasgow's Central Station. Trains initially make their way through the Glasgow suburbs stopping at suburban stations before leaving the city behind for the journey to the coast. The lines divide at Port Glasgow Station with the Weymss Bay line heading west and then south while the Gourock line goes a little further west to the port at Gourock.

Journey Summary:

Route:	Glasgow Central – Port Glasgow – Weymss Bay – Rothesay on the Isle of Bute OR Glasgow Central – Gourock – Dunoon (by ferry).
Operator:	Scotrail.
Trains:	Standard class accommodation.
Trip Length:	41 minutes to Gourock, 53 minutes to Weymss Bay.
Frequency:	Hourly service to Weymss Bay and up to four trains per hour to Gourock.
Links:	Caledonian MacBrayne ferries to Rothesay and the Isle of Bute.

To Isle of Bute (Rothesay) and Dunoon

The first stop of interest to visitors on this route is at **Port Glasgow**. The station at Port Glasgow (Princess Street, PA14 5JH) has a ticket office, waiting room, toilets and a taxi rank. The town was originally known as Newark but was renamed in honour of its role as Glasgow's port. The town grew in the 19th century as a centre of shipbuilding and many of the famous River Clyde shipyards were once located here. Today the only shipyard left is Ferguson Shipbuilders which is now one of the last shipbuilders on the River and the only remaining non military shipbuilder. Its main business is the construction of ferries, some of which you may use to reach the Scottish islands. The town centre is unremarkable but does have one interesting feature, a replica of the paddle steamer Comet. PS Comet entered service on the River Clyde in 1812 and was the first commercially successful steamer service in Europe.

The main attraction at Port Glasgow is **Newark Castle**. The Castle has a wonderful location overlooking the River Clyde. In recent times it has been hidden behind shipyards but with their decline it is now in full view again in a specially created park which has been developed around it. The Castle is the result of the Maxwell family who lived here for hundreds of years. Highlights of this 15th century Castle include its Jacobean external details, complete downstairs servants quarters and an original 16th century bedchamber. Unfortunately there is a dark side to the history of the Castle. It was built on the instruction of Sir Patrick who may have had a beautiful house but was a murderer who abused his wife. Thankfully he is long gone and the visitor may simply enjoy the Castle and its fine views. It is a 12 minute walk from the railway station and is open from April until October with an admission charge. See the Historic Scotland website or call 01475 741858 for details.

Return to the station and either select a train for Weymss Bay or Gourock. Each journey is described in turn now.

To Weymss Bay and Rothesay

Trains head south west and through the stations at Whinhill, Drumfrochar and Branchton. There are attractive hills to the left of the train. Continuing by the Spango Valley hills, the train calls at IBM Halt station. It is named after the computer manufacturer which had a facility here. It is now owned by other companies and only visitors to the factory complex may use the station. A short stop is also made at **Inverkip Station**. The station serves the town which now has a popular marina. The next section of the line is through a short tunnel and then some cuttings before arrival shortly afterwards at Weymss Bay Station.

Weymss Bay

Weymss Bay can trace its history back to the 15th century but came into its own in Victorian times as a settlement for the wealthy merchants and business people from Glasgow. The Chairman of Cunard shipping line was one such person who had a villa here. It also developed as the steamer departure point for several locations on the Clyde.

Weymss Bay railway station (Greenock Road, PA18 6AA) incorporates the Caledonian MacBrayne ferry terminal for ships to Rothesay on the Isle of Bute. The railway was opened in 1865 but the present station, designed by James Miller, was opened later in 1903 by the Caledonian Railway. James Miller was notable in that he wished his stations to add to the travelling experience for the passenger. They continue to give pleasure to passengers on the West Highland Railway as well as at Weymss Bay. This station is worth visiting Weymss Bay for alone. It is category A listed and a remarkable building. Inside there is a beautiful curved glass roof which continues down a walkway to the ships. The exterior is equally impressive with its white and black timber framing and its own tower. Photographers can have a lot of fun at this station. The station has a staffed ticket office, waiting room, toilets, café, luggage trolleys and pay phones.

Caledonian MacBrayne Ferry from Weymss Bay to Bute

The ferry from the Weymss Bay station takes 35 minutes to cross the sea to the heart of Rothesay, the main town on the Island of Bute. The service is very regular with up to 16 rail connected ferry crossings in each direction daily. Reservations are not required for this route, but can save time. Combined rail and ferry tickets are available from Scotrail stations. The route is currently operated by two new vessels, the MV Argyle and MV Bute which provide high quality accommodation on this service. These ships have open deck space, indoor lounges and a café on board. During the crossing the land that appears close to the ship on the right is the Cowal Peninsula, go to Gourock to reach this location. There is a minimum ten minute check in time on this route so if you do find yourself missing the sailing you had planned, then there will be another ship along shortly with departures almost every half hour. Arrival on the Isle of Bute is at the Rothesay Ferry Terminal in the heart of the town.

Bute and Rothesay

The Island of Bute is large and mostly uncultivated or inhabited, with many Forestry Commission plantations. The only town on the Island is Rothesay. Most of the interesting places for the visitor are also in the Rothesay area.

Practicalities

Tourist Information is provided in Rothesay at the Discovery Centre in the Winter Gardens, Victoria Street, PA20 0AH. It is open seasonally from Easter until October. Telephone 08707 200619.

Local Transport is provided by West Coast Motors who have an excellent bus service all over the Island. The main departure point is located close to the ferry arrival point. See their website at www.westcoastmotors.co.uk or telephone 01586 552319.

Rothesay

Rothesay is the splendid Victorian holiday resort on the Island. With its promenade and fine buildings surrounding the romantic Rothesay Bay visitors today arrive as the Victorians did - by sea - and are treated to countryside and fine buildings not unlike their previous counterparts. The shoreline is dominated by the impressive 1920s Art Nouveau Winter Gardens now restored as the Isle of Bute Discovery Centre. The circular structure of cast iron and glass incorporates a cinema, theatre and many interactive displays as well as showcasing the best of Bute. No less impressive are Rothesay's Victorian public lavatories! Located on the Pier these facilities were not only practical but also built to impress. There are many local cafés, restaurants and shops to delight the visitor as well as a good selection of places to stay in the town, which is probably the most convenient location for island visitors to stay.

Places of Interest

Rothesay Castle (Castlehill Street, Rothesay, PA20 0DA). Rothesay Castle is everything that might be hoped for from a castle with its moat, unique round curtain wall and a remarkable place in Scotland's history. Built by Walter, 3rd High Steward of Scotland (1204–41) it was long associated with the Stewarts. However the Castle had a key role in the Norwegian and Scottish wars. In 1098 King Edgar of Scotland formally ceded the Hebrides, including Bute, to Norway. But Walter wanted to reclaim the land for Scotland which prompted a Norwegian war and siege of the Castle in 1230. The Norwegian forces were defeated but returned in 1263, with King Haakon himself at their head. They retook the Castle, but lost a subsequent battle at Largs, resulting in their retreat. Haakon died in the Bishop's Palace, Kirkwall, on his return voyage which you can read about in the Orkney section of this book (Chapter 8). As well as the moat and curtain wall, the other highlight is the gatehouse with its Great Hall, completely restored in 1900. To reach the Castle, follow the signs from the Ferry Terminal. It is a three minute walk. The Castle has an admission charge and is open year round but with restricted opening during the winter. See the Historic Scotland website or call 01700 502691 for information.

Canada Hill (or Common Hill). From Rothesay Castle walk through the streets to the Serpentine Park and then past Skipper Wood (marked on Ordinance Survey maps as Bogany Wood) to the top of the hill and the viewing platform. It is possible to return through the wood or continue down the opposite side and return by the seafront. There are views over Rothesay, the Cowal Peninsula, the Great and Little Cambrae Islands and Firth of Clyde. The walk is three and a quarter miles long and takes between one and two hours.

Bute Museum (7 Stuart Street, PA20 0EP). Bute Museum is an independent museum housed in an attractive building on Stuart Street, behind the Castle. There are displays on the history, archaeology and natural history of Bute. The Society also has an active publications programme covering local history. See www.butemuseum.org for information. It is open all year with restricted hours in winter and there is an admission charge.

Open Top Bus Tour of Bute. An excellent way to discover not only Rothesay but also the entire Island is the open top bus tour. The double decker bus used on this special tour has an open upper deck for full viewing, not to mention enjoyment of the summer sun. Starting in Rothesay, it passes the Isle of Bute Discovery Centre, Ardbeg point, Port Bannatyne, Kames Castle and Ettrick Bay. Following the coast road south it pauses at Scalpsie Bay to savour its peace and tranquillity before heading towards Kingarth, Kilchattan Bay and Ascog Bay and then ending back at Rothesay Pier with ample time to catch the ferry back to Wemyss Bay.

Tickets on the bus may also be used on all West Coast Motors services for unlimited travel to explore the Island over two days. See www.west coastmotors.co.uk or telephone 01586 552319.

Ardencraig Gardens. (Ardencraig Lane, High Craigmore, Rothesay, Isle of Bute, PA20 9EZ). The Gardens were originally linked to Ardencraig House but the walled garden was acquired by Rothesay Town council in 1970, and has been developed to create a propagation, education and show garden. There are also a number of aviaries housing a range of exotic bird species to create further interest. The gardens are open from May to September, have free entry and are a five minute bus journey from the town centre.

West Island Way. Scotland's first long-distance island walk, is this 26-mile route meandering across Bute and covering a wide variety of landscapes. The walk is very beautiful and embraces a variety of landscapes including seashore, moorland, farmland and forest. It passes St Blane's Chapel, the abandoned townships in Glen More and the outskirts of Rothesay. It has minimal road-walking and can be taken as two day-long walks from Rothesay as a central starting or finishing point. As such it is an ideal beginner's long distance walk. To take the walk, check an Ordnance Survey map for a diagram of the route. The starting point is Kilchattan Bay and the ending point is Port Bannatyne in the north with Rothesay in the middle. All three locations are served by buses 90 and 490 of West Coast Motors allowing maximum flexibility. The village of Kilchattan Bay (walk starting point) lies in a sheltered bay at the southern end of Bute. You could spend a day here on the pink sands or walk around the south end of the island. Port Bannatyne is a beautiful small village which is now a popular location for yachts people.

Nearby Places of Interest
During the summer a special tourist bus service south from Rothesay takes visitors for a short journey to several more places of interest on Bute. Consult West Coast Motors for details.

Ascog Hall Victorian Fernery and Gardens is the first stop of interest to visitors on the bus route. In 1986 Ascog Hall was purchased by the Fyfe family who discovered a long neglected treasure in the garden in the form of a Victorian Fernery. Dating from 1870 it was long disused but an original description of the plants which once formed the Fernery still existed and with the help of the Royal Botanical Gardens in Edinburgh and a great deal of hard work, it was recreated. As well as the Fernery there is also a restored three acre garden at the Hall. It is open from Easter until October (except Mondays and Tuesdays) and there is an admission charge. See www.ascoghallfernery.co.uk or call 01700 504555 for details.

Mount Stewart House. This amazing Victorian Gothic mansion looks as if it might be more at home in India than Scotland, but it is a style that works. The visitor feels as though they have gone to the ends of the earth, and a very beautiful part of the earth at that, but this was the creation of the Marquis of Bute and the architect Sir Robert Rowand Anderson. Inside there are many amazing rooms including the hall, staircase, marble chapel and gallery. Outside there are more delights with 300 acres of vibrant gardens, wilderness and woodland which were started by the 3rd Marquis who was a founder of Kew Gardens in London. It is open during Easter and then from May until September. There is an admission charge. See www.mountstuart.com or telephone Tel: 01700 503877 for information. To get there take the bus from Rothesay which is operated regularly throughout the day on days when the house is open by West Coast Motors, see www.westcoastmotors.co.uk or telephone 01586 552319.

Kingarth Trekking Centre. Scotland is a great place to go horse riding. However some locations are better than others with opportunities to ride for miles off road. Kingarth is one such location. It is seven miles south of Rothesay on the bus route and is located a five minute horse ride from the vast sandy beach of Kilchattan Bay. There are also many hill and woodland rides available. It is the ideal location to ride if you are looking for off road riding without being restricted to a paddock. As an added benefit, all children attending the Centre are met off the ferry at Rothesay. It is of course also an ideal day out for families, couples and others. See www.kingarthtrekkingcentre.co.uk or call 01700 831673.

This concludes our tour of Bute and we return to the Port Glasgow station line for the alternative route to Gourock and the Cowal Peninsula.

Glasgow to Gourock and Dunoon or Kilcreggan

The train departs Port Glasgow Station and splits from the Weymss Bay line to continue close to the River Clyde towards Gourock. The suburban stations at Bogston and Cartsdyke are briefly called at before arrival at Greenock Central Station, not to be confused with Gourock our destination.

Greenock Central

Greenock Central Station (Station Avenue, PA15 1DH) was opened in 1841 by the Glasgow, Paisley and Greenock Railway. Unfortunately the original station buildings along with the glass platform canopies were demolished in the early 1990s. At least the new building has a traditional stone roof and is not too unattractive. The station has a staffed ticket office, waiting room, toilets and pay phone. It is located a few hundred metres from Custom House Quay, which the paddle steamer 'Waverley' still sometimes calls at. See the Waverley Steam Navigation Company website for details of cruises from Greenock and other Clyde locations: www.waverleyexcursions.co.uk.

Greenock is a large town on the River Clyde with fine views across the River to the hills on the opposite shore and further west on to Cowal. There are eight railway stations in the town, with Central serving the town centre area. The town has long been a port and early trade with the Americas and the import of sugar from the Caribbean made the town wealthy. Custom Quay is close to the Station and is dominated by the magnificent Custom House. This is the official office of the HM Customs & Excise in the area and was designed by William Burn in 1818 and is considered by many to be the finest in Britain. It was refurbished in 1989 and now also contains a very interesting museum which is open year round on weekdays to visitors. Unfortunately the customs service has announced plans to close the building in 2011.

Another outstanding building in the town centre is the municipal town hall named Victoria Tower. With the town's increasing wealth and importance it was possible to construct this set of Italianate Municipal Buildings with their centrepiece Victoria Tower, built in 1886. Standing 245 feet (74.7 m) tall it is actually higher than the city hall in Glasgow itself. However if it looks incomplete it is because local businessman Robert Cowan refused to sell his land and therefore the entire right wing is missing having never been started.

Returning to the train, stops are made at Greenock West with its neat Renaissance style red sandstone building and Fort Matilda with its unused but attractive station before arrival in Gourock.

Gourock

Gourock railway station (The Pier, PA19 1QR) once had 18 platforms with glazed canopies and significant ticket hall. It is hard to believe today with the small modern replacement building and what little remains of this once grand station. However while lacking any form of charm the station has good passenger facilities, while the views over to the Cowal Peninsula remain as impressive as ever. It has a ticket office, waiting room, toilets, pay phone and taxi rank. The Caledonian MacBrayne ferry terminal is within the railway station.

Gourock is a former resort town with a fine promenade along the sea front. It also has an outdoor heated public swimming pool. Continue along the road from the station for three minutes (Albert Road) to find the pool, which is open from May until September.

However it is for the shipping links that most rail passengers come to Gourock. There are two routes from Gourock both of which are of interest to visitors. By far the most popular is the Dunoon service, but the Kilcreggan route is also worth mentioning and is detailed first here.

Strathclyde Passenger Transport Ferry to Kilcreggan and Helensburgh

From Gourock Ferry Terminal catch one of Britain's last passenger only ferries. Until 2007 this service was operated by the MV Kenilworth, a historic 1936 vessel. It has now been replaced by a modern ship which of course is good news for the future of these routes. The routes cross the Firth of Clyde and the Gare Loch to Kilcreggan and Helensburgh. There are up to 15 sailings daily and four between Gourock and Helensburgh. The journey time is 15 minutes to Kilcreggan and 25 to Helensburgh. Strathclyde Passenger Transport Zonecards and Day-tripper tickets (also valid on rail routes) may be used on these services. See www.spt .co.uk/ferry/ or telephone Traveline on 0871 2002233 for sailing information.

Kilcreggan is located at the end of the Rosneath Peninsula, between the Gare Loch and Loch Long. Although Kilcreggan is on the north shore of the Clyde River and in no way an island, the journey by road on the north shore is quite long, plus the sea option is more enjoyable for most people. Kilcreggan has the last Victorian pier on the Clyde and it is still in use for the ferry. The town itself does not have a lot of interest for the visitor but there are some cafés and good views. It is dominated by large Victorian villas from a time when this was where the well off from Glasgow lived.

Helensburgh is mentioned in chapter 12, the West Highlands. However it is worth nothing that this ferry link can provide an interesting circular tour returning from Helensburgh Central Station to Glasgow or continue north on the West Highland Railway from Helensburgh Upper station.

Return to Gourock for the main ferry route to Dunoon.

Caledonian MacBrayne Ferry to Dunoon

By far the most popular route from the Gourock terminal is the Caledonian MacBrayne ferry to Dunoon. Dunoon is the main town on the Cowal Peninsula. Although it is possible to reach the location by road (take a Citylink coach to Inveraray and then connecting West Coast Motors service to Dunoon) the quickest and most direct route is by rail and sea via Gourock. Western Ferries also operates a competing service with their distinctive red boats but these depart from terminals outside both Gourock and Dunoon and are therefore not so convenient for the rail traveller. The Caledonian MacBrayne route is a twenty three minute crossing. Check in closes ten minutes prior to departure. On board there are toilets, a lounge and a café. There are up to 17 rail connected sailings in each direction daily and fares may be purchased as part of a rail ticket or are included in Freedom of Scotland explorer tickets.

The sailing has excellent views of the hills of the Cowal Peninsula and arrival is at the beautifully restored 1895 Dunoon Pier. The buildings of the pier are worth a closer look on arrival and must be some of the most attractive pier buildings in existence.

Dunoon and the Cowal Peninsula

Dunoon became a popular location for wealthy Victorian Glasgow people to build their villas that may still be seen on the hillside behind the town. The town centre itself is attractive and has a selection of cafés, restaurants and services for the visitor. The Pier is the focal point of the town and the paddle steamer Waverley is still a regular visitor continuing a link with the past when steamers were constantly bringing day drippers from the city. On the hill above the Pier are the remains of the old Dunoon Castle.

Practicalities

Tourist Information. There is a Tourist Information Centre at 7 Alexandra Parade (PA23 8AB), telephone 01369 703785. It is a three minute walk from the Pier.

Local Transport. Dunoon is easily explored on foot. Local transport along the Cowal Peninsula is provided by West Coast Motors who provide a good quality bus service on all their routes. See www.westcoastmotors.co.uk for timetables and a route map or telephone 01586 552319. Service 486 from Dunoon to Inveraray connects with Scottish Citylink services 926 (Campbeltown – Glasgow) and 976 (Oban – Glasgow). Service 926 is included in Freedom of Scotland Travelpass tickets. Also of interest is bus 479 to Rothesay from where you may connect with the Caledonian MacBrayne ferry and rail service back to Glasgow.

Places of Interest

Castle Gardens. The Gardens have been the property of the people of Dunoon since 1893. These municipal Gardens are located opposite the Pier in the town centre and offer a nice place to relax or enjoy a picnic.

The Bishop's Glen is a favoured beauty spot and a delightful walk can be entered either from the top of Nelson Street, the bridge at the head of Auchamore Road, or Kilbride Road. For the more energetic, there is a track leading on and upwards to the Bishop's Seat Hill (1655 feet high).

Castle House Museum. In 1824 Lord Provost Ewing of Glasgow bought the land around the ruined medieval castle and built himself a holiday home. In 1998 the House became a museum and now has an excellent set of displays on local history. It is open from Easter until October and has an admission charge. See the website at: www.castlehousemuseum.org.uk for details. It is located in the Castle Gardens, opposite the ferry pier.

Nearby Places of Interest

The seasonal bus Route 485 from Dunoon visits three excellent places of interest. **Botanic Garden**. These gardens are one of Cowal's highlights and are not to be missed, even if you don't think you are a garden lover. Set in 150 acres of mountainside beauty the gardens were laid out in 1820. There are over 250 species of rhododendron and a spectacular Avenue of Giant Redwoods planted in 1863 which are now over 40 metres (130 feet) high. However the tallest trees in the garden are the Douglas Firs which are now over 55 metres high. Opening times are from Easter until October and there is an admission charge. See www.rbge.org.uk and follow the link to Benmore Garden or telephone 01369 706261. There is an all inclusive, rail, ferry, bus and gardens ticket available from Scotrail stations.

Alight at Kilmun for **Kilmun Church** and **Kilmun Aboretum**. The Church was founded in 1422 and still has a Sunday service at 12 noon. The ruins of the old church are still present while the new church on the site was built in 1841. Dr Elizabeth Blackwell, the first woman to graduate as a MD (medical doctor) in the USA, is buried here. Nearby is the Kilmun Aboretum (owned by the Forestry Commission). Set up in the 1930s to monitor the growth of exotic tree species in Scotland there are over 160 varieties of tree on display which may be viewed in large groups of each species.

14. Kintyre: a Scenic Coach Route from Glasgow to Campbeltown via Loch Lomond, Inveraray and Lochgilphead

This scenic coach journey is operated by West Coast Motors and is included in Travelpass railway tickets of Scotland. Starting at Glasgow's Buchanan Street Bus Station, service number 926 travels via the famous Loch Lomond, Inveraray, Lochgilphead and Tarbert to the Kintyre peninsula and the community of Campbeltown, which while accessible is also probably one of Scotland's most remote areas of mainland. The route is also useful for people wishing to visit the islands of Gigha and Islay, as it serves the Caledonian MacBrayne ferry terminal at Kennacraig. This journey can also be combined with a rail and sea crossing to Dunoon as a coach links with this service at Inveraray from Dunoon. Take the time to enjoy this wonderful journey and one of Scotland's best coach routes and a real complement to the rail network for those wishing to really get to know the west coast.

Journey Summary:

Route:	Glasgow Buchanan Bus Station (next to Queen Street railway station) – Loch Lomond – Inveraray – Lochgilphead – Campbelttown.
Operator:	West Coast Motors. Coaches may operate in the livery of West Coast Mortors or Scottish Citylink Coaches.
Trip Length:	4 hours 25 minutes.
Frequency:	Three coaches daily in each direction.
Links:	Connecting coach service from Inveraray to Dunoon. Caledonian MacBrayne ferries to the islands of Islay and Gigha.

Glasgow

For the main Glasgow entry see chapter 11, Central Scotland.

Buses on this route are service number 926 and depart from Buchanan Street Bus Station. The Bus Station is located behind Queen Street Railway station and Buchanan Street Subway Station in Glasgow, both of which are about a six minute walk. Because it is located on the opposite side of the 'Buchanan Galleries' shopping centre, it is not possible to see the bus station from the railway, so head towards the shopping centre instead. The bus station has a ticket office, Strathclyde Transport information centre, waiting area, café, cycle racks, left luggage, post box, public telephones, toilets and a taxi rank.

Departing Glasgow the coach makes its way through Dumbarton which is served by Glasgow to Helensburgh trains, and Glasgow to Fort William or Oban trains. It then starts the journey north and along the shoreline of Loch Lomond. For those wishing to visit the Loch, use the Glasgow to Balloch rail service which will take you to the southern shores of the Loch. The coach however takes in the beautiful views of Loch Lomond as far as the villages of Tarbet and Arrochar, where a stop is made. These villages lie only a mile and a half from each other with Tarbet on the shores of Loch Lomond and Arrochar at the head of Loch Long. Arrochar was until 1986 a torpedo testing station for the Royal Navy. Today it is only the fine views that people head here for. The West Highland Railway is crossed here at the Arrochar and Tarbet station, which is halfway between the two villages. It is possible to join the coach here if using the railway. The coach sets out west now through the winding roads of Argyll on the journey west along Loch Long for a few miles before heading up the glen past Ben Arthur / The Cobbler (884 metres) on the right of the coach. After the bus stop at the 'Rest and Be Thankful' viewpoint, the mountain of Beinn an Lochain (901 metres) is passed on the left behind the small Loch Restil. The bus then turns to the west again and heads along the wooded Glen Kinglass alongside Kinglass Water River. The coach heads steeply downhill now until Loch Fyne. This water will be viewable now for much of the rest of the journey to Campbeltown. Travelling along the shores of Loch Fyne with the mountains towering above on all sides, Dunderave Castle is passed on the left side of the bus. This attractive Castle was built in 1596 and rebuilt in 1911–12. The coach arrives at Inveraray on the shores of the Loch.

Inveraray

Arrival is at the shoreline bus stop. Change here for West Coast Motors services to Dunoon. This classic 18th century planned town on the shores of Loch Fyne is one of Scotland's visitor hotspots. Inveraray was established in 1745 by the 3rd Duke of Argyll and is one of the best examples of Scottish Georgian architecture in the country. The Duke's home, Inveraray Castle, in neo-gothic style, is also open to visit and is only a short walk north from the town centre. The reason for this new town being built at all was the new Castle of 1745. The Duke decided to replace the tower castle with this modern building and in doing so create parkland stretching down to the Loch. To create the parkland, Inveraray had to move, and the new town was constructed making one of the finest small towns of its kind in Scotland at the time. Many of the important buildings in the town are open to the public through the summer months. Look out for the old Town House near the Jail, the All Saints Church, and the Bell Tower. The free standing Bell Tower was built between 1923 and 1931 as a war memorial and has ten working bells inside. It is often open for visitors to climb to the top and enjoy the views. The town has its own website with local information and accommodation details at www.inveraray-argyll.com.

Tourist Information. The Tourist Information Centre is located on Front Street (PA32 8UY) and is open year round. Telephone 08452 255121.

Places of Interest

There are three unmissable attractions in Inveraray which each require at least half a day to fully enjoy.

Inveraray Castle. The Castle incorporates Baroque, Palladian and Gothic styles and could be equally at home in France as Scotland. With four turrets, one at each corner, interesting arched windows and a central tower, the Castle has a unique appearance. The interior, while still a family home, is open to the public, as are the gardens, which are worth a visit in their own right with many opportunities for photography or finding interesting plants. The Castle is open from Easter until October and there is an admission charge. See www.inveraray-castle.com or telephone 01499 302203.

Inveraray Jail. This family day out begins in the restored 1820 courtroom where life-size models and actors re-create a court scene. Visitors may then visit the old and new jails to see what life was like for the prisoners in this typical Scottish prison of the time. There are lots of opportunities to try out prison activities and experience jail life. The buildings are also some of the best preserved of their type anywhere and offer a fascinating look into our recent past. There is an admission charge and the Jail is open all year, see www.inverarayjail.co.uk.

Inveraray Maritime Museum. Located on the pier, close to the Jail, is the Maritime Museum. The Museum is set on board the iron sailing ship 'Arctic Penguin'. This 1910 ship has displays on everything from Victorian steam yachts to the emigrant ships. Visitors are encouraged to try hands on experiences such as knot tying. Also at the museum is a 'puffer' ship – 'Vital Spark'. These small ships were lifeline supply ships for the Clyde and Hebrides communities and became famous through the stories of Neil Munro set on the 'Vital Spark'. The Museum has an admission charge. See the website www.inveraraypier.com or call 01499 30 2213 for details.

Returning to the coach, the journey heads inland for a short distance before returning to the Loch at the village of Furnace, after which the coach heads slightly inland again through the forest. The road swings round the head of Loch Gilp and makes a stop at Lochgilphead.

Lochgilphead is an attractive village on the shoreline of Loch Gilp. Its streets were laid out as a planned village in 1790 and retain their basic layout to this day. About a 20 minute walk from the village centre is Kilmory Castle, which is now used as council offices, but still has attractive gardens and a woodland park that is open to the public. The village is in fact surrounded by woodland walks. The main attraction in the town is the

Crinan Canal which passes right through the village. It continues for a further two miles along the shore of the Loch before finally joining it at Ardrishaig. Lochgilphead is the starting point for those without boats who still wish to enjoy what is probably Scotland's most beautiful canal. The canal cuts through the Kintyre peninsula and is still used by thousands of boats each year while in the past it was often used as a short cut for 'puffer' boats to the Hebrides. At only seven miles in length to Crinan it is easily explored on foot or bike. It is possible to take a bus to Crinan and walk back, or walk both ways. Find out more at www.scottishcanals.co.uk.

Rejoin the coach for the scenic journey down Loch Fyne as far as the village of Tarbert, not to be confused with Tarbet which was passed back on Loch Lomond.

Tarbert

This tiny village is nestled in the hills and overlooks its natural harbour. It is known as the gateway to Kintyre and is an ideal place to stop on the journey. If you are heading to Islay, most B&Bs will provide an early breakfast and transport to the ferry terminal so that you won't need to rejoin the bus. It is of course equally easy to stay on the coach and stay overnight on Islay, personal preference will dictate which one you choose. There is a seasonal Tourist Information Centre on Harbour Street (PA29 6UD) and plenty of cafés and restaurants as the area has become very popular with sailing enthusiasts who stop off here. The village is also the starting point for the Kintyre Way long distance walk. The village has a website at www.tarbertlochfyne.com.

Returning to the coach, the peninsula is now crossed as the bus heads down the west coast for a time and joins West Loch Tarbert. Only ten minutes after leaving Tarbert, the Kennacraig Ferry Terminal is reached for ferries to Islay.

Islay

Kennacraig Ferry Terminal is surprisingly well appointed for such a remote location. The service to Islay usually has either the vessel MV Isle of Arran or MV Hebridean Isles (although a new ship is currently under construction). Ships to Port Askaig continue to Colonsay and in summer on to Oban, where there is a rail connection back to Glasgow, or ferries to the Western Isles. Facilities on board include a passenger lounge, café / restaurant, bar, shop, open deck space and toilets. The journey takes about two and a half hours to Islay.

Islay has a good bus service on the Island and you can find out about timetables and other aspects of island life including accommodation at www.islayinfo.com. There is also an airport on the Island with flights to Glasgow (see www.hial.co.uk).

The Island was once much more densely inhabited than it is today with almost 18,000 inhabitants compared just over 3,000 today. It is mild for a Scottish location, being right on the Gulf Stream and it has some amazing scenery. There are three main villages on the Island, Bowmore, Port Ellen and Port Charlotte, with ferries arriving into Port Ellen.

Visitors head to Islay mostly for the activities on offer. The small 25 mile long Island has over 130 miles of coastline which are ideal for walking, fishing or bird watching. There are numerous other activities including walking, golfing, bird and nature watching, sea safaris and cycling. See the Islay website for details.

Returning to the mainland, the journey continues for the short journey across the peninsula to Campbeltown.

Campbeltown

Campbeltown is probably Scotland's most remote mainland town and is ideal for exploring the Kintyre area. There are places to stay, eat and some local shops and businesses. Although the town is quite plain, the surrounding scenery, including Campbeltown Loch, is stunning and there are some interesting buildings in the town itself. Look out for the pure white spire of the town house and the huge bell tower of the **Lorne and Lowland Church**. It was completed in 1872 to the design of John Burnet in a style influenced by Italian Renaissance design. The main places of interest are the local **Picture House** (www.weepictures.co.uk) which is Scotland's oldest cinema, and **Campbeltown Heritage Centre** which has excellent displays on local history and culture. It is open from April until September and has an admission charge.

Practicalities

Tourist Information: The Tourist Information Office is located in MacKinnon House, The Pier, Campbeltown, PA28 6EF or call 08707 200609.

Transport Links: Campbeltown Airport has regular flights to Glasgow. See the airport website, www.hial.co.uk or telephone 01586 553797 for information.

15. Southern Clyde Coast Rail Lines and the Island of Arran

This journey starts at Glasgow Central railway station and takes in the Isle of Arran, the resort of Largs and the popular Great Cumbrae Island. The places along the route are not nearly as interesting as the travel links to these two popular and accessible Scottish islands which may be enjoyed as day trips or longer excursions.

Journey Summary:

Route:
:   Glasgow Central – Ardrossan Harbour for the Island of Arran or – Largs for Great Cumbrae Island.

Operator:
:   Scotrail.

Trains:
:   Standard class accommodation.

Trip Length:
:   50 minutes to Ardrossan Harbour and 65 minutes to Largs.

Frequency:
:   There are multiple departures daily on this fast electrified railway. To Ardrossan Harbour there are four trains / ships in each direction all week with five on Fridays. Trains either go to Ardrossan or Largs as Ardrossan is on a separate branch line from the Largs railway.

Links:
:   Caledonian MacBrayne ferries from Ardrossan Harbour to the Island of Arran. Caledonian MacBrayne ferries from Largs to Great Cumbrae Island.

Glasgow to Ardrossan and the Island of Arran

The journey begins at Glasgow Central railway station. Once through the city's suburbs look out for Lochwinnoch on the right of the train which is an attractive Loch with good bird life. There is also a station at this point. Several stations are called at before arrival at Ardrossan. Ardrossan South Beach Station is the first Ardrossan stop and is on South Beach Road (KA22 8AU). The station has a ticket office, waiting room and information point. As the name suggests this is the most useful station for visits to the South Beach, although you may end up walking into town and returning from the Town Station. Ardrossan Town station (KA22 8DU) is the town centre. It is unstaffed but has an information point and waiting shelter. Ardrossan itself is not a resort town and most visitors continue a few more minutes to Ardrossan Harbour Station for the ferry to Arran.

Ardrossan Harbour Station. The station is unstaffed but has an information point and waiting shelter. Trains are timed to connect with the Caledonian MacBrayne ferry service to the Island of Arran. There is a walkway between the ferry terminal building and the station. The Terminal is a modern building with ticket office, toilets and a comfortable seating area.

Caledonian MacBrayne Ferry to Arran

The ferry can be booked at Scotrail ticket offices or telesales for integrated travel without needing to buy a separate ticket. The MV Caledonian Isles usually operates on the crossing. This modern 1000 passenger ferry has comfortable passenger lounges, observation lounge, open deck space, bar, cafeteria serving snacks and main meals, a play area for children, information desk and shop. In the summer some sailings are operated by the MV Saturn which has a bar, café and passenger lounge. This smaller vessel has fewer facilities so it is better to travel on Caledonian Isles if possible. The sailing takes an hour and has fine views of the Clyde coast and the hills of Arran.

On arrival at Arran, there is a small ferry terminal and buses to all parts of the Island. Make sure you catch a bus to the part of the island you wish to visit rather than waiting at the terminal as once the buses leave there isn't usually another one until the next ferry arrival. Ferries arrive in Brodick, the main village on the Island.

The Island of Arran

Arran is known as 'Scotland in miniature' with its mountains, woodland, cliffs, beaches and quiet coastal villages. Naturally, the Island is divided in two with the northern half being rugged, mountainous and rural. The peak of Goat Fell Mountain dominates the Island. The southern half is forest, farmland and has the Island's resort towns. It is where most of the population live and is very mild with the occasional palm tree growing thanks to the warming of the Gulf Stream. In the middle is the village of Brodick (where the ferry arrives). It is a beautiful village with all the facilities a visitor will require and makes an excellent base for exploring the Island with buses leaving from here. Arran is one of the most accessible Scottish Islands, being only an hour by train followed by an hour's ferry journey from Glasgow. It is therefore not only feasible as an extended visit but also a day trip from much of central Scotland.

Places of Interest

Brodick is the Island's main village and is attractively situated on a small bay with wooded hills forming a backdrop to the rear. It is ideal for activities such as angling, horse riding, cycling, golfing, walking and climbing. Equipment for such activities can usually be hired locally. The town itself could not be in finer scenery, so although lacking any particularly attractive architecture it is a pleasant place to be based with fine views from its streets. The waterfront has the potential to be very nice although it has a functional feel, being a long car park rather than a proper promenade to be enjoyed. Look out for the little stone harbour next to the Ferry Terminal. This type of harbour was to be found all around the coastline. There are also nice sandy beaches in the town which are usually quiet. The Tourist Information Office is located at the Pier (Ferry Terminal

– KA27 8AU) and is open seasonally. It contains details of where activities may be undertaken and equipment hired.

Brodick Castle and Country Park (Brodick, KA27 8HY). Over 600 years of history are on display at Britain's only island country park. The Castle is the ancient seat of the Dukes of Hamilton and has been a fortress since Viking times. The present castle's tower dates from the 13th century and was extended and developed in the 16th and 17th centuries to form what is seen today. The last Duchess to stay here was Lady Mary Louise, the 6th Duchess of Montrose, who lived at the Castle until 1957. Internally there are displays of 17th century furniture, paintings, porcelain and silver. Outside, the Walled Garden dates from 1710 and has now been restored as an Edwardian garden. There is an audio tour of the plant collections. Out with the Walled Garden the Country Park offers way-marked trails, woodlands, waterfalls, gorges, wildlife ponds, a nature room and wildlife garden. To fully appreciate the Park, visitors might need two days, one for the house and one for the outside attractions. For serious walkers, Goat Fell Mountain is a half day's climb and is part of the Estate. Start from the House and follow the marked path. At 874 metres, it is the highest peak on the Island and has amazing views from the summit. As with all hill walks, take sensible precautions even in summer. For all visits either take a picnic or make use of the on site café. The Castle is located in Brodick, two miles from the Ferry Terminal. It is possible to walk or take the connecting bus which departs shortly after the ferry's arrival. Through rail, ferry and bus tickets are available from staffed Scotrail stations. The House and Park are open from March until October and are owned by the National Trust for Scotland. See the Trust website or telephone 0844 4932152 for details.

Island of Arran Heritage Museum (KA27 8DP). The museum maintains artefacts and records of island life, including archaeology, geology, mineralogy and social history. The Museum is open seasonally and is a short five minute bus journey from the Ferry Terminal. Call 01770 302636 for details.

Four miles south of Brodick is **Lamlash** on the east coast of the Isle of Arran. This is the main town on the Island and has an attractive village feel along with plenty of places to eat and drink, or to relax away an afternoon. There is a cycle trail between Lamlash and Kilmory, providing mountain bikers with miles of off-road tracks and forest trails. There are also many walking routes from the village into the glens and hills that provide a backdrop. Buses to Lamlash depart from the Ferry Terminal. It is also possible to walk to Lamlash through woodland trails. A few miles further south of Lamlash is **Glenashdale Falls**. These are located behind Whiting Bay (a village) and again may be reached on the Lamlash cycle trail, by woodland walk or by bus followed by woodland walk. There are many miles of walking and cycling trails on Arran which may be found on good Ordnance Survey maps.

Return to Brodick Pier for the journey back to Glasgow. We now look at the alternative route to Largs.

Glasgow to Largs and Great Cumbrae Island / Millport town.

The alternative route is to take a train which continues on the main line to Largs further up the coast. On departure from Ardrossan the train passes the neglected remains of Ardrossan Castle and heads along the cliffs for a short distance with views across to Goat Fell and the Isle of Arran before heading inland to West Kilbride. West Kilbride station (KA23 9BP) is an unstaffed halt with waiting shelter and information point. The former station is an attractive timber frame building, now used a restaurant. **West Kilbride** has few visitor attractions but is a pleasant coastal town. The train departs past Law Castle (not open to the public), built in the 15th century for King James III's sister Mary. Kaim Hill at 374 metres is passed on the right at the same time as the Hunterston Coal Terminal comes into view on the left. The Terminal imports coal which travels by rail to Fife and Yorkshire and was a large part of the reason for the reopening of the Alloa rail line. Cumbrae Island has now come into view on the opposite shore of the Clyde with Arran just to the south.

The train makes a short stop at **Fairlie Station** before continuing along the coast with views of Cumbrae to Largs. Fairlie was the home of Fairlie Yachts in the early part of the 20th century and was the departure point for ferries to Cumbrae until they were moved to Largs.

Largs

Largs is a wonderful seaside resort town overlooking the hills of the Great Cumbrae Island. Surrounded by hills itself, which give the town its name (Learg is Gaelic for hillside), it also has a pleasant sandy beach. The town is famed for a battle in 1263 when the Vikings, attempting to land from a fleet of longboats, were repulsed by the army of Alexander III. Today it is everything one would expect from a Victorian resort with traditional promenade, ice cream parlours, cafés and restaurants. Great Cumbrae Island is only a mile off shore and a regular ferry service departs from the town throughout the day. In the summer you can also often catch the paddle steamer 'Waverley' for trips around the amazing coastline.

Largs railway station (Main Street, KA30 8AN) is a functional and rather ugly building located a few minutes walk from the Ferry Terminal – follow the signposts. The station has a staffed ticket office, waiting room, luggage trolleys, pay phone, toilets and taxi rank. The original 1885 station with glazed canopies over the platforms was badly damaged in 1995 in an accident when a train overran the buffers; the station was subsequently demolished. In 2005 after many years of temporary station facilities a new station was built.

For those interested in activity there is a Viking themed leisure centre, Vikingar (40 Greenock Road, KA308QL) with family friendly swimming pool, fitness suite and sports facilities. See www.naleisure.co.uk or call 01475 689777 for details. It is an 11 minute walk from the station on the seafront.

Great Cumbrae Island

Make your way to the Ferry Terminal (five minutes walk from the Largs Station) for the crossing to Great Cumbrae Island. The ferry is operated by Caledonian MacBrayne with a basic vessel which provides open and covered accommodation for the short ten minute crossing. There is no need to book in advance for this service, although doing so will save queuing for tickets. As with all Caledonian MacBrayne services these journeys are included in Freedom of Scotland rail tickets. Arrival on Great Cumbrae is at Cumbrae Slip. A connecting bus operates from here to the Island's town, Millport. Alternatively, those with bikes may prefer to cycle.

Great Cumbrae is a small island only 2.4 miles long by 1.2 miles wide. It has been inhabited since the end of the last Ice Age. Legend has it that St Mirren, on his return to Scotland from Ireland around 710 AD, arrived in Cumbrae and following the example of St Patrick, rid the island of snakes and Cumbrae to this day remains snake-free. There is a round the island road which is popular for family cycling outings. The route is 11 miles long. Thankfully Cumbrae with its small size and bus service to Millport means that few people take a car and the island's roads are still a pleasure to cycle or walk on. There is one town, Millport, which hugs the bay on the south end of the Island. In the centre of the land is 'The Glaidstone', a 127 metres high hill. It is possible to walk or cycle up from the Slipway, although take a map as it is not well marked with signposts.

Millport is the Island's only village, situated on the wooded land surrounding the bay. There are wonderful views out across to the Island of Arran and to Ayrshire, although if you look a little too hard in this direction you will still see the power station and coal terminal. The town has an attractive promenade, Victorian villas, cafés and an old style harbour to enjoy. Look out for the now ruined grand house, 'The Garrison'. This was the home to a customs clipper Captain who was based on the Island in the 19th century to patrol the Clyde. The building is thankfully now being restored.

The most significant building in Millport is the **Cathedral of the Isles** and a 'must see' for anyone visiting. The Cathedral and its associated college were built in 1851. The beautiful stone for the buildings was quarried on site giving the site its sunken appearance. The Cathedral itself is actually very small, seating only 100 people. See www.island-retreats.org

for details. By the shore is the **Robertson Museum & Aquarium** which is part of the Marine Biology Centre. There are displays on the local area's marine life inside.

Millport and Cumbrae make an ideal day out but they can also be enjoyed for longer by taking up accommodation on the island.

16. Southwest Scotland – Glasgow to Stranraer

For details of Glasgow city see Chapter 11 and the Edinburgh to Glasgow route guide. The southwest railway line to Stranraer is not only a connection to the Irish ferries but is also one of the scenic rail journeys of Scotland in its own right. Highlights of the route include the rural southwest, the Ayrshire coast, Southern Upland hills and the opportunity to visit Culzean Castle & Country Park.

Journey Summary:

Route:	Glasgow Central – Paisley Gilmour Street (or Barrhead – Kilmarnock) – Troon – Prestwick – Ayr – Maybole – Girvan – Barrhill – Stranraer.
Operator:	Scotrail.
Trains:	Standard class accommodation. Most trains have a trolley catering service.
Trip Length:	2 hours 15 minutes.
Frequency:	Eight trains in each direction daily over entire route, with an additional intensive local service between Glasgow and Ayr.
Links:	Stranraer Harbour to Belfast with Stena Line Ferries.

We start the description of this route at Troon having come through the Glasgow suburbs.

Troon

Situated in the Ayrshire countryside and on the Clyde coast with views across the Isle of Arran, Troon has been a popular holiday destination since the 1880s. Most visitors concentrate on the esplanade and marina area which forms the centre of the town in between the North Sands and South Sands beaches. There are many hotels and B&Bs together with restaurants, cafés and bars to choose from. The town is also famous for its Royal Troon Golf course which hosts the Open Championship every seven years.

Troon railway station (St. Meddars Road, KA10 6JY) has a ticket office, waiting room, toilets, payphone, shops and taxi rank outside. The station was opened by the Glasgow and South Western Railway on the 2nd of May 1892 replacing an earlier station on the same site. It is an unusual light coloured traditional building which somehow has a seaside feel to it.

Troon Beach is a long sweeping sandy beach alongside the esplanade with a children's play park nearby. The yachting marina is nearby and dogs are banned from the beach between May and September. The beach is also popular with windsurfers and kite enthusiasts. The view from Troon beach is towards Arran which creates a silhouette of 'The Sleeping Warrior'. It is a five minute walk from the station.

Barassie Beach is the other sandy beach in Troon. Located on the north side of the harbour it is also a five minute walk from the station. With views to the Isle of Arran and the Firth of Clyde it is a relaxing place to spend time with the family. It is also popular for windsurfing and sailing.

Departing Troon Station the train makes its way alongside the shoreline and sand dunes. On the right is the Royal Troon Golf Club immediately followed by the Prestwick Golf Club, which is alongside **Prestwick International Airport station**. The station is located inside the airport area and has a walkway into the main terminal. It was opened in 1994 to serve the airport and although unstaffed, tickets are available on board trains. There are waiting areas and toilets and a wide range of shops in the airport terminal building. Prestwick International Airport has flights to a range of European destinations. A few minutes later the train arrives into Prestwick Town Station.

Prestwick

The Town Station (Station Road, KA9 1AQ) is a traditional station building and is a fully staffed station with ticket office, waiting room, toilets, café, payphone and taxi rank.

Prestwick is one of Scotland's oldest towns, becoming a burgh as far back as 1170. This gave the town the right to hold markets, and the Mercat cross, which dates from 1777, may still be seen today (look out for them in many Scottish towns) outside the Post Office. The Old Parish Church was established in 1163 and it is possible that some of the ruined remains date from then. Unfortunately most of the buildings in Prestwick are not nearly as old as the town itself, although there are some notable buildings. Look out for the 1908 St Nicolas Church in attractive red sandstone Romanesque style and bordered mature trees. The town itself grew especially in Victorian times when it became a popular resort on the Clyde coast. There are several local golf courses and plenty of services for the visitor.

The train departs Prestwick but stays in urban surroundings as Prestwick and Ayr are effectively joined now. Local trains will make a stop at the Newton on Ayr Station which serves the north suburbs of the town, while long distance trains continue to the main Ayr station.

Ayr

Ayr is also situated on the Forth of Clyde and is probably most famous for its association with Scotland's national poet Robert Burns who was born in Alloway on the town's outskirts. It is one of the most visually appealing towns of the coastline with its attractive architecture, coastal views and many fine buildings.

A walk through the centre of Ayr is an architectural delight. The River Ayr flows through the town and forms an attractive walk starting from close to the railway station. Heading into town and towards the sea, the New Bridge (1877-79), with five stone arches and iron lamps along its length, frames the views of the town nicely at this point. Although a listed building in its own right, the New Bridge is overshadowed by the nearby Auld Brig. The Auld Brig is a 1470 stone bridge crossing the River Ayr in the town centre. It appeared in Robert Burn's poem Brig's O' Ayr but was almost demolished in the 20th century but for a successful campaign to save it. Wallace Tower at the corner of High Street and Mill Venal is a baronial tower. It was first recorded in 1673 and rebuilt in the present gothic style in 1834. The County Buildings, located in Wellington Square, are a beautiful set of municipal buildings completed in 1931. Near the River Ayr and the High Street on Boat Venal is Loudoun Hall. Built for James Tait, a wealthy merchant in the late 1400s, it later became the townhouse of the Campbells of Loudoun in the 16th century, before being rescued from demolition and restored by the 4th Marquis of Bute.

Practicalities

Ayr station on Smith Street, KA7 1TH, is this coastal resort's main station. This is a full service station with ticket office, ticket vending machines, waiting room, pay phone, toilets, café, shops, cash machine and taxi rank. The station is in the town centre close to the River Ayr. It is the third station to have been built in Ayr and was completed in 1886 by the Glasgow and South Western Railway as a replacement for its smaller predecessor. The platforms are covered by a traditional glazed canopy while the large and attractive red sandstone station building is largely occupied by the Station Hotel. Originally owned by the Glasgow and South Western Railway, the hotel was sold to a non railway hotel company in 1951.

Places of Interest

Ayr Auld Kirk. Opposite Lorne Arcade on the High Street is the Kirk. The church has existed on this site by the River for 800 years and in the present building for 350 years. See www.auldkirk.org for details.

Fort Wall. By the Harbour is the remaining wall of Cromwell's Citadel built in 1650 and at one time housing over 1000 troops. Although dismantled in 1660 much of the site can still be traced today by walking around the streets in the area.

In the south end of Ayr there are four excellent attractions worth visiting. They are about a six minute bus journey from the station and the bus fare is included in Plusbus tickets to Ayr. All are located within a few streets of each other in the village of Alloway (now part of the town of Ayr). The attractions are Burn's Cottage, the Tam O' Shanter Experience, Rozelle Estate and Belleisle Park.

Burn's Cottage. The Cottage is the birthplace of Scotland's national poet Robert Burns who was born here in 1759. It is now the centrepiece of the Burns Heritage Park owned by the National Trust for Scotland. The Cottage of 1757 is not only Burn's birthplace but also typical of the kind of house people lived in at that time. Adjacent is the Museum where Burn's poetry and original manuscripts and personal artefacts are on display. Also within the Park is the Burns Monument of 1814, Kirk Alloway which featured in his work, and the Tam O' Shanter Experience which details the poet's most famous work. There is an admission charge and the Park is open year round. For information see www.burnsheritagepark.com or telephone 01292 443700.

Rozelle Estate is a 37 hectare park located in Ayr and gifted to the town in 1968 by Commander J. Hamilton. The pond has swan, mallards and heron while the parkland is home to many types of bird and the native Scottish red squirrel. The gardens of Rozelle combine mature woodland, rhododendron walks, parkland and ornamental ponds, while Rozelle House has an art gallery. To get there take a bus from near the station for a six minute journey to the Estate on Monument Road next to the Seafield Golf Course. The bus journey is included in Plusbus rail tickets to Ayr. Telephone the Estate on 01292 616100 for details.

Belleisle Park is one of South Ayrshire's most popular family days out. The Council-run Park has woodland, gardens, parkland areas and a 'Pets Corner' which is home to ducks, doves, rabbits, guinea pigs, chipmunks, aviary birds and pigs, with deer, ponies and donkeys in the park.

Returning to the station for the journey south, Ayr marks the end of the electric railway and the start of the scenic and rural line to Stranraer. The train heads inland and through pleasant hilly South Ayrshire for the short journey to Maybole. Look out for the River Doon which you may have seen earlier if visiting Burn's Cottage in Ayr.

Maybole

Maybole station on Culzean Road (KA19 8DS) is in the town centre. The station is unstaffed with a waiting shelter and information point as the building is no longer used by the railway.

The town has an important history which is evidenced by the many important buildings to be found. On the High Street is Maybole Castle which comes as something of a surprise on its street corner position. Not open to the public, it is the oldest inhabited house, dating from 1560. Most notable buildings are located along Cassilles Road, near the station, which is worth walking along. Look out for the unusual orange coloured stone church of 1808 with its stepped stone spire. The 1887 Town Hall looks much older and was the town house of the Lairds of Blairquhan at Straiton. Also close to the station is the Maybole Collegiate Church. The chapel of St Mary was founded by John Kennedy of Dunure in 1371 and the associated college 11 years later. It is now cared for by Historic Scotland. The town has many small shops, cafés and restaurants for the visitor. Maybole (or Ayr which is a slightly longer bus journey but has a more frequent service) is also the stop for Culzean Castle, one of Scotland's most impressive country houses and parks. Buses to Culzean depart from close to Maybole station for the short four mile journey. Check with Traveline for details of bus times.

Nearby Places of Interest

Culzean Castle & Country Park. Culzean Castle and Country Park is one of Scotland's top attractions. The Castle seen today is largely the result of additions constructed in the 18th century by Robert Adam. With a cliff top position and unique style it is instantly. The Eisenhower Apartment is now available for hire and was the holiday home of President Eisenhower of the USA as a thank you from Britain for his command of troops in Europe during the Second World War. Eisenhower artefacts are still on display inside, together with amazing art, furniture and Adam's masterpiece oval staircase. Outside there is 600 acres of wood and parkland, and three miles of cliff-top coastline to be enjoyed. A full day is required to fully appreciate the grounds and castle. The Castle is open from Easter until October, with the Gardens open year round until sunset. See www.culzeanexperience.org (or the National Trust website) or telephone 0844 4932149 for details of times and admission charges.

Crossraguel Abbey. Founded in the 13th century by Duncan of Carrick, the Abbey is ruined but complete. Visitors may view the church, cloister, chapter house and domestic premises. There is an admission charge and the Abbey is open from Easter until October. See the Historic Scotland website or telephone 01655 883 113 for information. It is a 34 minute walk from Maybole station, mostly along the A77 road. There is a footpath along the entire length and about two thirds of the way along the ruin of a castle is passed on the left. The Abbey is right beside the road once you reach it.

On departure from Maybole the train crosses the Ayrshire countryside which is generally pastoral with small patches of trees and gently undulating hills. On the left of the train is the Waters of Girvan River. Travelling down the valley, the Maxwellston Hill is on the left. Traces of an early fort have been found on top. The line turns to head south and arrives at Girvan.

Girvan

Girvan is a pleasant coastal resort town popular with day trippers from Glasgow. There are lots of cafés, restaurants and shops and a great beach. The views from Girvan are spectacular, with the Isle of Arran and Ailsa Craig rising 339 metres out of the Clyde Firth. There are some attractive buildings in the town. Look out for Auld Stumpy, a clock tower and the former town jail built in 1825. A hall was added to the spire but it burnt down leaving 'Stumpy' as it looks today and as a local landmark in the town centre.

Girvan Station (Vickarton Street, KA26 9HF) was originally opened in 1877. However in January 1946 the station caught fire and was destroyed. The London, Midland & Scottish Railway who owned the station by that time did not rebuild it, as the government was about to nationalise the railway system, so it remained like that until 1951. The nationalised British Railways then rebuilt the station but did so in the Southern (south of England) style of station building! This therefore explains why Girvan has an art deco brick station building more commonly found in the south of England. The station is still well appointed with a staffed ticket office, waiting room, toilets, payphone and taxi rank.

McKechnie Institute (Dalrymple Street, KA26 9AE) is a local museum. Opened in 1889, it was designed in the Scottish Baronial style with some Renaissance detailing by the Glasgow architects McKissack & Rowan. The Institute has a collection of memorabilia from Girvan and the surrounding Carrick area. Telephone 01465 713643 or email Rozelle.House@south-ayrshire.gov.uk for opening times. It is a ten minute walk from the station.

Ailsa Craig. Situated ten miles off shore from Girvan is Ailsa Craig. At 338 metres tall this rock rising sheer out of the sea is a volcanic plug from a long extinct volcano. There is a lighthouse on the rock, and some local boat owners offer trips out from Girvan Harbour.

Return to the station to continue your journey. Behind Girvan are the Galloway Hills which are clearly seen from the station. Immediately upon departure the train starts the long two and a half mile 1 in 54 climb of these hills. The line travels high in between Laggan Hill and Cairn Hill. In the days of steam trains, it was hard work to pull the trains south through this difficult geography. The train then enters the 543 yard Pinmore Tunnel and emerges to follow the Water of Asset River. The line winds between hills in narrow valleys and crosses four viaducts on this highly scenic section to **Barrhill Station** (KA26 0QF). There is a waiting shelter and information point at the station. It serves the community of Barrhill, which is about half a mile or a 20-minute walk away. There are miles of walking and cycle tracks to be explored through Arecleoch Forest the entrance to which is at Barrhill station.

Departing Barrhill the train now runs direct to the Port of Stranraer through some beautifully Galloway scenery. Shortly after departure, Chirmorie Summit is reached, the highest point on the line. From here Merrick (843 metres high), the highest mountain in the Southern Uplands, is clearly visible. The landscape is bleak, remote, heather covered but not unattractive at this point. Some have likened it to the interior of the Falkland Islands. The line negotiates a tight 's' curve known as the 'Swan's Neck' where the curve is so tight that you can see it from the train window before reaching it. The train then descends into the more fertile valley of the Water of Luce. The Southern Upland Way walking route is crossed before passing Glenluce Abbey on the left of the train.

The line curves past Luce Bay to head west for the final run into Stranraer. The old abandoned 'port road' railway which once took trains directly from the west coast mainline is passed on the left. The Upland Way is crossed again at Loch Magillie before the train heads through Stranraer town centre and to the Harbour Station.

Stranraer

Stranraer station (Ferry Terminal, DG9 8EJ) is located in the Ferry Terminal and is about a ten minute walk from the town centre. The station is an interesting mix of old and new with its traditional wooden station buildings now hidden by the modern additions. There is a ticket office, waiting room, pay phones, luggage trolleys and toilets available in the building. There is currently a plan to move the ferry terminal. Should this happen a bus link to the ferries will be provided and it is likely that a new station will be built in the town centre. Presently however the station is ideally located next to the ferry terminal for Stena Line ferries to Ireland. Through rail and ferry tickets are available from Scotrail.

Stranraer is a bustling town at the start of the Southern Upland Way and has more to it than simply a ferry port. If you have the time it is worth having a look round the brightly painted streets and enjoying a meal in some of the local restaurants and cafés. The town is located at the head of the sea loch, Loch Ryan. It is actually very mild in this part of the country and it is not unusual to see palms and exotic plants. Although the modern Port dominates transport, the old 19th century harbour still exists and is used by small boats and yachts. Families enjoy Agnew Park with gardens, boating lake and miniature railway, located next to the Harbour.

The town centre is dominated by the **Castle of St Johns**. This 1510 tower was built by Ninian Adair of Kilhurst and has had many uses over the years and is now a museum and visitor centre. It is located on Charlotte Street (DG9 7EJ) and is a ten minute walk from the station. Telephone 01776 705544 for details of opening times. **Stranraer Museum** is housed in the historic Old Town Hall built in 1776. The displays tell the story of Wigtownshire from the earliest times and include archaeology, farming and local history. There is also a section on Stranraer-born John Ross, one of the pioneers of Polar exploration. It is located on 55 George Street (DG9 7JP) and is a 14 minute walk from the station. Telephone 01776 705088 for details.

Stranraer concludes this journey. Either return to Glasgow or catch the ferry to Ireland.

17. Southwest Scotland – Glasgow to Carlisle

There are two railways from Glasgow to Carlisle. The main route is the West Coast Mainline that goes via Carstairs and the famous Beatock Summit (1016 feet). It provided a real challenge to train crews in the days of steam. Today's high-speed electric trains take the same route with ease but passengers still enjoy the wonderful scenery of the southern upland hills. InterCity trains from England use this route while local trains from Carlisle (some start in Newcastle) take the slower route via Dumfries. This is the best route to take if wishing to get off at some of the more interesting destinations along the route, or for a more leisurely journey through the area.

Journey Summary:

Route:	Glasgow Central – Barrhead – Kilmarnock – Auchinleck – New Cumnock – Kirkconnel – Sanquhar – Dumfries – Annan – Gretna Green – Carlisle (and then onwards to Newcastle)
Trains:	Scotrail with standard class accommodation. Most trains have a trolley service.
Trip Length:	2 hours 15 minutes via Dumfries.
Frequency:	Regular services over the entire line. Additional trains over parts of route.
Links:	Connecting rail services in Glasgow to the rest of Scotland and from Carlisle to the rest of Britain.

The description of this route begins in Kilmarnock, which is reached once through the Glasgow suburbs where several stops will be made.

Kilmarnock

Kilmarnock was a textile town, first with weaving and then a greater range of textile products, including carpets, which led to the rapid expansion of the town. In 1840 Andrew Barclay established his railway locomotive building workshops in the town. Over the years the company became famous for building simple little locomotives for use in industrial sites. They were also the largest builder of fireless steam locomotives and exported their products to railways in Australia, New Zealand and Fiji. Over 100 of their engines remain preserved in the UK. Amazingly the company still exists and is now known as Brush-Barclay. The workshops may be seen from the train before Kilmarnock station. The town today does not have much of interest for the visitor but there are some attractions which are worth mentioning.

Practicalities

Kilmarnock Station (Hill Street, KA1 2AF) is staffed with a ticket office, ticket vending machine, waiting room, luggage trolleys, café, toilets, pay phone and taxi rank. The railway first arrived in Kilmarnock in 1812, being one of the first railways in Scotland. The present impressive Scots Baronial red sandstone building with its Italianate tower and large canopied platforms was completed in 1878.

Local buses are operated by Stagecoach, see the Traveline website for information. These buses are included in the Kilmarnock Plusbus rail ticket.

Places of Interest.

Dean Castle and Country Park, Dean Road, KA3 1XB. Dean Castle was built in 1350 and sits in a beautiful 200 acre park. The name 'Dean' simply means wooded valley and this is exactly what the Castle is built in. Constructed by the Boyd family this wonderful location can with a little imagination be pictured as it was. However, happiness did not last long as Sir Robert Boyd was murdered around 1290 at the Castle. This resulted in his son, also Sir Robert, joining with William Wallace to fight for Scottish independence. The Castle now has displays of armour, weapons and musical instruments. Outdoors, the Country Park has a ranger service, pets' corner, adventure area and woodland walks. The Castle and Country Park are a 25 minute walk from the station. Alternatively take a bus from the station which is included in Plusbus tickets to Kilmarnock. The Castle and Park are open all year and have free admission. See www.dean castle.com or call 01563 522702 for details.

Burns Monument (Demolished) and Kay Park. Still appearing on many maps is the Burns Monument in Kay Park. Close to the station, this park with its 29 landscaped acres may be enjoyed all year round. It was gifted to the town by Alexander Kay and its highlight was the Burns Monument, opened in 1879. It was built from red sandstone, was highly ornate and offered wonderful views. Burns fans were angered in 2004 when it was burnt down in an arson attack and subsequently mostly demolished. Although Grade B listed, the building will not be rebuilt as it was.

Dick Institute (1 Elmbank Avenue, KA1 3BU). Two art galleries and three museum galleries house permanent and temporary displays of fine art, contemporary art and craft, local and industrial history, and natural sciences. It was opened in and is operated now by East Ayrshire Council. It is open Tuesday to Saturday with free admission, telephone 01563 554343 for information. It is a 13 minute walk from the station.

Departing Kilmarnock the railway makes its way through southwestern farmlands and passes the junction of the freight-only line to Ayr on the right, a few miles south of the town. Auchinleck station is an unstaffed halt serving the town of the same name. It is now the nearest station for the nearby town of Cumnock which has lost its station. The train passes over the River Lugar as it heads past Cumnock. The scenery becomes more interesting at this point with the train passing through some hills, the first of which is Avisyard Hill (330 metres) on the left before entering a narrow valley with two small lochs on the approach to New Cumnock.

New Cumnock railway station (KA18 4DG) is located at the one end of the village and is an unstaffed halt with waiting shelter and information point. This is a former coal-mining town and has little to offer the visitor, however, the stop is useful for visiting the **Knockshinnock Lagoons**. This former industrial site has become a nature reserve with young birch woodland, open grassland and water areas which attract a range of bird species. Spring is best for birds and flowers, summer for plants, butterflies and black-headed gulls and autumn/winter for waterfowl and waders. Walk through the town and up Castlehill lane, following the Community Pathway signs to Knockshinnoch to reach the reserve.

Departing New Comnock the train makes its way along the base of Hare Hill (575 metres) with the large wind farm. If you have a bike there is a path to the top of the hill from about three miles outside New Cumnock station. The River Nith flows alongside the train for the next part of the journey. It rises in East Ayrshire and is the seventh longest river in Scotland, flowing through Dumfries and Galloway before entering into the Solway Firth south of Dumfries. Corsencon Hill (475 metres) is on the left of the train as it makes its way through the narrow valley and into Kirkconnel. **Kirkconnel Station** is a small unstaffed station serving the village. There is a plaque on the platform commemorating 'The Surfaceman'. Alexander Anderson was a platelayer or surfaceman on the railway. Self taught, he became an excellent poet and wrote under the name 'Surfaceman' and eventually went on to be the Chief Librarian at the University of Edinburgh. From the station there is a day-long walk towards Kirkland and then up a path beside Kirkland Hill to follow back to Todholes Hill (481 metres). See an Ordnance Survey map for details. Departing Kirkconnel the train has fine views of Todholes and Black Hill (483 metres) on the left of the train as it curves round their base to enter Sanquhar.

Sanquhar Railway station was reopened in 1994 and is an unstaffed halt with waiting shelter and information point. The former station buildings are of substantial stone construction dating from 1850 and while still in existence are disused and derelict.

Located in the heart of what was once Scotland's wool country, the annual July wool fair regulated the prices for the entire south of Scotland. This market town has existed since the earliest settlers arrived here in the 9th and 10th centuries. Sanquhar Post Office, founded in 1712, is said to the oldest working Postal Office in the world. The other most notable building is the Tollbooth. Dating from 1731 this is the only surviving such building built by famous Scottish architect William Adam. This elegant Georgian building with double sided forestair and tower is now the town's museum. It is open year round and has displays on local life, the knitting industry and mining. Telephone 01387 253374 for details of opening times, admission is free. It is located on the town's High Street, close to the station.

Sanquhar Castle (13th century) is located just outside the town on the Southern Upland Way walking route. It was the home of the Crichton family and was visited by many notable people including Robert the Bruce, William Wallace, Edward I, Mary Queen of Scots, and James VI. There are no signposts, directions or information when you get there. Yet it is a fascinating and interesting ruin. An attempt was made between 1895 and 1900 by John Crichton-Stuart, 3rd Marquess of Bute to restore the Castle but it ended on his death. Today it is sadly crumbling away and targeted by vandals. Although not worth a special visit, it is a notable feature if using the Southern Upland walking route.

Departing Sanquar the valley narrows and the hills become steep on either side of the train. On the left is Thirstane Hill (583 metres), and the Southern Upland Way walk. A tunnel is entered before emerging into the wider valley near Carronbridge. The former Carronbridge Station is now a house and is still visible from the train. The village of Thornhill is passed on the right with the huge Forest of Ae on the left of the train. Not a 'real' forest, this is rather a plantation of Sitka Spruce first planted in the 1920s by the Forestry Commission to provide timber. It has however became an important Red Squirrel habitat.

The River Nith is rejoined and the scenery of this part of the Southern Uplands may be enjoyed for miles now with little human interference in the landscape. The train crosses the River Nith on the Portrack Viaduct. A realignment of the railway at this point has resulted in a new, and attractive, viaduct. Look out for the little preserved railway shunting locomotive and parts of the old viaduct which have been cleverly incorporated into a new ornamental garden. The scenery stays beautiful as the train speeds its way towards Dumfries. The sharp eyed will also see the remains of the old Cairn Valley Light Railway to Moniaive. The old wooden terminus at Moniavie still stands although it is derelict and in very poor condition. The line then passes a junction which was the old line to Stranraer along the coast. Although it looks intact the tracks in fact end just outside of Dumfries.

Dumfries

The town has an attractive town centre with many fine red sandstone buildings and the River Nith, which has followed the train down to this point. Being a crossing point of the River, there has been a town here for many hundreds of years. The Devorgilla Bridge was built in 1432 and although rebuilt many times over the years still exists and is one of the country's oldest bridges. Being on the boarder with England for a long time, the town was the point of many battles and changed hands many times. In fact it was only secured as part of Scotland during Alexander II's reign in 1234. In later years it has become the largest town in the southwest and the administrative centre of the Dumfries and Galloway local authority area. Among the notable buildings in the town is the Globe Inn. This 1610 pub has long been associated with the area and Robert Burns. It was once complete with stabling for horses but today still retains much of its charm.

Practicalities
The 1859 Glasgow & South Western Railway building with impressive glazed platform canopies still serves the town. Dumfries station (Lovers Walk, DG1 1NF) has a ticket office, waiting room, luggage trolleys, toilets, pay phones, café and taxi rank outside.

Local Transport. Buses are operated by Stagecoach Western. See www.stagecoach.com or telephone Traveline on 0871 2002233 for bus details. Local buses are included in Plusbus rail tickets to Dumfries.

Places of Interest
Burns House (Burns Street, DG1 2PS). Visit the house that poet Robert Burns spent the last years of his life in and where he wrote some of his most famous works. The house is restored to the condition it would have been found in Burn's time. It is open year round and admission is free. Telephone 01387 255297 for information and opening times. The Museum is a 12 minute walk from the railway station.

There are two other excellent places of interest within a 30 minute bus journey from Dumfries, making them ideal for day trips. Take bus number 6A to Caerlaverock for the **Caerlaverock Wetland Centre** or Caerlaverock Castle. The Wetland Centre is a 20 minute walk from the bus stop at Eastpark Farm, Caerlaverock, DG1 4RS. It is open all year and has information and advice to best explore the wetlands, which are famous for their visiting flocks of barnacle geese (seen between October and April). The reserve consists of 1,400 acres of wetlands with hides and observation towers linked by a network of screened approaches and seasonal nature trails. Other highlights include the ospreys between April and August, and the barn owls. Being located on the shores of the Solent makes this area an excellent place for watching wildlife and wildlife photography. Visitors arriving by bus or bike receive a discount on admission. Telephone the Centre on 01387 770200 or visit the Wildfowl and Wetland Trust at www.wwt.org.uk for more information.

Stay on the bus for **Caerlaverock Castle**. Again this is about 30 minutes by bus and will let you off at the end of the Castle driveway which is five minutes walk from the entry point. With its huge battlements, twin towered gatehouse and moat, Caerlaverock is the epitome of the medieval castle. Although ruined, the Castle is remarkably complete from many angles. However the Castle's outer wall is badly damaged on the southern side and this was due to the 1640 siege when those defending the Castle held out for 13 long weeks. Inside, the main attraction is Nithsdale Lodging, a remarkable 17th century residence in the castle courtyard. There is also a nature trail taking visitors around the moat and nearby woods to the site of an earlier castle. The Castle is unique for being built in a triangular shape, although it is not known why this design was used. Today it is cared for by Historic Scotland. There is an admission charge and it is open all year. Telephone the Castle on 01387 770244 or visit the Historic Scotland website for details.

Return to the station at Dumfries to continue the journey. The train makes the short dash to Annan, the next stop, through forestry plantations and the hills of Rockhall Moor on the right. The line turns to make its approach to Annan, and the Solway Firth comes into view. The mountains on the other side of the Firth are the hills of the English Lake District, another very popular holiday destination. The coastline itself was designated an Area of Outstanding Natural Beauty in 1964. The train crosses flood plains and then the viaduct over the River Annan before stopping at Annan station.

Annan

Annan station (Station Road, DS12 6AR) was built in 1848 in the Italianate style and using red sandstone. It is now used as a restaurant and B&B. As recently as the 1980s, the station was busy with fish trains transporting fresh Solway fish to London. The station has waiting areas under the platform canopies and a pay phone. There is also a free train information phone.

Annan is a pleasant small town with the River Annan flowing through its town centre. Look out for the attractive stone road bridge taking the High Street over the River with its graceful arches. Beside the bridge is Bridge House (not open to the public) of 1780 which is considered one of the finest Georgian town houses in Scotland. The other building worth seeking out is the Town Hall of 1878. Built in Gothic style with a huge centre clock tower, the Hall is still an amazing piece of architecture.

While in Annan, visit the **Annan Museum** (Bank Street, DG12 6AA). The first floor of the museum houses a permanent exhibition on the history of Annan and its surrounding area. This is a fascinating walk through time from the prehistoric period right up to the Second World War with interactive, and children's activities. The town's location on the shoreline has also led to the development of walks which offer fine views of the Solway Firth.

Shortly after the stop at Annan the train arrives at Gretna Green, after a short section along the shoreline of the Solway.

Gretna Green

Gretna Green railway station (DG16 5HF) was originally opened in 1848 as Gretna but closed in 1965. The station was re-opened in 1993 but having lost all its original features, this new station has little of historical or aesthetic interest.

A 1753 Marriage Act of Parliament in England resulted in the legal age of marriage being 21 without parental consent, and only 14 north of the border, although this was later changed to 16. For this reason many young people wanting to get married headed north and the first village they came to was Gretna. The village has since developed as a bit of a wedding centre with several wedding locations still operating to this day. However for those expecting a real rural Scottish village, people usually find the tourist areas of Gretna to be lacking any charm. Expect to see the 'historic' blacksmith's shop (the traditional wedding venue) in the middle of a family entertainment and shopping area. The station, for those wishing to visit, is located on a footpath a short walk from the Blacksmith shop (to the north) and village of Gretna (to the south).

The train departs Gretna to join the West Coast Mainline (the main route from Glasgow to Carlisle) and then immediately crosses the small River Sark, which is also the border between Scotland and England. The line then almost immediately crosses the larger River Esk. This small area of marshy land between the two rivers was known as the 'debatable lands', and was formerly a haven for criminals who wished to exploit the weakness of the two countries' border defences. Shortly after the Esk the train arrives at its destination, Carlisle.

Carlisle

Although in England, Carlisle receives a mention in this book for being an excellent place to visit at the end of this journey. Carlisle has existed since before Roman times when it was developed to serve Hadrian's Wall. Situated on three small rivers, the Eden, Caldew and Petteril, the town has a very pleasant environment. In the past it has been an important industrial centre for textiles and iron, but today is more popular with visitors stopping off on the journey between Scotland and England

Practicalities

Carlisle railway station (Court Square, CA1 1QZ) is in the heart of the city. The attractive station was opened in 1847 and later extended in 1875 and remains much as it was from that time. Take a walk outside to view its imposing façade designed by Sir William Tite (who also designed the Bank of England) in a Tudor Gothic Style to match the Citadel. The station has a ticket office, ticket vending machines, waiting rooms, toilets, luggage trolleys, pay phones, café, refreshments, shops and a taxi rank. Carlisle is a

Plusbus city, so ask about adding local bus travel to your train ticket on booking.

Tourist Information. The Tourist Information Centre is housed in the Old Town Hall (CA3 8JE), built in 1717. Telephone 01228 625600 or Email: Tourism@Carlisle-City.gov.uk.

Places of Interest

On leaving the station, the **Citadel**, which in actual fact was until recently the town's court, is an attractive building constructed on the site of the former citadel. Follow the road up between the buildings to enter the city centre. These buildings were also built to accommodate the town's jail and the one on the right is now open to the public. Occasionally visitors can look round the West Tower, and see the oak panelled Number One Court, the Number Two Court, the Grand Jury Room and the cells. For information about booking tours, enquire at the Cumbria County Council office in English Street (telephone: 01228 606336).

Carlisle Cathedral (Cathedral Office, 7 The Abbey, CA3 8TZ) is one of the most important, historic and attractive buildings in the town. With its traditional, attractive construction and detailed wood and stonework, the Cathedral is impressive yet tasteful. Founded in 1122, services have been held daily here for 900 years. Visitors may view items of silverware and the many stained glass windows which date from the 14th to 20th centuries, while volunteer guides are on hand to answer questions. The Cathedral is a ten minute walk from the station, has a restaurant and free admission. For information call 01228 548151 or visit www.carlislecathedral.org.uk.

Guildhall / Tullie House Museum (Castle Street, Carlisle, Cumbria, CA3 8TP). The Guildhall is one of Carlisle's oldest buildings, being almost 600 years old. Originally it was a row of shops attached to a merchant's house with a large hall in the upper storey where the city's Guilds met. The eight Guilds (butchers, merchants, shoemakers, skinners and glovers, smiths, tailors, tanners and weavers) began as specialist trade associations. Today the town's museum is also held within the building, detailing the history of Carlisle and Cumbria. Guildhall is ten minutes walk from the station, and is open year round with free admission. For information, see www.tulliehouse.co.uk.

Carlisle Castle (Castle Street, CA3 8UR). This huge medieval fortress with its imposing battlements and huge square keep is everything one might hope for from a castle. Visitors enter through the outer bailey and into the inner bailey and the keep. The 12th century keep was constructed by William Rufus, who also founded the Cathedral, and is the oldest part of the structure. Also inside the Castle is the King's Own Royal Border Regiment Museum and the Carlisle Roman Dig – displaying finds from Roman excavations in the town. The Castle is owned by English Heritage and is open year round. There is an admission charge and it is a 15 minute walk from the station. See the English Heritage website for details.

Also in the town centre is **St Cuthbert's Church**, a 1778 building on Blackfriars Street. Inside, there is a unique moving pulpit and some interesting stained glass. It is open on most days during daylight hours and has free admission. See www.stcuthbertscarlisle.org. uk for information.

Settle and Carlisle Railway. Carlisle is the starting point of England's most scenic railway. Talking an alternative route south though the Yorkshire Dales and over the 24 arch Ribblehead Viaduct, the line has long been a favourite with walkers and those seeking beautiful views. There are regular services over the line using modern trains stopping at all stations along the route, or you may wish to take a special train hauled by steam which operates from time to time. The Friends of the Line have a website at www.settle-carlisle.co.uk which has extensive details on services, places to visit and days out ideas. The website also has free MP3 guides to the line which you may download to take with you on your journey.

This concludes the journey to Carlisle and you may return to Glasgow on the same route, or the faster West Coast Mainline.

18. The North East – Aberdeen to Inverness

For Aberdeen details see Chapter 7, the East Coast.

This journey starts in the 'Granite City' of Aberdeen and ends in the capital of the Highlands, Inverness. The journey takes a little over two hours and passes through some pleasant pastoral scenery along the route. The line is not nearly as rural as many, though, with a string of small north east towns along its length. Baedeker's Great Britain 1890 describes the route as 'uninteresting'. However tastes may well have changed and with rapid urbanisation in many areas of the country, this line is perhaps more enjoyable than it once was with its unspoilt small towns and pleasant farmland.

Journey Summary

Route:	Aberdeen – Dyce (for Aberdeen Airport) – Inverurie – Huntly – Keith – Elgin – Forres – Nairn – Inverness.
Trains:	Scotrail. Standard and limited first class accommodation. Most have a trolley service.
Trip Length:	2 hours 10 minutes.
Frequency:	11 trains each way daily over entire route. Additional trains over parts of route. Five trains on Sundays.
Links:	Northlink Ferries from Aberdeen to Orkney and Shetland. Coaches from Inverness to Fort William. There are also many bus routes to rural Aberdeenshire from the bus station in Aberdeen, located outside the railway station.

On leaving Aberdeen's Guild Street station the train travels through the suburbs of the city and shortly arrives at Dyce.

Dyce Station

Dyce is an Aberdeen suburb and the location of **Aberdeen Airport**. There is a free shuttle bus from the station to the air terminal. Dyce is an unstaffed station although there is an attractive former Great North of Scotland Railway signal box on the platform for those interested in railway architecture.

Departing Dyce the train gets its first taste of Aberdeenshire countryside, which is for the most part a mix of pastoral and arable farmlands. The line is unusual in that every ten to twenty minutes the train seems to arrive at another significant small town with lots of people getting on and off the train. This first part of the journey is along the valley floor and alongside the River Don. The River rises in the Grampian Mountains and makes its way through Strathdon and down to the sea at Aberdeen. Its main tributary is the River Urie, which is crossed just before entering the town of Inverurie.

Inverurie

The original Great North of Scotland Railway (GNSR) station is still in use, together with signal box. The station (Station Road, AB51 9TN) is perhaps the closest thing to the traditional station on any part of the British rail network, even retaining its goods yard. The attractive stone built station is fitting for this small town. Look out for the Alexander Gill station clock and small, wall-mounted decorative cast-iron water fountain situated in bays beneath canopy. The interior of the station is equally pleasant with decorative plasterwork, coomb ceiling of ticket hall and broad segmental arches with part-glazed timber screen walls. The former Earl of Kintore's waiting room is entered through a two leaf part glazed timber door and has a parquet floor, timber fireplace and decorative plasterwork. Practically, the station is staffed with a ticket office, ticket vending machine, waiting room, toilets, public phone and information point.

The heart of Inverurie is close to the railway station where the High Street broadens out into the Market Place. Here is a small wooded park with the town's war memorial in the centre. Look out for the Town Hall with its decorative spire at this location. Inverurie used to be home to a huge locomotive works for the railway. The derelict building may still be seen although its future must now be uncertain after so many years of disuse. The works were so significant to the town that the local football team is still known as 'Inverurie Loco Works', having been set up by workers of the GNSR in 1902. The **Carnegie Inverurie Museum** is located in the town square and is open year round with free admission. The Museum has displays including flint arrowheads and bronze swords, Beaker folk and Pictish carved stones, Aberdeenshire canal and railway links and details of the Broomend of Crichie Henge & Stone Circle excavation. For opening times telephone 01467 621945.

Between Inverurie and Insch, the railway travels alongside the River Urie and passes the remains of the abandoned railway to Turriff. The little white station at **Insch** (AB52 6PU) was opened in 1854. Although almost all trains still stop here, the station is no longer staffed. However, the building has found new use as the community museum. The **Insch Connection Museum** is volunteer run and has displays which encompass the story of Insch and the railway connection and include a scale model of the station, photographs, artefacts and everyday stories of how life used to be in Insch. Call 01464 821354 or email inschmuseum@aol.com for opening details.

After Insch the train continues through the wooded countryside to Huntly. Look out for the small community of Kennethmont. On the left there is an old disused railway station, a signal box (still in use) and a distillery with the traditional and distinctive kiln roof. The large white castle type house on the right of the line is **Leith Hall** (AB54 4NQ), a National Trust property. Set in over 200 acres of grounds and a six acre garden, it is a typical Scottish laird's residence. It has seasonal opening hours and an admission charge. If you wish to visit take the train to either Insch or Huntly stations, and then a short 11 to 17 minute bus journey to the Hall. The train continues alongside the River Bogie until Huntly is reached.

Huntly

Huntly is a small town on the edge of the Speyside whisky trail. On the east side of the town is the River Bogie, flowing through Strath Bogie. Surrounding Huntly is farmland typical of north east Scotland. These rolling hills are in contrast to the heather filled Highlands south of Inverness. Visitors will enjoy exploring the shops, and the ruins of Huntly Castle, on the banks of the Deveron River.

Practicalities

Huntly railway station (AB54 5HS) has a ticket office, ticket vending machine, waiting room, pay phone, toilets and post box. Huntly station was a traditional wooden Great North of Scotland Station with wooden platform canopy opened in 1854. Unfortunately the station buildings were demolished in 1999 and replaced by a modern station building.

Huntly is easily explored on foot. Simply leave the station and cross the river into the town. The surrounding area is served by Stagecoach Bluebird buses of Aberdeen. There are also plenty of back roads that can be explored by bike and the typical surrounding farmland of rural Aberdeenshire is attractive in all seasons.

Places of Interest

Huntly Castle. This impressive ruined castle is open to visitors. The motte dates from the 12th century while the main building was erected in the 16th and 17th centuries by the Gordon family. The architectural details and heraldic enrichments are particularly impressive. The setting of the castle can also be enjoyed in these more peaceful times with its riverside views. The castle is situated in the town and is signposted from the station which is a 15 minute walk. It is under the care of Historic Scotland. See www.historic-scotland.gov.uk or telephone 01466 793191 for information. It is open all year and has an admission charge.

Brander Museum. Visit this recently refurbished museum and view displays of local history including civic regalia, an extensive collection of communion tokens and displays on the Huntly textile industry. You can also learn about the Huntly born author George Macdonald, 19th century arms and armour from Sudan, and the archaeological finds from Huntly Castle. Telephone 01771 622807 for information. The Museum is ten minutes walk from the station and located in the town square.

Huntly Nordic and Outdoor Centre. All weather cross country ski track, tea shop, bike hire, and Nordic ski hire in the winter.

Walking from Huntly. There are several pleasant walks from Huntly. Starting in the town centre there is a walk up Clashmach Hill behind Huntly. There are fine views through the countryside from the top. Alternatively there are woodland walks through Battle Hill and Kinnoir Hill. See an Ordnance Survey map for walk details.

Departing Huntly the train travels alongside the River Deveron and through a narrow valley for a few miles. The Deveron rises in the high hills above the Cabrach and slows as it meanders through the lower Aberdeenshire countryside before ending its journey at Banff, on the coast, after sixty miles. It is popular with salmon fishers as it is less well known than the neighbouring Rivers Dee and Spey. Having crossed the Deveron the river which now appears on the right of the train is the Isla which flows into the Deveron. The train follows the Isla all the way to the town of Keith.

Keith

The small but well appointed station at Keith (Station Road, AB55 3DR) is staffed with a ticket office, waiting room, toilets, public phone and information point. There are plans for the Keith & Dufftown Railway to use a platform at this station in the future. The town is easily explored by foot.

Keith is a market town serving the local agricultural industry – the annual agricultural show is held every August. It boasts one of the oldest bridges in Scotland, this being the 'Auld Brig', a packhorse bridge built in 1609, and now close to the Town Station. Scotland's only post-Reformation saint, John Ogilvie, was born here in 1579.

Places of Interest

Keith & Dufftown Railway. A short walk through Keith takes you to the Keith & Dufftown Railway station. This independent railway uses railcars to transport visitors through the wooded valley scenery to Dufftown. See the description below for details of this attraction.

Strathisla Distillery With its distinctive pagodas, cobbled courtyard and picturesque buildings, Strathisla Distillery is arguably the most beautiful distillery in Scotland. It was founded in 1786, and as such is the oldest operating distillery in northern Scotland.

Connecting Independent Rail Service – Keith to Dufftown.

When the railway is not in operation an alternative bus service is available from Keith or Elgin: refer to Traveline Scotland for details.

The Keith & Dufftown Railway Association reopened this railway in August 2001. Today visitors may enjoy a trip on this very scenic railway linking Keith with Dufftown, 11 miles to the south. It is ideal for exploring an area filled with traditional malt whisky distilleries, paths and wildlife. The journey is one of ever changing colours and rivers flowing through farmland and woodlands. To find out details of running times and fares contact the Railway at: Dufftown Station, Dufftown, Banffshire, AB55 4BA, or see the website at www.keith-dufftown.org.uk.

Trains presently depart from Keith Town station – a short walk from the mainline Keith station served by Scotrail trains. As this is an independent line, national tickets, railcards and rail passes are not valid on these services. Keith Town station is in the heart of the town and close to attractions. The split level station keeps out the noise of modern life and is a perfect replica of the original Great North of Scotland Railway station which once stood on the site. The present station was opened in 2003.

Having got on board, the train departs Keith for the journey down the valley. The first stop is at the small halt of Drummuir. The platform is sheltered from the village in a small wooded valley and passengers getting off here can enjoy the woodland and birdlife that lives here. Also in this peaceful setting is a walk through the wood to the gardens of **Drummuir Castle**. The Castle is not open to the public but the grounds and walled gardens may be explored. The Castle was built in 1847 by Thomas Mackenzie for Admiral Archibald Duff, whose distinguished career included service with Lord Nelson. The Castle is a splendid example of the Scottish Victorian architectural style. The 60 feet high central lantern tower, notable for its Gothic tracery dominates the interesting roofline, with its battlements, turrets and chimneystacks.

The line continues to the village of **Dufftown**, otherwise known as the malt whisky capital of the world – being the largest exporter of whisky from Britain. The village of Dufftown not only has some excellent distilleries to explore but also has its own castle. The town is a small market town in the heart of Speyside which takes its name from its founder James Duff, the fourth Earl of Fife.

On arrival look out for the Clock Tower standing in the centre of Dufftown which was completed in 1839. It was originally built as the town jail, later used as the burgh chambers and now houses the Information Centre.

The main attraction in Dufftown is **Balvenie Castle**, now cared for by Historic Scotland and is set in the attractive hills surrounding Dufftown. King Edward I of England was an early visitor to the Castle. Of particular interest today is the curtain wall – a rare example of 13th century military architecture in Scotland. Also of note is the Atholl Lodging – a fine example of Renaissance architecture, showing the layout of a noble residence and containing an iron yett – the two-part iron cross-barred gate behind the main entrance which is unique in Scotland. The Castle is a short walk from the Dufftown railway station. See www.historic-scotland.gov.uk or telephone 01340 820121 for details. It is open from Easter until October and has an admission charge.

If you wish to spend longer in Dufftown there is a bus service from Keith run by Moray Council. Otherwise there is a more regular service between Elgin (on the Aberdeen to Inverness railway) and Dufftown.

Returning to Keith and the train journey north, the train departs Keith and makes its way through hills and woodlands on its way to the next stop at Elgin. Roughly half way between the two towns the train crosses an attractive bridge over the River Spey and curves around the valley. This is a particularly scenic location for photographs. The Spey is Scotland's second longest river and its fastest flowing. The Speyside Way long distance walk also crosses the railway at this point on its way to the sea.

Elgin

Elgin is a former cathedral city and Royal Burgh in Morayshire. Today it is still the administrative and commercial centre for the area. The town originated to the south of the River Lossie on the higher ground above the flood plain. Elgin is first documented in the Chatulary of Moray in 1190. It was created a Royal Burgh in the 12th century by King David I and by that time had a castle on top of the present day Lady Hill to the west of the town.

A notable citizen of Elgin was William Dunbar (1749–1810) born in Thunderton House, Elgin. He emigrated to America arriving in Philadelphia in April 1771. President Thomas Jefferson appointed him and fellow Scot Dr George Hunter to explore the Ouachita River region and travel all the way to the source of the Red River. Dunbar became the first man to give a scientific report of the hot springs, and his journal of the exploration was later published in 'Documents Relating to the Purchase and Exploration of Louisiana'.

Visitors today will enjoy the busy shopping areas, culture and history. While having all the services of a small town, it has retained much of the charm lost by its larger neighbour, Inverness.

Practicalities

The modern station at Elgin (Station Road, IV30 1QP) is functional and comfortable. It has a ticket office, toilets, information, snacks, waiting room, pay phones, ticket vending machine and luggage trolleys. There are two platforms, and signs direct passengers which one to use. The old Great North of Scotland railway station with its attractive architecture is still in existence, next door. It is now used as offices and you will view the rear of the station from the train. Elgin's rail facilities were rationalised after the closure of many lines in the Moray area in the 1960s. The town was once the heart of an intensive local rail network of branch lines which are sadly no longer in existence.

There is a Tourist Information Office located at the east end of the High Street (17 High Street, IV30 1EG), telephone 01343 542666.

Local Transport. Local buses depart from the bus station on the High Street and are operated by Stagecoach. Plusbus rail tickets to Elgin include local bus travel. Although Spynie Palace is close to Elgin it does fall out with the Plusbus area so you will need a separate ticket if travelling by bus to that attraction.

Places of Interest

Elgin Cathedral (King Street, IV30 1HU). The Cathedral is a ruin, but don't let this put you off a visit to this amazing building. The Cathedral was founded in 1224 and rebuilt after a fire in 1340. The remaining sections are more complete than St Andrews and contain some richly decorated stonework. The best preserved parts of the Cathedral are the chapter house and two west towers. The chapter house is still roofed and glazed and gives a true reflection of what the entire building would have looked like when complete. The west towers still stand over the entrance to the Cathedral and are for the most part intact. Visitors may climb the stairs to the top to obtain fine views over the town. The rest of the cathedral has not fared so well. The neglect began after the Reformation. In 1711 long before conservation efforts began the central tower collapsed causing considerable damage to the main portion of the Cathedral. It is open all year and has an admission charge. A joint ticket with Spynie Palace is available. See the Historic Scotland website or telephone 01343 547171 for details. The Cathedral is a ten minute walk from the station. Outside the Cathedral look out for the Biblical garden. This quiet spot has examples of every plant mentioned in the Bible.

Spynie Palace. The Palace was the official residence of the Cathedral Bishops. For five centuries the Palace was the residence of the Bishops of Moray. The last Bishop left in 1689 and the Palace fell into disrepair. However it is still an impressive building today, and half a day can be spent exploring its ruins. Set in attractive Morayshire countryside there are excellent views from the top of the Palace's tower. However the scene was quite different in the past as it was then located next to a medieval town and a sea loch. Nothing remains of either and today it is birdsong that the visitor enjoys. The most intact part of the complex is David's Tower, one of the largest such structures to have been built. The Palace has a joint ticket with Elgin Cathedral. As in the days of its use, it is quite possible to walk to the Palace and there is now a joint walking and cycle path from central Elgin near the Cathedral and station. The walk takes about 50 minutes, or you can take a bus from outside the bus station which drops you off at the end of the Palace's driveway (about a five minute walk). Visit www.historic-scotland.gov.uk or call 01343 546358 for details. It is open year round and there is an admission charge.

Town Centre and Architecture. Elgin has a wonderful town centre only minutes from the station. While shops tend to be national chains there are some local shops of interest. The High Street is dominated by the unusual architecture of St Giles Church. Further along the High Street is Dr Gray's Hospital (not open to the public). The building dates from 1819 and stands at the head of fine gardens. Dr Alexander Gray, a doctor who worked for, and made his fortune with the East India Company, endowed £26,000 for the provision of the hospital. Nearby is the 80 foot high Duke of Gordon tower dedicated to the fifth Duke.

Elgin Museum (1 High Street, IV30 1EQ). Elgin Museum was opened in 1842 and was privately built by the people of Elgin for the display of 'objects of science and virtue'. It remains an independent museum and opens each year from Easter until October to members of the public. The main collections are the fossil collection, archaeology, local history and art, in addition to special exhibitions. The Museum is a eight minute walk from the station, on the way to the Cathedral. Opening hours are seasonal and there is an admission charge. See www.elginmuseum.org.uk or telephone 01343 543675 for details.

Returning to the station and the train, the journey continues westward. Shortly after Elgin on the right side of a train a branch line is visible. This is freight only railway to Burghead. Immediately afterwards is the Royal Air Force base at Kinloss. In front of the base is the ruin of what appears to be an old church. This is Kinloss Abbey. Founded in 1150 by King David I the Abbey is now a ruin although a conservation trust has been established to preserve the remains (see www.kinlossabbey.co.uk). Just before entering Forres station look out for the tall chimney of the Benromach Distillery (IV36 3EB) on the right. Opened in 1898, it fell into disrepair but was saved and reopened in 1998. On the left is the traditional white signal box controlling the signals around Forres station.

Forres

The Royal Burgh of Forres is an ancient burgh situated in the north of Scotland on the Moray coast, approximately 30 miles east of Inverness. Forres has been a winner of the 'Scotland in Bloom' award on several occasions in the past for its impressive floral displays. Nearby are many historic and natural attractions for the visitor. The River Findhorn provides many beautiful woodland walks, while historical artefacts and monuments can be found all over the town. Also look out for St Laurence Church on the High Street. It is a beautiful stone building completed in 1906. With is 120 foot tall spire it would cost over £6 million to build today.

Practicalities

The town's 1950s railway station (Tytler Street, IV36 0EL) constructed of brick would look more at home on the London suburban rail network. There is a staffed ticket office, ticket vending machines, waiting room, luggage trolleys, pay phone and toilets. There is a taxi rank outside and buses nearby (operated by Stagecoach Bluebird).

The Tourist Information office is located at 116 High Street, Forres, IV36 1NP, telephone 01309 672938.

Places of Interest

Falconer Museum (Tolbooth Street, IV36 1PH). Hugh Falconer was a distinguished geologist, botanist, palaeontologist and paleoanthropologist who left a legacy for the founding of the Museum. The Museum is housed in an attractive building and before going inside have a look at the exterior to see a number of carved heads depicting eminent scientists. Amongst some you might pick out are James Watt, Sir Walter Scott and Hugh Miller. Check with www.falconermuseum.co.uk for details and opening times or call 01309 673701. Admission is free. It is a 13 minute walk from the station.

Nelson's Tower and Grant Park. Both are located a 17 minute walk from the station at the east end of the High Street. Admission is free. The Grant Park lies on the east side of Forres High Street and was gifted to the town by Sir Alexander Grant. Its traditional gardens and floral sculptures form the centrepiece for the Forres entries in the 'Britain and Scotland in Bloom' competitions. The large animals formed of flowers are an excellent way to interest children in flowers. The Park is the venue for many local events. On the hill in the Park is Nelson's Tower. Opened in 1812 to commemorate Admiral Nelson's victory at the Battle of Trafalgar in 1805, it was the first memorial in Britain to be built in honour of Lord Nelson. It is open May to September and a flag is flown from the roof to show when it is open.

Brodie Castle (Brodie Village, IV36 2TE). Brodie Castle was home to the Brodie family until the late 20th century. It is an attractive tower castle with later 17th century wings increasing the size and comfort of the residence. Set in attractive parkland which is nice for walks and bird watching on the lake, it provides a peaceful and interesting day out. The gardens are most famous for their daffodil fields, perhaps the largest in the country. Visit in Spring to take beautiful pictures of these flowers around the Castle. The Castle is just outside Forres but if you are not cycling the access is via a busy road so it is better to take a bus to the Castle entrance driveway. The bus leaves from close to the station and takes ten minutes to reach Brodie Village and the Castle footpath. It is open from Easter until October and the grounds year round. There is an admission charge to the Castle, while access to the grounds is free. See www.nts.org.uk or call 0844 4932156 for details.

Dallas Dhu Distillery. The Distillery was opened in 1898 and is perhaps the last not to be modernised and so was taken into the care of Historic Scotland upon closure. It is now preserved and visitors can explore the entire site to see how whisky was traditionally produced. The bonded warehouses are also open to the public together with the peat kiln. To get there it is a 40 minute walk from the station. Having walked through the town centre the walk takes you along the Dava Way (see below) for a short distance to the Distillery. There is also an optional woodland walk to enjoy along the way if you wish. For Distillery opening times and admission prices see www.historic-scotland.gov.uk or telephone 01309 676548.

The Dava Way is a long distance off road walk along the old railway line from Forres to Grantown on Spey. It is 23 miles long and takes in the beautiful Speyside scenery. You can find out about the route and download a leaflet and map from www.davaway.org.uk. If going the whole way to Grantown you can pick up a bus from there to Inverness railway station or Aviemore station. In a few years time the Strathspey Railway hopes to return rail service to Grantown and it will once again be possible to travel by train from Aviemore.

On departure from Forres the train crosses the River Findhorn and skirts close to the Moray Firth with views across to Ross Shire and the Black Isle.

Nairn

Nairn is a coastal town on the Moray Firth. With fine views across to the Black Isle peninsula and with a nice beach it is popular with families (follow signs from town centre). The town's old harbour is now an active sailing club and you can often view boats arriving into the busy harbour. When at the beach or harbour area, look out for the dolphins which live in the Firth. These are the most northerly population of bottlenose dolphins in Britain. The town itself is split between the former 'fishertown' with its old fishing cottages and the later Victorian part of town with its fine houses, churches and town centre.

Practicalities

The large attractive stone built station at Nairn (Cawdor Road, IV12 4QS) is staffed with a ticket office, ticket vending machine, pay phone, toilets and waiting room. There is also a public pay phone, information and taxi rank. The station is situated on the town's main street. It was built in 1855 by the Highland Railway and the original building is still in use with its glazed wood canopy over the platform. The station used to have two signal boxes with the signal man provided with a bike to get between the two. The boxes still exist although they are no longer in use.

Tourist Information is available at the Library, High Street, Nairn, IV12 4AU. Telephone 08452 255121.

Places of Interest

Culbin Sands RSPB Reserve. The highlight of Nairn is the Sands. The area was part of an estate until it was overrun by sands in 1694. It was not until the Forestry Commission planted trees in 1922 that the area was stabilised. Today it is a great place to view wildlife and get away into the countryside. There are many walks and places to relax. It is especially good for watching birds, with the RSPB looking after the site. For information see www.rspb.org.uk or call 01463 715000. It is a 30 minute walk from the station.

Nairn Museum. Located in Viewfield House (IV12 4EE) the Museum is open from Easter until October and has displays on local history. Find out more at www.nairnmuseum.co.uk or by calling 01667 456791.

Departing Nairn the train makes the short sprint to Inverness. Around half way between the two towns is Inverness (Dalcross) airport on the right of the train. There is a regular bus service from Inverness station and Nairn to the Airport. Following the Airport, the Moray Firth again comes into view along with the Black Isle. On the approach to Inverness, the large suspension bridge over the Firth is the Kessock Bridge, opened in 1982 by the late Queen Mother.

Inverness

Inverness is described in Chapter 10, the Highlands. This is a major transport interchange. You can transfer here to trains for Wick, Thurso, Kyle of Lochalsh, Edinburgh, Glasgow and London. There are also bus links to Ullapool and Fort William.

19. The Far North – Inverness to Thurso and Wick

Along with the railway to Kyle of Lochalsh, the railway to Thurso, known as the Far North Line, is one of Britain's most scenic. The line is a scenic feast in four parts. From the fertile farmlands of the Cromarty Firth the line heads north through the sparsely populated Lairg loop with its remote communities and hills. Then it returns to the North Sea coast and the coastal communities before heading inland for one of the most remote sections of railway in the country as it crosses the famous flow country, a landscape of peat bogs that are unique in the United Kingdom. The train visits Thurso, Britain's most northerly railway station, before continuing to Wick, former herring port and the journey's end. The route is also popular with those wishing to visit Orkney, as trains connect with ferries near Thurso.

Journey Summary

Route:	Inverness – Beauly – Dingwall – Invergordon – Tain – Culrain – Lairg – Golspie – Brora – Helmsdale – Forsinard – Thurso – Wick.
Trains:	Standard class accommodation only. Most have a trolley catering service.
Trip Length:	4 hours 25 minutes.
Frequency:	4 trains daily over entire route with one train on Sundays. Additional local services run over the Inverness – Ardgay section of the route.
Links:	Northlink ferry service from Scrabster (on Thurso Bay) to Orkney. Bus link from the station at Thurso to the ferry. Bus from Tain (near the station) to Dornoch. Bus links from Lairg station to the far north west.
Stations:	Stations on this route are unstaffed with the exception of Inverness, Dingwall, Thurso and Wick which have booking offices. Other stations have waiting shelters and train information.

Inverness (See chapter 10)

On leaving Inverness station, trains head north west and across the River Ness. The modern bridge is a replacement for the original stone structure which was brought down during a flood in 1989. During that time the terminus of the railway was moved to Muir of Ord with buses provided between there and Inverness.

The train quickly makes its way through the town and slows to cross the northern end of the Caledonian Canal. The Canal is described in Chapter 12 in the Fort William section. Along with other bridges over the canal, this is a swing bridge and the small signal box to your left alongside the canal operates the bridge when ships require through. The train now makes its way along the shoreline of the Moray and Beauly Firths. Passengers gain excellent views of the Firth and the Black Isle on the opposite shore. To the left of the train in the distance is Ben Wyvis, the highest hill in the area and often snow covered even well into the Spring time. Crossing the River Beauly the train slows for its first stop in the village of Beauly.

Beauly

Beauly is an attractive village which has only recently regained its railway station. The original station was closed and converted into a house. The new station is at the west end of the village on Station Road (IV4 7EF). It is unstaffed and occupies part of the former station area. There is a waiting shelter and telephone link for train information and a pay phone. Cross the bridge at the end of the station and make your way along Station Road to enter the village.

The village has a selection of unique small stores, a river and a historic priory. It has often won the 'Scotland in Bloom' competition. There are good local services, with grocery stores, banks, a post office, bus stop, library, hotels, restaurants and other local services. The main place of interest is **Beauly Priory**. It is open year round and has free admission. The Priory was one of three founded in Scotland by the monks of the Valliscaulian order, who came from France around 1230. It was rebuilt and repaired in 1430, the local landowner Sir Hugh Fraser having written to the Pope to say that it was falling into disrepair. After the Reformation the Priory began its decay, first with lead being removed from the roof. It then became nothing more than a 'quarry' as local people removed its stone for other buildings. Today the building is a ruin, however most of the main chapel remains, if roofless. The North Transept is the best preserved section of the Priory and retains its roof to give an idea of how the structure would have looked when complete. The Priory is in the village square and it is suggested you contact the gate keepers to gain admission, see the Historic Scotland website for contact details.

Return to the train for the short journey on through farmland to **Muir of Ord.** This was formerly the junction for the branch line to Fortrose on the Black Isle, of which nothing now remains in the town. Today those wishing to visit the Black Isle take a bus from Inverness. The train has views of Ben Wyvis again and then follows the River Conon for a short section, crossing on an attractive stone bridge then heading through the village of Maryburgh before arrival in Dingwall.

Dingwall

Dingwall is the largest town on the line. This market town and seat of local government still has a farmers' market and town hall (although no longer used as such). It is a busy place with local government offices, the Sheriff

Court, a hospital and theological college. There are walks into the surrounding countryside, while the nearby former spa resort of Strathpeffer may be reached from here by bus. Opposite the station is the Highland Theological College. The College occupies the former Hydro Board buildings, the organisation that built and still operates the hydro electric dams throughout the Highlands.

Practicalities

Arrival is into the original 1862 station built by the Highland Railway (Station Road, IV15 9PZ). The attractive building is constructed from red sandstone. The station is staffed for most arrivals and has a booking office, waiting room, café, bookshop, public telephone and nearby taxi rank. Buses for nearby Strathpeffer depart from outside the station at the bus stop on Station Road.

Places of Interest

Dingwall Museum. The museum is situated on the High Street in the former town hall, about five minutes walk from the station. There are interesting displays on local history and visiting exhibits. There is an admission charge and the museum is open during the summer months from mid May until October. The building is worth having a look at in itself. The former tollbooth with its square spire is an attractive building and once housed the town council until it moved to the new premises.

Strathpeffer. The village of Strathpeffer is filled with Victorian villas, grand hotels, and mature gardens. A regular bus service leaves from near the Dingwall railway station and from Inverness bus station (near Inverness railway station). There is a Victorian Pavilion which has recently been restored, the spa waters and the restored Victorian railway station now has some interesting small shops and a museum of childhood.

The train leaves Dingwall and continues north now following the shoreline of the Cromarty Firth. On the left is Foulis Castle (a private house) and the Teaninich and Dalmore distilleries are also passed. On the hills to the left of the train, look out for the Fyrish Monument.

Alness station is a small halt in the town centre (just off the High Street at IV17 0SE). The station has an information point and waiting shelter. This stop is the best route to reach the nearby **Fyrish Hill**. It is famous for the distinctive monument on its summit. Built by Sir Hector Munro in 1782, it represents the Gate of Negapatam, a port in Madras, India, which General Munro took for the British in 1781. Make your way to the back of town and then take either route towards the B9176 road. There are a number of paths but none require anything more than a short walk along this reasonably quiet road. You then make your way through forest tracks and start the ascent up Fyrish. The walk is easy and won't take more than a few hours.

A few minutes after the train departs Alness, Invergordon is reached, again on the shoreline of the Cromarty Firth.

Invergordon station is a traditional station but sadly no longer staffed. However the building has recently been restored and has some very interesting and colourful paintings. Look out for people waiting for trains, comical station staff and people running to catch their train – all depicted on amazing paintings on the station walls. The station has a help point and waiting shelter and a canopy over the main platform. It is located just off the High Street at Station Road, IV18 0NJ.

Invergordon has yet another whisky distillery and you will pass right along side it on this journey. In fact you will probably smell the production process from the carriage. This small Highland town is situated on the shores of the Cromarty Firth, which the train travels alongside at this point of the journey. The Firth has particularly deep water and is an ideal natural harbour. At the time of the First World War Invergordon was developed as a base for the Royal Navy. After the Navy facilities had been removed there was a period of decline. This was halted in the 1970s when heavy industry came to the town in the form of the oil industry and an aluminium smelter. The smelter was short lived, however the oil industry, although itself now not nearly as large as it was, remains. You will probably see oil rigs in the Firth from the train and there may be one close to the line being repaired at the repair facility in the town. More recently the town has developed as a cruise liner terminal, and visitors have included the Norway, QE II and the Queen Mary II.

The train departs Invergordon past the huge former Navy oil stores and into farmland again overlooking the Cromarty Firth. The sands of Nigg Bay may be seen to the right of the train. This is an important area for birds and iscared for by the RSPB. It is possible to visit the area and it is four and half miles from **Fern Station** (IV20 1RS). It is best to go by bike although the road is quiet if you wish to walk. Unfortunately the Bay is somewhat spoilt by an oil fabrication yard (now closed). It is also possible to cycle to the coastal village of Portmahomack or Loch Eye, a small loch near the station.

On the opposite shore, and visible from the train, is the pleasant village of **Cromarty** with its historic pre-Reformation church, former courthouse museum and the cottage of Hugh Millar. Hugh Millar was a historian, writer and stonemason. The house is now owned by the National Trust for Scotland and is open to the public. If you are cycling, there is a ferry (seasonal for a few weeks during summer) from Nigg to Cromarty. The ferry website at www.cromarty-ferry.co.uk has details. If not cycling, it is easier to detrain at Inverness to catch a bus if you plan to visit the village. There is a frequent service from Inverness to Cromarty six days per week.

The train now heads inland and up to Tain. On the right there is a military bombing range which ironically means that the area is untouched by development and appears remarkably natural.

Tain

Tain is a pleasant small town with attractive architecture and gardens in the town centre. Another important administrative centre, it also has a court and town buildings. Many of the fine buildings in the town centre were designed by the Maitland firm of architects and once you know what you are looking for it can be rewarding to pick out the many notable buildings bearing their style. It was the destination of what become known as the 'King's Route'. Between 1493 and 1513, James VI travelled on pilgrimage to the shrine of St Duthac at Tain at least 18 times, using the ferry route from Cromarty.

The town centre is dominated by the tower of the Tollbooth. Originally built in 1630 it was destroyed when Oliver Cromwell's troops were stationed in the town in 1656. The present Tollbooth was built as a replacement in 1708 and functioned as court, jail and local tax collection point.

Practicalities

Tain railway station (Station Road, IV19 1JA) is an attractive stone building originally built by the Highland Railway Company. It has been recently refurbished and has an information point and waiting shelters. Unfortunately for such an important town it remains unstaffed at this time. From the station, you are in the centre of the town and beside the shoreline, with park and picnic area overlooking the Dornoch Firth.

Tourist Information is available from the Tain Through Time museum on Tower Street (IV19 1DY).

Places of Interest

Tain Through Time. Opened in 1966 to coincide with the town's 900th anniversary of its first charter, the museum has accumulated an impressive collection of local artefacts. Especially of note is a collection of locally produced silverware from the 18th and 19th century, which is always on display while another important part of the display is the collection of Clan Ross items. Balnagown Castle, built for the Earl of Ross in the 15th century and home to the senior branch of the clan until 1711, is situated just a few miles south of the town. Tain is famous as birthplace of St Duthus in around 1000 AD. His remains were returned here and it then became a place of pilgrimage. On leaving the museum, visitors are encouraged to visit the St Duthus Church and then take a self guided walking tour of Tain.

The Museum is open from Easter until October and there is an admission charge. Telephone 01862 894089 or visit www.tainmuseum.org.uk for visitor details. It is located a five minute walk from the station.

St Duthus Church. The early ruined St Duthus Chapel (1246) was a popular place of pilgrimage during the Middle Ages, and is situated in the cemetery of Tain by the seashore. It is close to the station and you can see the Chapel from the train. The later collegiate church (14th century) is behind Tain Through Time. It became a place of pilgrimage for the remains of St Duthus until after the Reformation in 1560. In 1815 it was replaced by a new church and fell into disrepair. It was later restored and has become a popular tourist destination.

Nearby – Dornoch

From Tain's Lamington Street take a bus north for 18 minutes to Dornoch. This small town of under two and a half thousand inhabitants lies on a beautiful stretch of the north Highland coastline. Famous for its golf links and as a tourist destination, today it is a quaint village with all the unique character one would hope for, together with all the facilities for the tourist. There are many hotels, shops, cafés and restaurants and, so, many people choose this as their holiday destination. The surrounding countryside is ideal for walking and cycling.

Buses arrive into the town square. The centre of Dornoch has a picturesque village feel to it and visitors will enjoy exploring its buildings and taking photographs. It is a conservation zone and as such its buildings are protected from change. There are a number of notable buildings to look out for, the most significant being the Cathedral (see below). The Castle (opposite the Cathedral) was the site of the original Bishop's Palace for the Cathedral. Although the Cathedral dates from the 13th century it is not known when the Castle was built, although the 15th century is thought likely. Since 1947 it has been in use as a hotel, known as Dornoch Castle Hotel (www.dornochcastlehotel.com). Almost all the sights of Dornoch are centred on the Square. On the south are the old police station, the jail, now a commercial enterprise, the court (1850), and Dornoch Castle. Between the Castle and Cathedral is the Green. King Haakon VII of Norway planted a tree here in 1942 as an expression of the gratitude of the Norwegian forces for the hospitality they had received while stationed in Dornoch. Also look out for the beautiful iron fountain in the Green with its four coats of arms.

Golfers will enjoy the Royal Dornoch Golf Club with its attractive coastal links (www.royaldornoch.com) while non golfers will enjoy attractive walks in the same area and the sandy beach. Both of these areas are just off the Square and about a five minute walk from the bus stop.

Places of Interest
Dornoch Cathedral. Occupying the prime site in the centre of the village, there has been a cathedral on this site since 1239. Its beautiful

appearance both externally and internally, together with the decorative stained glass windows make it a stunning building despite its comparatively small size for a cathedral. The building was unfortunately seriously damaged in 1570 when it was burnt during a clan feud. Rebuilding was not completed until 1835 by which time much of the original fabric was lost. It has been a parish church ever since. It is usually open for visitors and there are regular services held there. See www.dornoch-cathedral.com for information.

History Links. Dornoch has an active historical society which has produced a number of local history books and runs a small museum in the town. There are displays from Viking history to the Cathedral, the light railway, military history and of course golf in the town. It is open from Easter until October and there is an admission charge. It is located in the Meadows (IV25 3SF), behind the Castle and about five minutes walk from the bus stop. See www.historylinks.org.uk for information.

Old Station and Walk. Dornoch had a railway line from the Mound (on the Thurso railway) to the town. Opened in 1902 it survived until 1960 with its downfall partly being that most people were travelling south and the railway connected to the north and the county of Sutherland. There have been many plans over the years to build a railway from the south (Tain end) through Dornoch and north to join the Thurso railway again as a short cut over the Firth but so far none have been successful. The former station in Dornoch may still be seen and you can imagine the little steam engine with its single coach preparing to take its passengers north with the Cathedral spire in the background. Trains were often a single coach with some goods wagons behind. The branch line was notable in that its locomotive was built in Inverness and survived working its entire life on the line until 1956. The former railway is now a scenic walk of only a few miles to the village of Embo. See www.dornochlightrailway.co.uk to find out more.

Returning to Tain and the station for the journey north we rejoin the train and make our way out of Tain past the Glenmorangie Distillery. The train now skirts the shoreline of the Dornoch Firth for this highly scenic section of the journey. The scenery is becoming less cultivated and more mountainous as the line turns to head west and makes its way inland. The train now stops at Ardgay. The station serves the village and also Bonar Bridge, a twenty five minute walk across the bridge.

Ardgay

Ardgay station (IV24 3AQ) has a waiting shelter and information point. It is attractively situated on the shoreline with pleasant views across the Dornoch Firth. On the opposite shore is the village of Bonar Bridge with its modern but attractive bridge over the Firth giving the village its name. Both have local services, shops and cafés for the visitor and are set in attractive scenery for bird watching, walking, cycling and photography.

Cyclists and keen walkers may wish to alight at Ardgay to visit Croick. Some ten miles west of Ardgay along a narrow single track road is Croick Church. The Church is a good example of a 'parliamentary church', constructed in 1823. Its simple white walls, plain glass windows and basic hard wooden benches have a certain appeal and remain timeless since its construction. However it became famous in 1845 when a Times newspaper reporter visited to expose a scandal that was representative of a shame which was sweeping the Highlands. Eighty people were living in the churchyard under a home made tarpaulin having being evicted from their homes. Across the Highlands in hard conditions people lived as tenant farmers on small crofts practising subsistence farming. However landowners decided to displace them in favour of more profitable sheep grazing and so in the space of a few years cleared the Highlands of thousands of people who had lived in their homes for generations. The names of those who sheltered at the church may still be seen as they etched their details into the glass panes of the windows providing us today with a tangible link with these people. These clearances became known as the 'Highland Clearances' and are still remembered as one of the most shameful episodes in Scotland's history.

Upon departure from Ardgay station the train leaves the Dornoch Firth and crosses the River Carron which flows down from a pleasant wooded valley. The line then rejoins the water, which is now the Kyle of Sutherland and is forested on either side.

Culrain and Invershin

The train shortly stops at Culrain (IV27 4ET). This halt has a pleasant wooden waiting shelter and is usually decorated with flowers. Alight here if you wish to stay at Carbisdale Castle. The Castle driveway is opposite the station. There are few street lights here, so take a torch if you plan to stay here. The Castle is a magnificent mansion which is now owned by the Scottish Youth Hostel Association (see www.carbisdale.org). The Castle is relatively modern being constructed between 1907 and 1917 for Mary Caroline Mitchell, Duchess of Sutherland. It is one of the last of such great houses to have been built. King Haakon VII of Norway and Crown Prince Olav were provided safe refuge at the Castle during Nazi occupation of Norway in World War II. Shortly afterwards it was gifted to the Youth Hostels Association and opened as such in 1945.

Culrain is also a wonderful location for hill walking and cycling. There are many tracks to be explored leading in all directions away from the station and Castle. The 'Castle Walk' passes Carbisdale Castle and goes through pleasant mixed woodland and Culrain Burn and some particularly good mature oak trees. Alternatively the 'Loch View' walk leads to an idyllic loch edged with old Scots Pine and then on to a battlefield viewpoint. This fine view east over the Dornoch Firth overlooks the site of the Marquis of

Montrose's last battle in 1650. Either take a map with you or consult some of the Forestry Commission information boards near the station for walk details. There is also a mountain bike trail starting from the station through Commission woodlands.

On leaving Culrain the train crosses the viaduct over the magnificent Kyle of Sutherland, so have your camera ready. Look out the left of the train to see the Carbisdale Castle. **Invershin station** (IV27 4ET) is at the end of the bridge is the next stop only two minutes after departure from Culrain, making it perhaps the shortest possible rail journey in the UK. It is also possible to follow a footpath between the two stations. Use Invershin station for walks through Balbair Wood (Forestry Commission).

The train curves around the end of the hill and makes its way north and steeply uphill. This particularly scenic section of the line rises sharply along the hillside to give magnificent views of the Kyle of Sutherland waters as they narrow and head off to the left and the north west. Branching off to follow the route of the train to the right is the River Shin. The train shortly enters a very narrow cutting with sheer rock faces on either side of the train and brushes past the occasional bush which encroaches into the train's narrow space. When the train suddenly exits onto the hillside again one finds the line has now gained considerable height and is on a ledge looking down over the River Shin and Falls of Shin. Down below is a scenic cycle route so cyclists may choose to bike between Culrain and Lairg stations rather than take the train. This amazing land formation continues for a few miles until Lairg station is reached. At this point the ravine has disappeared as the surrounding land has levelled out into gently sloping hills.

Lairg

Lairg station (Station Road, IV27 4EX) is a small stone building (not open to the public) which now houses the offices of the Highland Rail Partnership, an organisation that was set up to develop railways in the Highlands. There is an information point and waiting shelters. Lairg station is not in the village and a bus operates between the station and the village – see www.macleodscoaches.co.uk or telephone 01408 641354. It is better to use this service rather than walking as the village is two and a half miles from the station along an unlit road. There are other longer distance connections from here to the remote north west coast of Scotland as Lairg is the railhead for the entire north west region. Two bus routes of interest to those wishing to explore this region are available. George Rapson Travel runs a bus from the station to Lairg, then to Kinlochbervie (north west coast) and on to Durness (north coast). This service is ideal for walkers and people wishing to get into some of the remotest parts of Scotland. See www.georgerapsontravel.com. There is also a Royal Mail post bus (post and passengers travel on the same bus) to the remote areas of Lochinver and Tongue. See www.postbus.royalmail.com or telephone 08457 740740 for details of this service.

Lairg Tourist Information. There is a seasonal office located at Ferrycroft Countryside Centre, Lairg, IV27 4AZ. Telephone 08452 255121.

The small village of Lairg fulfils an important role serving the community in central Sutherland. It is attractively situated on the shores of Loch Shin. Although the Loch is natural, its height was raised by nine metres when a dam was built next to the village.

Departing Lairg the train makes its way through the heather covered hills and sheep farms which are typical of this part of Sutherland. The line is also turning to face east again, making its way back towards the sea. At this stage the line is also running alongside the River Fleet in the narrow valley of Strath Fleet. There is little in the way of human habitation except for the occasional house as the line passes alongside Ben Doula.

Rogart

Rogart station (IV28 3XL) has a waiting shelter and information point. The station building is now a house and the garden has become something of an outdoor railway museum with a collection of old trains and other railway items. The old signal box has been restored and there are a number of old railway carriages which used to run this railway. They have now been converted into camping coaches for those wishing to holiday here. See www.sleeperzzz.com or telephone 01408 641343 for details. Rogart itself is a hill farm village and you can still see the cattle pens which were formerly used for loading sheep onto trains alongside the line.

The line continues down Strath Fleet and meets Loch Fleet at the mound. The remains of the platforms which once formed the junction station for the line to Dornoch may still be seen from the train as you rush through to meet the North Sea again. On the left of the train is the hill of Ben Bhraggie. The statue on top is to the 1st Duke of Sutherland who was notorious during the Highland Clearances. It is a popular walk to climb the hill and you can do so by following directions from the village of Golspie, the train's next stop.

Golspie

Golspie Station (Station Road / Main Street, KW10 6SZ) has a waiting shelter and information point. The station building is now a house and the former goods yard has given way to more houses. Golspie is a pleasant village on the shores of the North Sea. There are all the necessary local services and places to stay and eat. The station is also useful if you plan to visit Dunrobin Castle when its own station is not open. Just walk through the village and walk up the driveway to the Castle (at the north end of the village). The driveway is marked 'no entry', but this only applies to vehicles and not pedestrians!

Golspie is the starting point for the walk up Ben Bhraggie, situated behind the village. The circular walk starts from Fountain Road in Golspie. From the summit there are views along the Sutherland coast and across the Moray Firth. It takes around two and a half hours to complete from the station and is just over nine kilometres in length. The summit is 415 metres above sea level.

The journey between Golspie and Dunrobin Castle Station follows the back of Golspie and only takes three minutes so be ready to alight if getting off. Also, let the guard know well in advance as it is a request stop.

Dunrobin Castle

During the summer the train makes a special stop on request at Dunrobin Castle station (KW10 6SF). This is the only remaining private railway station in Britain and was opened in 1874. The building is not a normal station, but rather was the private waiting room for the Duke of Sutherland. The attractive wood framed building is now a small museum and is set in fields and mature trees. It is located at the end of the driveway to the Castle. Continue along the driveway and into the Castle itself which you can actually see from the station.

The Duke of Sutherland paid for much of the construction of the Sutherland Railway which is still in use today as the Far North Line. As such in addition to having his own station he was one of the few people in Britain to have his own private train. The locomotive built in 1895 was named 'Dunrobin' and worked with a private parlour carriage. Both have survived and are now located at the Fort Steele heritage site in British Columbia, Canada (see www.fortsteele.ca).

This fairytale castle is the largest private residence in the north of Scotland and is set in its own woodland overlooking the sea. Home to the Earls and Dukes of Sutherland since 1401, the Castle was firstly a heavily protected tower. It was encased by a series of additions from the 16th century, but the original castle still survives surrounded by its newer and more impressive additions. It was the 1845 rebuild however which gave the Castle its present day appearance. Largely the result of Sir Charles Barry, who worked on the Houses of Parliament, he created a Scots Baronial style building in keeping with the most popular styles of the time. The gardens were also extensively remodelled to the design they retain today. Most of the interior of the Castle is opened to the public and a substantial amount of time should be allowed to view the many rooms and treasures they contain. Outside, the formal gardens are amazing in summer and provide an excellent opportunity for photography. The gardens are also the location for falconry displays. A resident falconer and his birds provide daily displays during the summer. While in the gardens, take some time to visit the Castle museum. With displays of natural history and archaeology including 1500 year old Pictish stones it is a nationally important private collection. To fully explore the Castle and grounds a full day should be allowed. The Castle is open from April until October and there is an admission charge for entry. For further information see the website www.dunrobincastle.co.uk or telephone 01408 63317.

Walk back along the driveway to the station to rejoin the train for the journey north. Departing Dunrobin Castle Station the train follows the shoreline. Look out for seals that often lie on the beach here. The next stop is at Brora where the train crosses the River Brora flowing down from Loch Brora in the hills behind the village.

Brora

Brora station (Station Square, KW9 6PY) is an attractive single storey stone building with decorative wooden canopy over the platform. Look out for the decorative tiles on the roof and the 'HR' carved into the stonework. HR stands for Highland Railway, the station's builder and original owner. Unfortunately it is now disused and boarded up. There is a waiting shelter and information point for passengers.

Brora lies on the east coast of Sutherland, in prime golfing country. Brora has two claims to Scottish uniqueness. It once possessed the only bridge in the region – which gave it its name, meaning River of the Bridge – and until the 1960s, had the only coal mine in the Highlands. For such a small town in a remote area it is was surprisingly industrialised with a coal pit, boat building, fishing, salt mining, fish curing, lemonade factory, distillery, wool mill, brick making and a stone quarry. Brick tends to be a building material more commonly found in England and the existence of the factory explains the brick houses in Brora. A woollen mill survived until recently while the stone from the quarry found its way into buildings as diverse as Liverpool Cathedral, London Bridge and the local Dunrobin Castle. Nowadays this small town between Dornoch and Wick is a good base for a number of superb golf courses in the area. It is also famous today for being the home of Capaldi's ice cream.

Three miles south of Brora is a preserved Iron Age broch, Carn Liath. You can walk there by the coastal path between Brora and Golspie, six miles away. As well as the seals can otters can also sometimes be spotted here. Also of interest for the visitor is the Brora Heritage Centre with displays on local history.

The train journey continues its coastal path alongside the North Sea. The line at many sections is only a few metres from the shore which seems to be pounded by waves even on calm days. On the left of the train are a series of hills including the 415 metre Creag Riasgain, all of which rise steeply from the shoreline. The train curves sharply around the base of Eldrable Hill

(416 metres) which can be walked by path from Helmsdale. On the right is the village harbour.

Helmsdale.

Helmsdale Station (Stittenham Road, KW8 6HH) has an information point and waiting shelters. The large white station building is no longer used and the signal box is also disused but still on site. Once this was a very busy station and even had its own engine shed which survived into the days of diesel locomotives.

Helmsdale was chosen as the location for a Scottish 'Emigrants Statue' to mark the thousands of people who were evicted from their homes during the Highland Clearances. Also in Helmsdale is the **Timespan Heritage Centre** which tells the history of the town and the area. It is open from Easter until October and is located on Dunrobin Street (KW8 6JX) about five minutes walk from the station. See www.timespan.org.uk or telephone 01431 821327.

On leaving Helmsdale the train parts from the coast and heads inland to the west. The route follows the Strath Ullie or Strath of Kildonan valley with the river flowing below the train on the right and hills on either side of the line.

Kildonan Station was the scene of a gold rush in 1868 when people flocked to this village to look for gold in the river Kildonan and Suisgill. Some people still try, although there is very little to be found. As the train leaves Kildonan, passengers should look out west for views of the hills Ben Grian (579 metres), Ben Loyal (762 metres) and Ben Hope (926 metres). The line is now entering one of the remotest areas of Britain. Stations are usually request stops only and are sometimes surrounded by only a handful of buildings.

The line continues through the Strath until the base of Creag nan Caorach where it turns to the north and makes a stop at **Kinbrace Station**. Set in unspoilt countryside the quietness is especially striking when having just come from a town or village. Look out for rare hen harriers and deer over this section of line. Beyond Kinbrace the line runs alongside Loch Ruathair with 580 metre Ben Griam Mountain behind. Turning to the right the line enters Forsinard Station.

Forsinard Station. The small station at Forsinard has two platforms, not for the level of traffic ever sustained here but to allow trains to cross at this point. The original station still exists and today is the welcome point for the **Forsinard RSPB Reserve** (Royal Society for the Protection of Birds). This area is known as the 'flow country'. It is a unique habitat of wetlands which is home to an array of birds both year round and migrating. The RSPB organises tours of the area from the station or you can go in and pick up a map to make your own exploration of the area. There is also a hotel here, although for a long day on the moor you may wish to take a sandwich lunch with you. In recent times the area was nearly destroyed by forestry plantations. While most of Scotland was at one time forested this is the one landscape that was naturally a moorland. The commercial tree plantations nearly drained this wetland and have left it scarred for years to come. However the RSBP is working to restore it. You can find out more about this work at their centre in the station. The reserve is open from Easter until the end of October, daily from 09.30 – 17.50. Admission is free but donations are accepted to help the Society's work. You can also reach here on the national cycle network or, as no bus operates, by subsidised Highland Council taxi from Melvich, Bettyhill or Thurso (telephone 01641 541297 by 18.00 the day before travel).

The train crosses the flow country where the remains of line side wooden fences may still be seen. These were designed to keep the worst of the drifting snow off the line in winter and were used in the past when keeping the line open in all weathers was given a higher priority. For some time trains in severe weather were equipped with food survival boxes in case they became trapped here.

Altnabreac Station. This is one of the remotest stations in Britain. At this point the Highland scenery gives way to the flat expanses of Caithness. This wide open space is surrounded by hills in the distance. Fields begin to appear as we re-enter agricultural land. The fields in this part of the country are unusual in that they are divided by flag stone fences rather than dry stone walls. The train briefly calls at **Scotscalder station**. This station has been restored to 1950s British Railways style as part of its conversion to a holiday home. The next stop is **Georgemas Junction**. The most northerly junction in Britain still has a station, although now unstaffed. The railway splits here continuing to Wick with a short branch line to Thurso. Various strategies have been tried over the years to serve Thurso. Recently trains were split at Georgemas with one section going to Thurso and the other Wick. Today the train makes its way to Thurso before returning for a second time to Georgemas for the journey to Wick. The detour doesn't add significantly to the journey. The short to run to Thurso is alongside the River Thurso.

Thurso

Thurso is Britain's most northerly town on the mainland. This is an irregularly laid out town of around 10,000 inhabitants. It is situated around Dunnet Bay with views across to the island of Hoy. The old harbour in town is too small for modern ships so most vessels use the nearby Scrabster harbour. Look out for Thurso castle to the east and Harold's Tower, built over the tomb of Earl Harold (1190), who ruled Caithness, Orkney and Shetland. Thurso dates back to Viking times as a settlement although the present town is much newer. It has wide streets, shops and accommodation and is the ideal base for touring the surrounding area.

Practicalities

Thurso railway station is the original Highland Railway building built from attractive stone and with a large slate roof covering the tracks. Trains come indoors into the station to protect passengers from the harsh Caithness weather. There is a staffed booking office, waiting room, public telephone, luggage trolleys, left luggage lockers, taxi link, toilets and information. The waiting room is decorated with various unusual items, including a painting of a Union Pacific (USA) 'Big Boy' steam locomotive.

Local Transport. The village is easily seen on foot. The ferry to Orkney departs from Scrabster just along the bay with a bus link from the front door of Thurso station to the ferry. The connection is listed in the railway timetable.

Tourist Information is provided at the office on Riverside Street (KW14 8BU), telephone 08452 255121.

Places of Interest

Surfing. Thurso is a popular surfing destination and equipment is usually available for hire locally. The beach at Thurso is also pleasant for walks.

The Castle of Mey. This castle was the former home of the Queen Mother. It is now open to the public and has become a very popular attraction. On display are the rooms just as they were during the time she lived here, including some of her personal belongings. You can get there by bus from Thurso. Many businesses in Thurso still display the Royal Warrant.

Orkney. Thurso (Scrabster) is the departure point for ferries to Orkney. Northlink Ferries operate this route and it is possible to return the same way or to take one of their alternative services south from Orkney to Aberdeen. The usual ship is the MV Hamnavoe which is very well appointed with comfortable lounges, a bar, restaurant and shop to keep you entertained on the one and a half hour crossing. During the summer (usually April until October) it is possible to book a cabin on the 06.30 sailing from Orkney, avoiding an early departure from your hotel. This can be booked with Northlink on 0845 6000449. See Chapter 8 for details on Orkney and Northlink Ferries.

Return to the train for the short journey through Caithness back to Georgemas Junction and on to Wick.

Wick

Wick has been a Royal Burgh for over four centuries. At one time it was the county town for Caithness, however it has been more famous for being

Europe's busiest herring port. The town and harbour were largely developed by the British Fisheries Society in 1808. During the herring season thousands of workers would travel to Wick from the surrounding area to work. Most would travel on foot, taking up to a week to reach their destination. These scenes continued until the early 1930s when herring became scarce.

Practicalities

Arrival is into the town's original stone built station which retains its character. The station is very similar to the attractive structure at Thurso. There is a staffed booking office, waiting room, public telephone, taxi link, toilets and information.

Places of Interest

Wick Heritage Centre. The award winning Heritage Centre is located near the harbour. It deals with the herring past and general history of Wick and has museum exhibits as well as recreations of significant everyday life. The Centre requires several hours to take it all in. It is open from Easter until October and has an admission charge. See www.wickheritage.org.

Wick Harbour. The harbour area developed by Thomas Telford can still be seen. Although not used as a fishing port today, the harbour is intact and remains along with many of the old fishing warehouses in the surrounding streets. The scene is not dissimilar to that which would have greeted visitors during the herring years. The harbour also at one time had passenger steamers to Aberdeen, Leith and Kirkwall.

John O'Groats. This is the most famous location in the Wick area. It is an increasingly popular place with cyclists wishing to do the John O'Groats to Lands End route (the two farthermost points on the British mainland). You can also take a bus here and return by Thurso.

Auld Man o Wick. About a one and quarter mile walk south of the town is the Auld Man o Wick, a square tower and the remains of Wick Castle. It is situated on dramatic cliffs overlooking Sinclair Bay. Although little remains it is a very historic site being the 12th century mainland base of Norwegian Earldom of Orkney.

20. Inverness to Kyle of Lochalsh, Skye and the Outer Hebrides

This is one of the great railway journeys of the world. The route begins in the Capital of the Highlands, Inverness, and ends in remote Kyle of Lochalsh, gateway to the Isle of Skye. Along the way travellers see the farmlands of the Moray Firth, the heather covered hills of the Highlands and the beauty of the west coast as the line makes its way along the sea lochs after Strathcarron.

Journey Summary

Route: Inverness – Beauly – Muir of Ord – Dingwall – Garve –
                Achnasheen – Achnashellach – Strathcarron – Attadale –
                Stromeferry – Duncraig – Plockton – Kyle of Lochalsh.
Trains: Standard class only. Summer trains have a catering trolley.
Trip Length: 2 hours 30 minutes.
Frequency: 4 trains each way daily over entire route, with one on
                Sundays.
Links: Coach link from Inverness to Ullapool for the Isle of Lewis
                ferry. Buses from Kyle of Lochalsh to destinations on Skye
                including Uig ferry terminal for connections to the Outer
                Hebrides.

For the Inverness to Dingwall section of the route, see Chapter 19, The Far North. The coach link from Inverness to Ullapool for the Island of Lewis is described at the end of this chapter.

Having arrived from Inverness, the train departs Dingwall station and makes its way through town and across three level crossings. The line quickly starts to take a westerly route and begins the long climb towards Garve. This is a journey of mountains as well as water and the train is soon in remote and beautiful scenery. Shortly after leaving Dingwall you may catch a glimpse of the village of Strathpeffer (see the Dingwall entry in Chapter 19) on the left of the train as it turns to climb the valley side. This Victorian spa town would have been the largest settlement on the line had it not been for a short-sighted landowner who refused permission for the line to cross his land. A branch line was later built to the village but as a branch it was uneconomic and closed in the 1930s. The train makes its way along the shoreline of Loch Garve with beautiful views of the loch and the hills before the first station at Garve.

Garve. Garve Station (IV23 2QF) has an information point and waiting shelter. This is a small village with a hotel. It is also the start of the road to Ullapool, however buses leave from Inverness and Dingwall if you plan to make the journey and these are better connections if coming from the South. People coming from Kyle can change at Garve or Dingwall for buses to Ullapool. On leaving Garve look to the right of the train to see views once more of Little Wyvis and Ben Wyvis (1045 metres). Ben Wyvis can easily be climbed leaving from Garve station and returning within eight hours, although it is a much shorter walk if getting there by bus (the Ullapool service) instead. Take the track behind the station and then through a low level woodland walk. Make sure to take a good map, food and appropriate clothing as conditions on top of the mountain can get severe even in summer.

The train now makes its way along the banks of Loch Luichart. This long narrow loch is picturesque with hills and trees surrounding the loch on all sides. One of the nice things about this line is that it is beautiful in all seasons. In spring and summer, flowers, heather and trees are in full bloom. In the autumn the unique colours are no less spectacular, while winter often results in the hills being snow capped along the entire length of the route.

Lochluichart station (IV23 2PZ) is a small request stop on the banks of the Loch and next to the hydro power station. The train is in rural Highland scenery now with an abundance of wildlife including birds of prey and deer which come right up beside trains. After Lochluichart the line rises up above Loch a Chuilinn on the right of the train before falling to cross Loch Achanalt. This is sometimes a popular spot for train photographers to alight at **Achanalt Station** to see the trains pass. On the left of the train are the five peaks of Sgurr a Mhuillin which are often snow covered until late Spring. The train travels through the narrow Strath Bran sharing the space with the River Bran. The valley eventually narrows so that rail, river and road share a space only a few metres wide before opening out again allowing the river to meander along the valley floor. Early morning trains are often treated to sun rises along this open valley with big hills and an even bigger sky to enjoy. To the west you briefly see the Torridon Peaks, which provide walks for hikers and nature enthusiasts.

Achnasheen station (IV22 2EJ). This was once a busy station although the building is now a house. However there is a waiting shelter, information point and public toilet. Achnasheen Tourist Information offers a limited service of free local information. It is open seasonally and is located inside the art studio. The settlement consists of only a few houses, however there was once a hotel here beside the station. It burnt down in the 1990s and the site was cleared. This was also the railhead for the west coast with buses to Gairloch. With road improvements, coaches now leave from Inverness and take a different route along the Ullapool road, with rail no longer featuring on that journey. The village and surroundings have changed little since this was a drovers' stop where cattle driven from Glen

Carron (to the south west) and Torridon, Gairloch and Poolewe areas to the north west would meet before being driven to markets at Dingwall. The line of the old drovers' road can still be seen about 100 feet above the main road on the north side of Loch a'Croisg (Loch Rosque) and with a little imagination you can still see what it must have been like in those days. During the summer a bus link connects with some trains (see Traveline) to offer day trips to **Inverewe Garden**. Inverewe is one of the world's great gardens and is run by the National Trust for Scotland. Overlooking Loch Ewe in the north west Highlands. There are plant types from around the world which enjoy the mild climate of their local area.

The mountains close in again after Achnasheen and the train passes Loch Gowan and then continues up to Drumalbain watershed. From here the streams and rivers flow west rather than east. Loch Sgamhain appears on the right as the train enters Glen Carron where the train winds its way slowly between the mountains on either side of the line. Glencarron Lodge is also seen on the right. It is the principal house on the Glencarron estate and was once served by its own private railway station, known as the Glencarron Platform.

Achnashellach Station (IV54 8YH) is the start point for the Coire Lair Horseshoe hill walk. The Coulin forests north west of Achnashellach are dominated by three wonderful hills which form one of the classic walks of Scotland. It takes in some great views together with two Munros and of the most impressive Corbetters, the Fuar Tholl at 907 metres above sea level. The walk starts from the station and takes around six to eight hours. It is a strenuous hill walk and shouldn't be attempted by anyone inexperienced or unequipped for such a journey. The train travels through Achnashellach forest. Little remains of the once great Caledonian pine forest, although efforts are being made to preserve these remnants. The train continues through Glen Carron following the course of the River Carron. The hills on the left of the train are Cairn Mor at 515 metres.

Strathcarron Station (IV54 8YR) is isolated although there is a hotel and post office at the location. A bus links the station with Lochcarron village. There are several hill walks from near the station to the hills behind the village.

On leaving the station the train travels alongside the waters of Loch Carron. The village named after the Loch, Lochcarron with its white cottages can be seen reflected on the water's surface. The journey has now dramatically changed from hills and mountains: the line now hugs the shoreline all the way to Kyle for one of the most spectacular and beautiful sections of railway in the world. **Attadale Station** is a tiny halt, but well worth getting off if you are a plant lover. This is the location of **Attadale Gardens**. These gardens are best visited in summer or in the spring when the magnificent rhododendron bushes are in full flower. There is also a sunken garden and a Japanese garden started in 2002. See the website www.attadale.com or call 01520 722603. They are open from April until October and there is an admission charge. The Gardens are located next to the railway station.

The train departs Attadale and crosses the River Attadale which flows down past the Gardens. The line winds its way along the shoreline right beside the sea loch. The hillside is so steep on the left of the train that an avalanche shelter has been built to protect trains from falling rocks and the train's wheels squeal out with every tight curve.

Stromeferry station (IV53 8UH). The small village of Stromeferry was once the terminus of this line. From here steamers left for the Island of Skye. However when a rival railway was opened to Mallaig (providing an alternative route to Skye), the Highland Railway pressed ahead with an extension to Kyle. There being very little room for the railway, the builders fitted it in between the hill and the sea by blasting their way through sheer rock. This remains the route of the Skye line to this day. This station had a revival in its fortunes in the 1970s for a few short years when a rail freight terminal to serve an oil construction yard was opened. Both yard and sidings have since gone. There are several woodland walks available from the village including a view point with stunning views along the Loch on the hill behind the village.

The train continues alongside Loch Carron, a sea loch which flows into the Atlantic Ocean, and will stop on request at **Duncraig station**. The halt is close to Duncraig Castle which provides a unique form of B&B accommodation in a family home and castle. The Loch is opening out at this point and the scenery increasing in beauty. The mild climate allows for incredible vegetation growth for a location this far north and west.

Plockton station. The village of Plockton is famous for its palm trees and of course its beautiful location on a sheltered bay. Surrounded by rugged hills and benefiting from the Gulf Stream flowing in to its waters, this Highland village really can grow tropical palm trees. This is a pleasant place to get off and spend some time. The railway station has been converted into a restaurant while next door a large building resembling an old signal box is in fact a backpackers' hostel. There are numerous places to eat and walk in this popular destination for tourists. Plockton is now an important village for the surrounding area, having had a High School constructed. Plockton Post Office provides tourist information.

The train continues beside the sea and makes a brief stop at **Duirnish**. This is a useful stop for the **Balmacara Estate & Lochalsh Woodland Garden** (National Trust for Scotland). The Estate is large and also covers the area of Plockton and Kyle so visitors may wish to use the train to travel within the Estate as well as to it. The Estate includes the woodland garden, an open air church at Plockton and miles of stunning coastal scenery with views across to the Cullin hills on Skye. See the National Trust website for details.

The train departs Duirnish to briefly head south. Look out for the Skye bridge on the right hand side of the train. There are spectacular views out to the Isles of Raasay, Scalpay, Longay, Pabay and Crowlin with seals sitting on the rocks. Kyle is now minutes away as the train heads through a steep rock cutting.

Kyle of Lochalsh

The train heads through a cutting in the rock and past the old Kyle signal box (now disused) and onto the platforms at Kyle. Until 1995 Kyle was the main ferry port for the Island of Skye. At that time the road bridge to Skye was opened. The bridge is a single span arch and since the land is relatively low on each side it has a very steep approach from both directions to gain enough height to allow ships underneath. There are frequent buses across to Skye from the bus stop near the station or you can walk across for free. The buses link all parts of the island and you can even take a ferry from Uig on Skye to the Western Isles or return via Armadale to Mallaig for the West Highland Railway to Fort William and Glasgow.

Kyle has some military establishments nearby and is the main village for the area with shops, banks, restaurants, hotels and local services. The small village is attractively situated on the shoreline and nestled amongst the rocky hills. It is an ideal spot for a picnic or walk. Many people enjoy the walk across the bridge to the Isle of Skye, but wrap up warm – it can be windy even in summer!

Practicalities

The station at Kyle is unusual in that it is actually built on top of the harbour. Steamers in the past departed from the train side. It is a pleasant two platform station with central building. The station retains services with staffed booking office, waiting room, toilets, restaurant, museum, telephones and information.

Tourist Information. The office is located at the Car Park, Kyle of Lochalsh, IV40 8AQ. Telephone 08452 255121.

Places of Interest

Skye Bridge. This is a very pleasant walk on a nice day. Or you can take a bus across. There is also a walk to a viewpoint overlooking Kyle and the bridge. Both are signposted from the village centre.

Eilean Donan Castle. Take a bus or taxi to the nearby Eilean Donan Castle. This may be the most famous and photographed castle in the world. There is a good chance you will recognise it as soon as you see it. The castle was originally built in the 13th century but had become a ruin and was rebuilt and opened in 1932. The Castle is open all year and has an admission charge. See the website, www.eileandonancastle.com, for details.

Coach and Ferry Links to Skye, North Uist and Harris

Kyle of Lochalsh is the northern railhead (Mallaig being the 'southern'!) for the Isle of Skye and the Outer Hebrides islands of North Uist and Harris. Kyle was also very conveniently the departure point for ferries to the Isle of Lewis until 1973 when the decision was taken to switch to the shorter crossing from Ullapool which resulted in passengers needing to take a coach connection from Inverness, as Ullapool was never on the rail network. Bus travel on Skye is good with multiple departures daily, even on the remote routes. Coaches are run by Scottish Citylink or Stagecoach. There are usually around three Citylink coaches which are rail connected between Kyle and Portree and one or two all the way to the ferry Terminal at Uig each day. Buses between Kyle of Lochalsh, Sconser (for the Raasay ferry), Broadford and Portree are quite regular with up to eight buses daily in each direction. People wishing to get to Armadale for the ferry to Mallaig should change buses in Broadford.

Departing Kyle, buses head over the Skye bridge and onto the Island. The bridge was completed in 1995 and in doing so ended the ferry route from Kyle to Skye which is thought to have existed since 1600. It is a large single span which is not unattractive to look at. Upon crossing many people are surprised at how high it is, this is simply to allow ships to pass underneath. Buses make a brief stop in the village of **Kyleakin** before heading into Skye. This village is directly opposite Kyle of Lochalsh and from either you will see the ruins of Castle Maol at the end of the village. Now little more than the remains of a few walls, it dates from 1400. The bus then travels along the rocky shoreline with the heather covered hills on the left of the bus and looking out to sea the tiny island of Pabay on the right. The hills rise up to the summit of Sgurr na Connich at 739 metres. Curving around the bay, the bus arrives into Broadford.

Broadford

Broadford is the largest village on the Island and stretches out along Broadford Bay. It lies on the foot of the Red Cullin Mountains with views across to Pabay Island and the Applecross mountains on the mainland in the distance. The village provides local services, has hotels and cafés and a supermarket. Change buses here if you wish to head down to the ferry at Armadale for Mallaig. It is a nice place to stop for something to eat and enjoy the views. The main attraction in Broadford is the Skye Serpentarium (The Old Mill, IV49 9PB) where you may have a close encounter with all kinds of snakes, frogs and lizards. The centre operates as a home for these creatures and the admission charge goes towards their good keeping. This worthy attraction has been privately established to provide a greater understanding of these animals and although those with a fear of snakes may be relieved to hear that snake handling is not compulsory, it is certainly possible if you wish! For information either telephone 01471 822209 or visit the website at: www.skyeserpentarium.org.uk.

Bus to Armadale. If changing buses at Broadford, the route south heads through the hills of south east Skye and crosses over to the shoreline, which the road follows all the way down to Armadale. The serious mountains all the way along this road are the Sleat Hills of Skye. This rugged and remote landscape is worth the journey to Armadale alone. Arrival in the hamlet of Armadale is at the ferry terminal. For details of Armadale and the Castle, see Chapter 12.

Departing Broadford the bus continues northwest through the woods and then along the coast following Loch na Cairidh, which is in fact a sea loch with the Isle of Scalpay on the opposite side. The road then turns inland and travels along the edge and to the end of Loch Ainort. The hills surrounding the road at this point are some of the steepest and most spectacular in Scotland. The road itself now has to cross these hills and a steep and twisting climb take the bus over the summit and through a valley before dropping down to the next loch, Loch Sligachan, and the tiny hamlet of Sconser. The bus will let you off at the ferry terminal which in fact is little more than a waiting shelter. This is the departure point for the regular ferry to the island of Rassay.

Raasay Island

The ferry to Raasay is operated by Caledonian MacBrayne (check the company website for details). The journey time is 20 minutes and there are up to ten sailings in each direction daily (two on Sundays) so you won't have to wait long from the bus arriving. On board there is a comfortable passenger lounge, open deck space and toilets.

Raasay is a small Island, only 14 miles long by 3 wide at its widest point. The only village is located at the new ferry terminal on Churchton Bay. Raasay is an idyllic Scottish island with only 200 inhabitants. Perhaps when you reach a Scottish island, from another Scottish island you know that you have gone somewhere remote and special. It is the perfect location for walking. On arrival the ferry will come into the island's only village where there are some local services. It is even possible to stay on the island as there are some B&Bs, an outdoor centre and hotel (see www. raasay.com). Starting at the village there is a walk back down towards the former ferry terminal along an old railway line. Or the most popular walk leads through the woods at the back of the village and up to the summit of Dun Caan hill (443 metres), where there are also two small lochs. If you plan to take a bike, the only small road on the island leads up to Loch Arnish, which is actually a bay, about 12 miles away near the north of the island. Although the road stops here, mountain bikers and walkers could continue right to the very top of the island. While there are no formal 'attractions' as such, for walkers who want to enjoy peace and tranquillity, Raasay is a very accessible and beautiful Scottish island.

Returning to Skye and the bus north, on departure from Sconser the bus heads along the lochside before venturing inland for the high road through the valley and hills to Portree. After a few miles the road passes between two mountains and passengers are given a wonderful view downhill to Loch Portree bay where the town of Portree is situated. This sheltered and beautiful bay allows vegetation which is almost tropical in nature compared to the contrasting bleak hills the bus has just travelled through.

Portree

This small, compact and attractive town is one of Skye's most popular locations due to its setting in the hills, by the shoreline and, for its beautiful vegetation. Many people choose to stay for a few nights here and enjoy day trips, walking, cycling or sitting down by the shore and enjoying the views and the food from local restaurants. There is cycle hire available in town and boat trips are also offered from the harbour. At the south end of the village is a small woodland with walks leading to some secluded waterfalls. Also at this location is the Aros Centre (www.aros.co.uk) which has live view cameras linked to sea eagle nests for visitors to enjoy. Sea eagles were once common on Skye but persecution and egg collecting meant the last birds were killed in 1916. Thankfully the species survived in Norway and in the 1970s they were reintroduced to Skye. The RSPB operates this camera facility for visitors wishing to get up close to the birds.

Day Trips from Portree

It is possible in two days touring to explore the entire northern half of Skye. There are two trips on most visitors itineraries from Portree.

Tour 1 - Portree to Dunvegan. Dunvegan and its Castle are probably the most famous locations on Skye. There is a regular bus service (no Sunday service) from Portree to Dunvegan village and the Castle. Separate stops are made for each location although it is easy to walk between them. Dunvegan is a pleasant village on a sea loch location in a sheltered bay. There are local services, places to eat and some walks around the village. At the northern edge of the village lies Dunvegan Castle. For over 800 years it has been the home of the Chiefs of Clan MacLeod and as such is the oldest inhabited castle in Scotland. Its position overlooking the sea Loch Dunvegan and surrounded by landscaped woodlands and gardens is stunning. In fact the gardens are as much an attraction as the Castle itself and you may enjoy the walled garden, water features, round garden and woodland areas. Sitting in what is essentially barren moorland of northern

Skye, these gardens laid out in the 18th century are like finding a hidden oasis in the desert. Due to the warmth of the Gulf Stream visitors are often amazed at the types of plants which thrive in these gardens. The Castle itself is a fascinating complex of six buildings, five of which are open to the public. Dunvegan Castle and Gardens are open daily from April until October and there is an admission charge for either Castle and Gardens or Gardens only. Boat trips to visit the seals are also offered as a supplement to visitors to either the Castle or Gardens. Telephone 01470 521206 or visit www.dunvegancastle.com for information.

Tour 2 – Portree to Flodigarry Circular. A service bus (number 57A) makes five daily circular journeys from Portree round the north of the island and then returning via Uig to Portree, allowing visitors to get on and off at attractions along the way. Ask your driver about the best ticket for touring. On this journey the bus travels over the remote northern half of the Island passing the Storr cliffs, peculiar cliffs which reach up from the land rather than the sea on the left of the bus. The path to the Storr from the road is very steep and might not be suitable for everyone. The Old Man of Storr is a single stack at the end of the cliffs and clearly visible from the road. Further along the road, just before Staffin village, is Kilt Rock. There is a short walk from there to the distinctive Kilt Rock cliffs which are just as impressive for their size as their strange 'tartan' appearance rock formation. The bus then crosses the top of Skye and passes the remains of Duntulm Castle, which is now little more than some very small remains of its walls, although it is possible to imagine how easy to defend this cliff top castle would have once been. The bus then makes its way down the west coast of Skye through Uig (where you can get off at the ferry terminal if you wish) and back to Portree.

For those wishing to continue from Portree north, coaches continue from Kyle of Lochalsh through Portree direct to Uig without changing. The coach departs Portree and crosses the spectacular hills north of Portree to descend back down into the secluded bay at Uig which is the ferry terminal for ships to North Uist and Harris. There are daily departures to both destinations from Uig and buses are timed to meet the ship's timetables.

Skye to North Uist and Harris

Many people expect Skye to be too rural and remote to have good public transport and are surprised to find how accessible and easy to get around it is. However turning to some of the Outer Hebrides a little more planning is required. There are no large towns on these islands and for much of even recent history, the sea has been the main method of transport. However there are some excellent and easy ways to explore these islands. The ferry operator, Caledonian MacBrayne, doesn't strand you at its terminals, but offers inclusive tours of many islands. To make best use of the day trips from Skye you are probably best to stay overnight in Uig. Check www.uigisleofskye.com for details of places to stay. It is of course also possible to take the rail – bus – ferry connection from Inverness to Harris or Uist in one day for a longer stay on the island. If staying for a while and wishing to explore, a bike is ideal, although car hire is available on both islands for the less energetic. The quiet roads are ideal for both cycling or driving. There are also bus services even to the most remote locations, check with Traveline Scotland.

Caledonian MacBrayne operates the Uig to Harris and North Uist routes which are usually covered by the MV Hebrides. Launched by HM Queen Elizabeth II in 2000, the ship accommodates 612 passengers and has a crew of 34. Facilities on board include several lounges, an observation lounge with electronic display showing the ship's position, restaurant / café, bar, shop, playroom and open decks. Packed lunches are also available for purchase from the coffee cabin for people intending to explore the islands. The ship's timetable usually allows two sailings each way on both routes daily, with one route having a single sailing in one direction on some days. The times change from day to day so that every route has a selection of sailing times offered at least some days each week. The crossing time on both routes is around one hour forty minutes.

To book any CalMac tour from Skye or to get more details see www.cal mac.co.uk/dayexcursions or telephone the booking office at Uig Ferry Terminal on 01470 542219. For railway travellers going through Fort William (Skye is accessible via the Mallaig rail route and then CalMac ferry to Armadale on Skye) there is a Caledonian MacBrayne ferry office in Fort William station which you may visit or telephone on 01349 705285. These tours operate from April/May until September/October. Out with these times, weather conditions and short day light hours would make them less enjoyable anyway. Remember that exact tour specifications and tours themselves are liable to change.

Non-Landing Cruises. Caledonian MacBrayne offer morning, afternoon and evening non-landing cruises from Uig to both North Uist and Harris. On these mini cruises you may enjoy a meal on board and spend time on deck taking in the stunning shoreline scenery of the Outer Hebrides. Sailings to Lochmaddy on North Uist enjoy coast views of Skye before passing by the tiny Ascrib Islands off Skye. The Skye shoreline then returns for a second time in the form of the Waternish peninsula before crossing the Little Minch to North Uist. North Uist itself is actually a collection of many small islands which the ferry will pass some of. The hills that come into view are uncharacteristic as arrival at the ferry terminal will demonstrate just how flat the wetlands of Uist are. The alternative voyage to Tarbert travels alongside the north Skye shoreline before crossing the Little Minch. Once over, the ferry negotiates tens of tiny islands as it makes its way up the narrow Loch Tarbert to the village itself. Both crossings offer different if still stunning scenery. Many passengers prefer to be on deck while these shorelines are in view and enjoy the on board restaurant when at sea.

Grand Tour of North Uist and Harris. This tour first takes in the beautiful beaches, dark hills and freshwater lochs. The tour then leaves North Uist by causeway to the Island or Berneray, which has been made famous as the favourite retreat of Prince Charles. There the MV Loch Portain takes visitors across the beautiful Sound of Harris to Harris itself. A leisurely journey is then taken through Harris, with photo stops, to the village of Tarbert for the ferry back to Skye. This particular journey can only be booked through the Uig Ferry Terminal Office.

Callanish Tour. This tour departs Uig for Tarbert on Harris, there a guided journey is taken through the Harris landscapes and on to the Island of Lewis for some amazing ancient history. A visit is made to the Callanish Standing Stones. Older than Stonehenge, this monument dates from between 2900 and 2600 BC and is interpreted at the on site visitor centre. The next stop is at Dun Carloway Broch. Brochs were family homes, with defensive features, which had accommodation for families and animals. The Dun Carloway Broch is thought to date from the last century BC and is remarkably well preserved on its hill top location. The final stop is at Gearrannan Blackhouse Village. This offers the chance to experience life as it was 300 years ago on this traditional croft village where you can see butter making, peat cutting and weaving in action. For anyone wishing to understand better the lives of perhaps even their ancestors this is a unmissable attraction. The coach then makes a stop at Stornoway for a couple of hours exploring before returning via Tarbert to Uig.

Independent travellers may prefer to make their own way through Harris and onto Lewis by bike or bus and then return via the Stornoway to Ullapool ferry and coach link to Inverness railway station. Regular buses operate between the ferry terminals on Harris and Lewis.

For all these cruises and tours, CalMac recommends you take your binoculars, camera, comfortable footwear, sunscreen, warm clothing and a waterproof jacket.

Inverness to Ullapool and the Island of Lewis

We return to Inverness to describe the coach link to the Island of Lewis. Coaches from Inverness bus station (next to the railway station) to Ullapool are timed to connect with ferries to the Isle of Lewis. There is a choice of either Stagecoach services or Scottish Citylink. Stagecoach buses also serve Dingwall, for train connections to the Far North Line, and both call at Garve for rail passengers from Kyle of Lochalsh. The journey time is approximately one and a half hours. Along the way the coach passes close to Ben Wyvis, travels alongside Loch Glascarnoch and views some remote and rugged Highland scenery before Loch Broom comes into view on the final approach to the village of **Ullapool**.

This north west town was built in 1788 by Thomas Telford for the British Fisheries Society which explains its rather uniform appearance and organised layout. Today it offers local services and a good base for exploring the surrounding countryside. It is also the ferry terminal for the Isle of Lewis. The terminal has a ticket office, waiting room, toilets and vending machines. The modern terminal in Stornoway has similar facilities.

The **ferry to Lewis** departing Ullapool is usually the MV Isle of Lewis. Passengers enjoy fine views of the Highland shoreline as the ship sets out on the two hours forty five minutes journey to Lewis. The ship accommodates 680 passengers and has a lounge, observation lounge, open decks, restaurant / café, bar, shop children's play room, toilets and offers packed lunches for sale. There are between two and three sailings in each direction daily. Check in for foot passengers closes 30 minutes prior to departure on this route. If travelling by Citylink bus from Inverness (but not Stagecoach), a checked baggage service is available so that you can collect your luggage again in the Lewis ferry terminal.

The Island of Lewis may be taken in with the Calmac 'Callanish Tour', described on page 194. However for visitors arrving into Stornoway (where the ferry terminal is located), there are scheduled buses to other parts of the island, although these are infrequent so you may find it eaiser to hire a car. The town is medium sized and has all the services a visitor requires, and a good selection of shops. The main attraction is the grounds of Lewis Castle. Although now disused, the parkland may be enjoyed for walks and picnics. The Island has a unique feel with Gaelic still spoken, peat cut, and a strong observance of Sunday as a day off. As such most shops and services will close on Sunday. Of paritular interest to visitors venturing into the countryside are the Golden Eagles that live on the island. Local tourist information may be obtained from the Tourist Tnformation Centre in Stornoway (26 Cromwell Street, HS1 2DD), who can also help with transport, accomodtion and bus times and car hire. It is a few minutes walk from the ferry terminal or can be called on 01851 703088.

21. Other Routes and Journeys

This section of the book describes some local rail journeys of interest to visitors. As the lines are short and not particularly scenic they are not described in detail, but interesting stations along the way are mentioned. These are short distance rail journeys so advance booking of tickets is not necessary and seat reservations will be unavailable. Trains will vary from route to route but all will have standard class seating and toilet facilities. Catering is not available on these services.

ROUTE 1: Edinburgh to North Berwick

This journey starts from Edinburgh's Waverley Station for a short trip down the start of the East Coast mainline. This is the express route south to Newcastle, York and London and has hosted many of Britain's most famous and fastest trains over the years. There are up to 18 trains in each direction per day from Edinburgh Waverley to North Berwick.

Musselburgh is the first stop, just east of Edinburgh. As with many of the surrounding towns it is often overshadowed by its more famous neighbour. However for those wishing to escape the busyness of Scotland's capital city, these small towns offer very attractive and unspoilt places to visit. Musselburgh is on the coast and has an old harbour and sandy beach. The town is built around what is known as 'Roman Bridge', the original having been built by the Romans. It was rebuilt on the foundations in 1300 and again 1597, and crosses the attractive River Esk which flows though the town.

Pleasant architecture is not in short supply in this town. Of particular interest is the ancient administrative centre of the Tolbooth. This castle-like structure was built in 1590. The town has developed from a fishing port to a centre of leisure with a golf course and racecourse (constructed in 1817).

Prestonpans. This historic town is located on the shores of the Firth of Forth. The town is actually an amalgamation of three adjoining villages. The name comes from Preston (one of the villages) and the old method of salt extraction using pans. The extraction of salt from the Firth was a major industry for the town, hence the name Prestonpans. Of interest to the visitor are the remains of Preston Tower, the attractive shore area, and the site of the Battle of Prestonpans. On the 25th July 1745 this was the site of the battle between the troops of Charles Edward Stewart and the Government forces. Although marked by a cairn the site has been altered over the years and is now somewhat spoilt by the overhead electric power lines coming from Cockenzie Power Station. Also notable is Prestongrange Parish Church which dates from 1596 and is one of the earliest post-Reformation churches in existence.

On departure from Prestonpans the train makes a stop at **Longniddry**. This is a former coal and weaving village. The original 1845 station is still in use and visible from the train. It is now a popular commuter town for Edinburgh.

Drem. During Second World War the former West Fenton Aerodrome (later Gullane Aerodrome) became RAF Drem, and the Drem Lighting System was developed to assist Spitfire landing. Today some of the outbuildings have become part of the Fenton Barns retail & leisure village and are used as studios by local craftspeople, particularly furniture makers. Chesters Hill Fort, one mile south of the village, is an example of an Iron Age fort. The branch line to North Berwick now leaves the East Coast Mainline for the last few miles into North Berwick.

North Berwick

The town is centred on its harbour which has existed since at least the early 1100s. For the next 500 years it was a ferry crossing to Earlsferry in Fife for pilgrims journeying to the Cathedral at St Andrews. The town today still has a busy harbour with the East Lothian Yacht Club based there. There is also a busy High Street with some unique locally owned shops. It is a popular golf resort with fine links overlooking the sea.

Practicalities

The station building at North Berwick was demolished in the 1980s and all that remains is a waiting shelter and telephone help point.

Places of Interest

North Berwick Law. This 187 metre high mound of volcanic rock overshadows the town. This is a pleasant walk with fine views over the Firth of Forth and the North Sea. At the top there is an arch made from a pair of whale bones.

The Scottish Seabird Centre. The Scottish Seabird Centre is an award winning wildlife visitor centre and one of Scotland's five star attractions. From its stunning location at the harbour overlooking the sea and islands of the Forth, visitors enjoy a close encounter with nature to remember. Over 300,000 seabirds, puffins, guillemots, shags and kittiwakes return to this haven for wildlife in early spring to nest each year. Don't miss the amazing spectacle of grey seals with their fluffy white newborn pups on the Isle of May National Nature Reserve from October to December. Find out more at www.seabird.org. There are often all-inclusive rail tickets available with Scotrail.

Nearby places of interest

From North Berwick, the village of **East Fortune** in East Lothian is within easy reach. It is served by bus service number 121 (First Bus Edinburgh), running between Haddington and North Berwick. The area is known for its airfield which was constructed in 1915 to help protect Britain from attack by German Zeppelin airships during the First World War.

In 1922, several buildings and an area of land were used to create East Fortune Hospital. This served as a tuberculosis sanatorium for the south east region of Scotland until the onset of the Second World War. The airfield was then brought back into service as a training base, and the hospital patients were transferred to Bangour Hospital in West Lothian. For a short period in 1961, East Fortune operated as Edinburgh's airport while facilities at the current Turnhouse Airport were being reconstructed.

In 1975, **the National Museum of Flight** was opened at the airfield, and has since become a popular tourist attraction. In 1919 the airship R34 left from East Fortune bound for Mineola, New York to make the first east to west crossing of the Atlantic by air. The collection includes a number of R34 relics. The aviation collections include aircraft (such as a Spitfire and Comet), engines, rockets, photographs, a reference library, archives, models, flying clothing and instruments. It is also home to a Concorde (number G-BOAA) from the decommissioned British Airways fleet, which forms the centrepiece of a major exhibition. The Museum is part of the National Museums of Scotland and there is an admission charge. See ww.nms.ac.uk.

If you continue on bus route 121 a few miles later you will reach the village of **Haddington**. You can also get here by express bus from Edinburgh city centre. The centre of Haddington comprises fine buildings centred on High Street and Market Street. The streets are attractive with wide pavements, fountains and statues. Of interest to visitors is the town house built in 1742. Also of interest is the post office which dates back to 1603 when it was one of the very first post offices in Scotland, servicing the mail between the newly unified capitals of Edinburgh and London.

ROUTE 2: Edinburgh to Berwick upon Tweed

Also starting at Edinburgh Waverley, passengers may journey a little further down the East Coast Mainline to Dunbar and Berwick upon Tweed. Trains run every at least every hour or more frequently.

Dunbar

The last stop before the English border is the town of Dunbar. The attractive town has had a castle for probably 2000 years with the town likely being just as old. It has had a violent past with the castle often under siege, and if the castle was not taken, the town was often burnt anyway! These days it is a picturesque town with charming High Street. The Parish Church is one of the highlights of a visit with its dark red stone and interesting features. At the end of the High Street is Lauderdale House. This is an unusual building for a town centre. It was a mansion house for the Earl of Lauderdale before being converted into army barracks in 1859. Today it has been converted into residential flats.

Practicalities

Dunbar's attractive railway station is staffed and has a booking hall and waiting room. There is a cash machine, customer toilets, luggage trolleys, a taxi rank and customer service information.

Places of Interest

Dunbar Castle. The Castle was probably founded by the Earl of Dunbar in the 1070s. Its most famous moment came in 1338 when 'Black Agnes', the Countess of Moray, commanded the defence of the Castle during a five month siege by the English. It was subsequently destroyed and rebuilt many times over the years. In 1567 Mary Queen of Scots was taken to the Castle. Her subsequent surrender lead to the destruction of the Castle. The ruins remained, however when the decision was taken to build a harbour at Dunbar, the very rock the damaged castle sat on was blasted apart. The explosives technique was developed especially for the job. What was left of the Castle suffered further in 1993 when part of the rock collapsed into the sea. The sad decline of such a historic site should not take away from its significance though. It can still be viewed from the harbour and with imagination, its size and importance can still be appreciated.

John Muir Birthplace Trust. John Muir's life and work has inspired people all over the world. Now the Dunbar birthplace of the pioneering conservationist has been transformed into a new visitor attraction. Born in Dunbar in 1838, John Muir emigrated with his parents to the United States where he campaigned for the preservation of natural environments through his work as an environmentalist, geologist and botanist. See www.jmbt .org.uk.

Dunbar Town House Museum. The historic Dunbar Town House is home to an archaeology and local history centre. A display of photographs of old Dunbar and its surrounding area, brought together by Dunbar and District History Society, gives a fascinating insight into the town's past. Copies of local history documents are available for study, and members of the society are usually on hand to help you in your research.

The journey continues through the spectacular scenery of Northumbria in northern England. The line travels through the centre of Berwick upon Tweed and over the spectacular Royal Border Viaduct which was opened by Queen Victoria in 1850.

Berwick upon Tweed.

Around 1120, King David made Berwick one of Scotland's four royal burghs, giving its freemen a number of valuable rights and privileges that allowed the town to prosper and become Scotland's greatest seaport and its largest and wealthiest town by the 13th century. The port thrived on the export of wool, grain and salmon, and traders from Germany and Flanders (modern day northern Belgium) set up homes and businesses in the town to make it a major international commercial centre, described by one medieval writer as the 'Alexandria of the North'.

This golden age came to a violent end in 1296, when King Edward I of England captured and sacked Berwick, beginning a period of some 300 years of warfare between England and Scotland. From the Middle Ages to the 1960s, Berwick was a garrison town. Cromwell's soldiers occupied it during the Civil Wars in the 17th century, Jacobites threatened it in 1715 and 1745, and the town's fortifications were again upgraded to ward off possible French assaults in the late 18th and early 19th centuries.

In 1882, Berwick Barracks became the depot of the King's Own Scottish Borderers, who still have their Headquarters there, though the Regiment has been barracked near Edinburgh since the mid-1960s. All around the town are reminders of Berwick's history as a border fortress town, from the ruins of its medieval castle and town walls, its unique Elizabethan fortifications and the 18th century barracks, to the emplacements for guns that defended Berwick during two World Wars.

Practicalities

The original Berwick upon Tweed station still serves the town. This busy two platform station has many express services daily from Edinburgh and London. The station is fully staffed with ticket office, waiting room, taxi rank, cash machine, customer toilets and first class lounge. Look out for remains of the town's 13th century castle on your way out of the station. The castle was demolished during the Commonwealth of Oliver Cromwell and the stones used to build the Parish Church.

North Northumberland and the East Borders are served with a rail-link bus, which departs from the station forecourt to Galashiels, Duns, Earlston & Melrose. The bus service is operated by Lowland Scottish Omnibuses.

Places of Interest

Berwick Barracks, among the first in England to be purpose-built, were begun in 1717 to the design of the distinguished architect Nicholas Hawksmoor. Today the Barracks hosts a number of attractions, including 'By Beat of Drum' – an exhibition on the life of the British infantryman. The complex is large and complete and is now under the care of English Heritage. It is open from April until September and there is an admission charge. See www.english-heritage.org.uk.

Town Wall. Much of the defensive wall around the town still survives. The remains of a medieval castle crucial to Anglo-Scottish warfare, superseded by the most complete and breathtakingly impressive bastioned town defences in England, mainly Elizabethan but updated in the 17th and

18th centuries. Surrounding the whole historic town, the entire circuit can be walked. The Main Guard is a Georgian Guard House near the quay: it displays 'The Story of a Border Garrison Town' exhibition.

Royal Border Bridge spans the River Tweed between Berwick-upon-Tweed and Tweedmouth in Northumberland. It is a Grade I listed railway viaduct built between 1847 and 1850, when it was opened by Queen Victoria. The engineer who designed it was the famous Robert Stephenson (son of George Stephenson). It is still in regular use today, as part of the East Coast Main Line. The bridge is 659 metres long and has 28 arches, constructed of brick but aesthetically faced with stone.

The Holy Island of Lindisfarne. At most times of the year a bus operates from the railway station at Berwick upon Tweed to the unique Holy Island which is linked to the mainland by a causeway. Lindisfarne is internationally famous both for its medieval religious heritage and its 16th century castle. These, together with most of the community, are located on the southern part of the island – the main focus for tourists and holidaymakers. Many are also attracted by the peace and tranquillity which pervades the Island and the remote northern conservation area, with more than its fair share of quiet beaches and unique natural history. See www.lindisfarne.org.uk.

Route 3: Glasgow to Balloch for Loch Lomond

This short journey from Glasgow's Queen Street Station is only 45 minutes long but a world away from Loch Lomond and the Trossachs National Park. Trains are operated by Scotrail and run every half hour. Passengers arriving at Glasgow Central Station may also buy a ticket for Balloch and take a train for Milngavie or Dalmuir changing to a Balloch train when you reach Partick Station.

Balloch and Loch Lomond

Loch Lomond and the Trossachs are Scotland's first National Park. This remote yet accessible location is an amazing landscape of mountains, lochs and forests which are packed with possibilities for days out and longer holidays. The West Highland Way walking route to Fort William has several days walking within the Park, while other shorter routes are also available. The National Park Authority produces a 70 page guide to all rail and bus services within the Park and it is available for download from the National Park's website at www.lochlomond-trossachs.org. In addition to Balloch station, there are several stations on the scenic West Highland Railway – Arrochar & Tarbet, Ardlui and Crianlarich – which are really useful for getting into the north of the Park which is less busy and has the best walking and cycling routes. For day visits to Loch Lomond for less serious walkers, Balloch is ideal as it has the Park Visitor Centre, the Loch and cruises. It is also the best starting point for serious walkers wishing to start the West Highland Way.

Practicalities

Balloch railway station is located in the village centre, a short walk from the shores of Loch Lomond. This new station is a replacement for Balloch Central which is next door and now houses the Tourist Information Centre. Until 1986 there was a small extension to the pier but this has now been converted to a walking route from the station. Balloch station has a ticket office, waiting room, toilet, pay phone and taxi rank.

There are numerous local bus services around the Loch and further into the Park and on to Stirling. Find out more from Traveline or the National Park Authority.

Places of Interest

Loch Lomond Shores. Most people head to Loch Lomond Shores on arrival. It is five minutes walk from the station, as the name suggests is located on the shoreline of the Loch. There are many shops located here which almost gives it the feel of a shopping centre. However there is also an information service about the Loch and Park and a hire service for canoes, bikes and pedal boats for you to get out onto the water. Also within the building is the Loch Lomond Aquarium (see www.sealifeeurope.com), places to eat and a children's play park. The centre is open all year, see www.lochlomondshores.com for information.

Maid of the Loch. The Maid of the Loch was the last British paddle steam ship to be built in 1953. Unfortunately it fell into disuse but a group of volunteers is now restoring the ship. At the moment there is a café and bar on board as well as free tours of the engine room and restoration progress. There are plans to restore the ship to working order and once again offer cruises. The 1902 steam powered slipway has now been restored and is open for viewing. The Maid is open year round at weekends and daily from May until September and is a five minute walk from the station. See www.maidoftheloch.com or telephone 01389 711865 for details.

Loch Lomond Bird of Prey Centre. The Bird of Prey Centre lets you get up close to Scotland's amazing birds of prey. The visitor centre is open year round, but check before visiting that it is open the day you intend to visit. There is an admission charge. It is on Stirling Road (G83 8NB), a ten minute walk from the station or take bus number 309. See www.loch lomondbirdofpreycentre.co.uk for information.

National Park. The Park has numerous walking and cycling routes. There are also bus routes throughout the Park for those less mobile. Check the National Park website for details of activities: www.lochlomond-trossachs.org.

PART 3. Reference Information

22. Overnight Trains – The Caledonian Sleeper

When travelling between Scotland and London the option of making the journey overnight is available on the 'Caledonian Sleepers'. The 'sleepers' are Scotrail's premier long distance services connecting 40 Scottish towns and cities with London Euston station. Euston offers easy access to central London and is close to the London Eurostar terminal. Trains leave in the evening and arrive early next morning at their destination. These trains provide leisure travellers with more time at their destination, savings in hotel bills and an enjoyable journey.

Routes

The Caledonian Sleeper services operate on five routes from London to 40 locations in Scotland. Additionally they call at Preston and Crewe in north west England for connections to Manchester, Manchester Airport, Liverpool, Lancaster and other locations. The routes are:

- London (Euston Station) to Glasgow
- London (Euston Station) to Edinburgh
- London (Euston Station) to Fort William
- London (Euston Station) to Inverness (and Stirling / Perth)
- London (Euston Station) to Aberdeen (and Dundee)

Passengers travelling to Stirling and Perth have the option of using the Edinburgh Sleeper and then a connecting day time train, thereby having longer in their berths. There is no extra charge for this option but it needs to be specified at the time of booking.

Travelling with the Sleeper

Standard class seated sleeper. Each sleeper train has a seated coach with air conditioning, comfortable seating, reading lights and footrests. While these coaches are sold as standard class the seating used is actually the same as in First Class in day services.   However, they are not as spacious or comfortable as seated coaches in other countries. A tip for new travellers is to take a travel pillow, light blanket, eye shades (unlike international trains the lights are not dimmed), and a small bottle of water. Coach passengers have access to a buffet counter throughout the night.

Standard class berths.   Standard class cabins feature two berths, a concealed washbasin with shaver point, individual air conditioning controls, reading lights and hand towels. Fresh cotton sheets and blankets are provided. In the morning a steward provides a snack and tea or coffee delivered to your room.   For a small charge, a light breakfast can be ordered. These cabins are ideal for two people travelling together. Single travellers may be required to share with someone of the same sex (or you can pay a supplement for single use of the cabin). For people travelling together or in small groups, adjoining cabins can be combined with an interconnecting door. This applies to both the first and standard class cabins.

First class cabins. First class cabins are similar to the standard however they only have one berth for privacy and therefore are also more spacious. In addition to the above features, there is a room service menu, complementary light breakfast, newspaper and toiletry packs. These cabins offer a peaceful and relaxing place to sleep and are ideal for the business traveller or the single leisure traveller wishing a bit of luxury.

Lounge car. First class passengers have access to the lounge car throughout the journey. Standard class passengers are also allowed in after departure subject to it not being too busy. This coach has comfortable lounge seating and it's a great place to socialise and meet fellow passengers. Stewards are on hand throughout the night to serve drinks, light meals and refreshments.

Station lounges. A private lounge area for sleeper passengers is provided at Inverness and Aberdeen. At Carlisle customers can wait in the Lakes Court Hotel (outside the station). In Edinburgh the Scotrail lounge is available while in Glasgow the train's lounge car is opened early. In London sleeper passengers with First Class tickets can use the Virgin Trains lounge, while standard class ticket holders can use the passenger lounge located on the main concourse.

Showers. There are no showers onboard the trains. Showers are available at Edinburgh Waverley, Glasgow Central, Fort William and Inverness. These are chargeable. First class passengers can use the showers at the Virgin Trains lounge in Euston station or at the Scotrail lounge in Aberdeen, free of charge. The journey is only one night so the use of a shower is not as important as some long journeys in other countries. However, if you were going on and you wanted a shower before your next journey, there are showers at Kings Cross station in London, only a short walk from Euston.

Luggage trolleys. These are provided at most stations along the routes for passengers to use. Sometimes a small charge is made (normally refundable on return of the trolley).

Tickets. Normal standard and first class tickets are usually valid on the sleeper on payment of a supplement. You should always book and reserve a place in advance as the sleeper can get fully booked at busy times of the year. Often the best value fares are specific to the sleeper, and are obtainable from ticket offices or direct from Scotrail through their web site www.scotrail.co.uk or from their telesales office on 08457 550033.

23. Scenic and Steam Railways

Scotland has many scenic railways to enjoy. Even if you are not on a rail holiday they are ideal for days out. Coastlines, mountains, rivers, farmlands and national parks are all enjoyed on these routes. Some scenic railways have the added attraction of using steam trains. Details of these routes may be found in part two of this book, however this page gives a useful summary of the routes to help you decide where you might like to visit.

West Highland Railway
Glasgow to Oban or Fort William and Mallaig

The West Highland Railway was voted 'Top Railway Journey of the World' by the 2009 and 2010 Wanderlust travel awards. Highlights of the journey are:

- Travel through the Trossachs National Park
- Cross Rannoch Moor
- The mountains, rivers and lochs of the West Highlands
- Visit the resort of Oban
- Take a ferry to Scotland's remote western islands including: the Small Isles, Skye, South Uist, Barra, Coll, Tiree, Lismore, Mull and Colonsay
- Travel by regular steam train during the summer on the 40 mile Fort William to Mallaig section of the route
- Walk the West Highland Way long distance walk or the Great Glen Way from Fort William

Kyle Line
Inverness to Kyle of Lochalsh

The Kyle of Lochalsh Railway has long been regarded as one of Scotland's most scenic lines taking in the coastline and farmlands of the east, the mountains and the rugged west coast landscapes. Highlights of the journey are:

- Travel alongside the Moray Firth and view Ben Wyvis
- Take a bus to the Victorian Spa resort of Strathpeffer
- Take a bus link to Inverewe Gardens
- Enjoy the mountains and wildlife between Dingwall and Strathcarron
- Enjoy the very scenic coastal line though typical West Highland scenery between Strathcarron and Kyle
- Visit Plockton village with sheltered bay and palm trees
- Visit Attadale Gardens
- Walk across the Skye bridge from Kyle of Lochalsh
- Take a day trip or longer stay to the Isle of Skye

Far North Line
Inverness to Thurso or Wick

The Far North Line makes a leisurely journey to the very top of Scotland. Although lacking the mountains of the Kyle line, the railway is also highly scenic passing the farmlands of the Cromarty Firth before heading through the valleys and huge expanses of wetlands of the far north. Highlights of the route include:

- Coastal views of the Cromarty and Dornoch Firths, and the North Sea
- Travel through the huge expanses of the Flow Country wetlands, a unique habitat in Europe
- Visit Dunrobin Castle, Scotland's most northerly great house
- Take a trip to John O'Groats or the Castle of Mey, the former home of the Queen Mother
- Take a day trip or holiday to the Orkney Isles

Strathspey Railway
Aviemore to Boat of Garten or Broomhill

The Strathspey Railway pass through the heart of the Cairngorm National Park, while on board the traditional steam trains offer an experience of rail travel in times gone by in Scotland. Highlights of the route include:

- Views of the Cairngorm Mountain range
- The River Spey
- Travel through the Cairngorm National Park
- Abernethy Forest, which passengers are able to explore on foot or bike
- Boat of Garten village, a traditional Highland village with golf course
- Enjoy afternoon tea, lunch or dinner on selected services

Highland Mainline
Glasgow and Edinburgh to Inverness

The Highland Mainline begins in Perth and takes in the beautiful green and forested Perthshire countryside before venturing through the some of the most mountainous and remote parts of the Highlands and the Cairngorm National Park before descending into the Highland capital of Inverness on the Moray Firth. Highlights include:

- Perthshire woodlands and hills
- The Grampian Mountains and the central Highlands
- Travel through the Cairngorm National Park
- Cross the Findon and Culloden Viaducts
- Britain's highest mainline railway
- Explore small Highland towns and villages including the resort of Pitlochry

24. Further Reading and Websites

There are many useful resources on the internet which can help in planning your trip. Some of the most useful websites are listed here.

Transport
Scotrail. Scotland's national railway: www.scotrail.co.uk
East Coast. Rail services from east England to Scotland: www.eastcoast.com
West Coast Railways. The Jacobite Steam Train from Fort William to Mallaig: www.westcoastrailways.co.uk
Railcards. Details of money saving Railcards: www.railcard.co.uk
Britain by Rail. Independent guide to British rail travel: www.britainbyrail.co.uk
BritRail. Rail passes for international visitors: www.britrail.com
Caledonian MacBrayne. Ferry services to Scottish islands: www.calmac.co.uk
Northlink. Ferries to Orkney and Shetland: www.northlinkferries.co.uk
Citylink. Road coach services throughout Scotland: www.citylink.co.uk
West Coast Motors. Bus and coach services in the west: www.westcoastmotors.co.uk
Stagecoach. Local bus services throughout Scotland: www.stagecoachbus.com
First Bus. Local bus services in towns and cities: www.firstgroup.com/ukbus/
Lothian Transport: Edinburgh area bus services: www.lothianbuses.co.uk
Plusbus. Joint train and bus tickets for local bus travel: www.plusbus.info
Traveline Scotland. Journey planner for all rail, bus, ferry and air travel in Scotland: www.travelinescotland.com
National Rail. Official website of Britain's rail companies: www.nationalrail.co.uk
Stena Line. Ferries from Northern Ireland to Scotland: www.stenaline.co.uk
Loganair. Air services within Scotland: www.loganair.co.uk or www.flybe.com
Heritage Railways. Steam trains throughout Britain: www.ukhrail.uel.ac.uk

Visitor Attractions
Local attraction websites are listed in the main text of the book.
Historic Scotland. Ancient monuments: www.historic-scotland.gov.uk
National Trust for Scotland. Historic buildings and gardens: www.nts.org.uk
Undiscovered Scotland. Independent website with visitor ideas: www.undiscoveredscotland.co.uk
Multimap. Print local maps on your PC before you leave: www.multimap.com

Accommodation
Local community websites can be an excellent source of accommodation information but change regularly – search on google.
Visit Scotland. Scottish Tourist Board with accommodation and visitor information – www.visitscotland.com
Scottish Youth Hostel Association. Budget accommodation – www.syha.org.uk
English Tourist Board. Official information for England – www.enjoyengland.com

Don't let your guidebook become out of date – free updates to download!

Unfortunately guidebooks soon become out of date. So to thank you for purchasing this book we are offering you free updates. Just log on to www.britainbyrail.co.uk and click on the 'Scotland by Rail' section to download and print maps, fares, times and general updates to keep your book up to date.

Visit www.britainbyrail.co.uk

From the author of Scotland by Rail, britainbyrail.co.uk is everything you need to know for days out and holidays by rail in Britain. From questions for the first time traveller to cheap fares, its all here!

Index